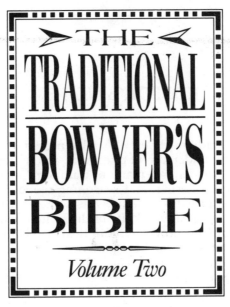

➤THE◄
TRADITIONAL
BOWYER'S
BIBLE

Volume Two

G. Fred Asbell
Tim Baker
Paul Comstock
Dr. Bert Grayson
Jim Hamm
Al Herrin
Jay Massey
Glenn Parker

THE LYONS PRESS

EDITOR'S NOTE

As Volume 1 of The Traditional Bowyer's Bible neared completion, there was, quite frankly, a lingering undercurrent of concern among the authors. We were concerned because we had slain so many of traditional archery's sacred cows; bow design, bow wood, tillering, and seasoning wood, just to name a few. Though we had slit the throats of these beasts somewhat reluctantly, the fact remained that we had the gleaming knife of the written word in our sweating hands, and we were unsure how such a radical departure from convention would be received by our fellow archers and bowyers, who, like us, pride themselves on keeping alive traditional ways and philosophies.

Our concern was wasted, it turns out, for readers immediately embraced the information presented, viewing it not as an assault on the conventions of traditional archery but as the opening of new doors, offering greater variety and avenues of expression in wooden bows.

We hope this present volume, too, will continue spreading the enjoyment and satisfaction of this most ancient form of archery.

Jim Hamm, Editor
Winter, 1993

ACKNOWLEDGMENTS

This book would be impossible without the assistance of many interested people. The authors would like to thank Doug Elmy with The Society of Archer Antiquaries, Frank Scott with the Fred Bear Museum, and Joe Cross with the National Museum of the American Indian, all of whom went far beyond the call of duty in researching background material and photos. Steve Allely, author of the Western Indian Bows chapter in Volume 1, provided the fine illustrations and line drawings used throughout. John & Geri McPherson shared their long experience with making cordage. Information and test materials, particularly dealing with strings, was supplied by "Neo-aboriginals" Dick Baugh, Jim Riggs, Steve Edholm and Tamara Wilder, Peg Mathewson, Jeff Schmidt, Joe DaBill, and Dave Wescott. All have science-embracing minds and hearts deeply immersed in the paleolithic.

In addition, Chuck Boelter, Ron Hardcastle, Malcolm Smith and John Strunk generously used their many years of bowmaking experience — combined with keen insight — to help shape this volume.

ABOUT THE AUTHORS

G. Fred Asbell began shooting a bow and arrow in the late 1950's and since that time has hunted most of the big game species throughout the U.S. and Canada. In 1991, he bowhunted for black bear in Alberta, mule deer, elk, and Rocky Mountain goats in Colorado, and whitetails in Minnesota, Wisconsin, Alabama, and Alberta. He started hunting in southern Indiana, but has called Colorado home for more than twenty years. He is perhaps best known for his philosophical approach to bowhunting and for his writing on bow shooting.

Fred is the President of the Pope and Young Club, Hunting Editor of *Bowhunter Magazine,* and a regular columnist for Professional Bowhunters Society. In 1986 he wrote *Instinctive Shooting,* which is now in its fifth printing. A follow-up book, also on instinctive shooting, will be available in the fall of 1992.

Tim Baker, like many others, first became interested in archery after reading about Ishi and the remarkable weapons he made with only stone tools. Upon reading the available archery texts, it became clear to Tim there was a great deal of contradiction and confusion about wooden bows and their design. He decided the only way to get reliable information was to make every conceivable type of bow of every conceivable material while keeping complete statistics on each one. By comparing stats, the qualities which produce superior bows slowly became apparent. Based upon his research, he has written articles on wooden bows and their construction, as well as teaching at archery meets and primitive skills workshops. Tim can be contacted at 6609 Whitney, Oakland, CA, 94609

Paul Comstock never used a hunting weapon he really liked until he started carrying a wooden bow. He earlier tagged whitetails and black bears using a center-fire rifle, muzzleloader, shotgun, compound bow, and glass-laminated recurve bow. Since switching to wooden bows, he has abandoned modern hunting weapons entirely. Where legal, he also uses stone-tipped arrows exclusively. His largest game so far with a wooden bow is a 300-pound black bear.

He began making wooden bows in 1984. From the onset he began experimenting with woods other than yew and Osage orange, curious because old bowmaking books ignored these woods almost completely. In 1988 he published the first edition of *The Bent Stick,* the first bowmaking manual to describe in comprehensive detail how to get the best results from some of North America's most common trees. Subsequent findings have been incorporated into updated editions of "The Bent Stick." Some of these findings stem from investigative projects conducted with Tim Baker. Paul sells the "The Bent Stick" for $11 a copy, postpaid. He can be reached at P.O. Box 1102, Delaware, OH 43015.

Charles E. Grayson, M.D., 82, retired, has been active in archery for 70 years in target, field, flight, hunting, history, and collecting of archery items, memorabilia, and literature. He is a life member of Sacramento Target Archery Club, installed into California Archery Hall of Fame, and a recipient of the Drake Flight Medal. He has made most of his own bows from the old English type to backed bows, laminated recurves, horn and antler bows. His extensive archery collection is now partly in the Archery Museum at the University of Missouri, Columbia, which opened in October, 1991. The remainder of the collection will be housed there in a new museum building now under construction.

Jim Hamm was born in Texas in 1952, and practically grew up with a bow in his hands, graduating from small game to deer hunting when only twelve. His interest in archery never faded, and about the time he married discovered bows made entirely from wood, a discovery which was to consume his adult life. Though spending his early years operating heavy equipment, working freight docks, and "becoming a promising young executive," Jim finally went into archery full-time. He has been, as he puts it, "self-unemployed" for the past twelve years: making bows, researching, writing about bows, and recently, teaching others the age-old skill of wooden bowmaking through intensive, hands-on seminars conducted at his home. He also owns and operates Bois d'Arc Press, publishing archery books both old and new. Jim's first book, *Bows and Arrows of the Native Americans,* is available for $16.95 postpaid. To order books or inquire about bowmaking seminars write; Bois d'Arc Press 4, PO Box 233, Azle, TX, 76020.

Dr. Al Herrin is a member of the Cherokee Nation and was reared near their capitol of Tahlequah, Oklahoma. He began shooting the traditional bow as a small child, and his interest in archery eventually attracted the attention of

several of the old Cherokee bowyers who taught him the secrets of their ancient craft. Al not only makes bows and arrows but uses them, regularly competing in archery tournaments (including the Cherokee sport of cornstalk shooting), and hunting big and small game. He has written extensively for newspapers and magazines on the topics of Indian culture and bowhunting. His book, *Cherokee Bows and Arrows,* is available for $14.95, postpaid ($15.62 Oklahoma, $20.95 foreign), from White Bear Publishing, Dept. H, Rt. 3 Box 172, Tahlequah, OK, 74464.

A native of Oklahoma, **Jay Massey** has lived in Alaska for the past 23 years and is a registered guide/outfitter and a former member of the Alaska Board of

Game. He operates an outfitting business, Moose John Outfitters, which caters to archery hunters, wilderness enthusiasts and salmon fishermen. He has written four archery books and is currently at work on a fifth which will combine fiction with fact to dramatize significant archery-related events of medieval England, the Steppes of Asia and pre-contact Indian America.

Jay's other books can be ordered through Bear Paw Publications, P.O. Box 429, Girdwood, AK 99587: *Bowhunting Alaska's Wild Rivers* ($15.95); *A Thousand Campfires* ($14.95); *The Bowyer's Craft* ($16.95); and *The Book of Primitive Archery* ($18.95). Add $2 for postage and handling.

Glenn Parker, M.D., began shooting an old lemonwood bow when only eight years old, and has had the good fortune to take many big and small game animals over the years. His interest in archery expanded to include the history behind the bows, arrows, and archers of the past and he became an avid collector of old archery items. His "hunting" now includes looking up old bowyers and bowhunters, and he travels across the country to personally meet these men. Hearing their tales of hunting in times past Glenn considers the most rewarding part of collecting. He has assembled one of the largest collections of historic archery tackle in the country, featuring items from Art Young, Saxton Pope, Ishi, Howard Hill, and a host of other well-known bowhunters.

Glenn currently manufactures a line of laminated recurves and longbows, each one hand-made with strict attention given to detail and performance. Contact him at Greywolf Bows, 11503 E. Jayhawk, Houston TX, 77044.

DEDICATION

The authors would like to dedicate this volume
to all of those in the modern world who still
harbor a touch of archery's magic in their souls,
whose bowmaking efforts are helping keep alive
the joy of a bent stick.

TABLE OF CONTENTS

Originally published in 1993 by Bois d'Arc Press
First Lyons Press Edition © 2000

Printed in the United States of America

10 9 8 7 6 5 4 3 2 1

The Library of Congress Cataloging-in-Publication Data is available on file.

ISBN 1-58574-086-1

TRADITION BEGINS WITH THE PAST

Jay Massey

In the autumn of 512 B.C. a great army of nearly 700,000 warriors — one of the largest armies of antiquity — was encamped on a rolling, grassy plain on the Steppes of southern Russia, somewhere north of the Sea of Azov. This vast army was under the command of King Darius I of Persia, an ancient kingdom in what is now Iran. At the time, Persia was the most powerful nation on earth, with an empire stretching from Egypt to India.

King Darius and his army — composed mostly of infantry — had embarked on the campaign two years earlier. His goal: subdue the Scythians, a fierce, nomadic tribe of Steppe herdsmen who were noted for their horsemanship and their skill with their powerfully-reflexed composite bows. The long campaign had been a disaster for the Persians; the skirmishes and running battles against the Scythians always seemed to end in frustration. The tactics of the nomads had been to retreat and attack and then retreat again. The Scythian horse-archers were excellent fighters, toughened from a harsh life on the Steppes and disciplined from the daily grind of making and breaking camp, forever moving in search of forage for their horses, sheep, and cattle.

Pressed by the huge Persian army, the Scythian horsemen led their pursuers deeper and deeper into the wilderness of the Steppes, periodically moving in with quick skirmishes to pick off the Persian infantry from long range with their horn-reinforced bows. As they retreated, the Scythians filled in the wells and springs, torched the surrounding grasslands and destroyed food supplies, depriving the Persians of food, water, and forage. Morale of the Persian army was at an all-time low.

The light of dawn on that autumn morning in 512 B.C. revealed a relatively small band of a thousand Scythian horsemen on a grassy hill two miles from the main Persian force. The Scythian horse-bowmen paused for a moment atop the hill and then charged directly down toward the great Persian host. The thunder of their approaching hoofbeats was instantly matched by a clamor from the Persian infantrymen as they realized they were being attacked by this puny force. The clamor became a roar as thousands of foot soldiers uttered battle cries as they hastily grabbed lances and swords and prepared to do battle.

Then came the inevitable deadly whistle as the attacking horse-archers closed, released their arrows in a black cloud and then wheeled about in unison and galloped away, leaving in their wake hundreds of dead and wounded Persian soldiers. The Persian infantry and some mounted lancers gave chase — and were ambushed by a force of ten thousand Scythian bowmen waiting on the other side of the hill. The Persians withered under the onslaught. The Scythians were too swift, too mobile. The extreme range of the Scythians' powerful horn-wood-sinew bows barely allowed the Persians to make contact.

This two-year campaign against the Scythians — a group of Indo-European tribesmen who had moved onto the Steppes of southern Russia two centuries earlier — ended in bitter defeat for the invading Persians. Those battles which took place between 514 and 512 B.C. are among countless others which were to occur on the Steppes of Asia for nearly two thousand years, as entire nations of horse-archers rose to power and then fell, like waves of grass rolling across the windswept Steppes.

The power of the Scythians was eventually broken on the Steppes — not by the army of any civilized nation, but by the Sarmatians, another group of nomadic horse-archers like themselves. The Sarmatians were in turn followed by many other nomadic tribes, including the Parthians, the Massagetae, the Hsiung-nu, the Avars, the Huns, the Bulgars, the Turks, the Mongols, and a host of other Indo-European and Turko-Mongol groups. All of these peoples were expert horsemen whose principal fighting weapon was the Asiatic composite bow.

These nomadic horsemen had a profound impact upon the entire civilized world — from the Roman Empire to ancient China. Echoes of their hoofbeats can even be found in the writings of the ancient prophets of Israel. Today we still use many phrases which date back to these horse-archer cultures. "Blood-thirsty" refers to the Scythians' and Hsiung-nu practice of lining human skulls with gold and using them — according to some reports — as drinking cups in which to drink the blood of their enemies to celebrate a warrior's first kill or to consecrate a treaty; "Parting shot" refers to the way the Parthian horse-archers turned to shoot arrows over the rumps of their horses as they withdrew from an engagement.

Today, the accounts of these ancient archer/warriors lie buried in dusty volumes, tucked away on the back shelves of libraries, forgotten by everyone except a few historians.

Few archers today have even heard of such peoples as the Cimmerians, the Scythians and the Sarmatians. Even the horn-wood-sinew composite bow used by these ancient archers has been ignored and neglected — as have the longbow used by the medieval English archer and the flatbow used by the American Indian. Though proven time and again on the field and in battle, these weapons are now looked upon as "inefficient" and "antiquated."

This biased view of ancient and traditional archery is a recent phenomenon; it did not exist in the time of Saxton Pope, Art Young and Howard Hill. The misconceptions about ancient archery have only become widespread since high-tech, mechanized archery became popular in North America a short twenty years ago. Ignorance of the cultural and historical significance of traditional archery can be found everywhere today. Furthermore, most archers who are fixated on modern archery show little interest in learning anything about the archery of old. To such people, "traditional" archery gear means a willow-limb bow and a cotton string.

Not long ago I visited a photo lab in Anchorage, Alaska to pick up some color prints of my archery hunting clients. One of the photos showed a great bull moose one of my hunters had killed with a recurved bow. The moose had an antler spread of 67-inches and had weighed approximately 1600 pounds on the hoof. One wood arrow tipped with a sharp broadhead had killed the moose within seconds; the bull had run but 35 yards after being hit.

A young man who worked at the photo lab said he was an archer. He expressed amazement when he saw the photo. "I didn't know you could kill a moose with a recurve bow!" he exclaimed with genuine surprise.

His ignorance caught me off-guard, for I thought every archer realized that ancient Assyrian archers had commonly shot African lions with their recurved bows. I was sure everyone knew that Howard Hill, Fred Bear and others had killed African elephants with both recurve and longbow.

And what American archer of Anglo-Saxon heritage didn't know about the great longbow battles at Agincourt, Crecy, and Poitiers, where the sky was literally dark with arrows? The very survival of medieval England had depended many times on the simple yew longbow and the clothyard shaft. Surely any archer of English heritage would be expected to know of such things, would they not?

You'd be surprised! Mention such historical events at a gathering of high-tech shooters and you'll likely draw blank stares. Crecy and Agincourt — who cares? — that's all ancient history.

Such disregard for the historical significance of traditional archery surprises me, for I found the accounts of such archery-related historical events fascinating long before I discovered that several of my ancestors were Cheshire bowmen who had fought in some of the great longbow battles. After learning this I now find historical events such as Hastings and Poitiers even more interesting.

I'm sure thousands of other archers would feel the same if they were to research their own family lines. Descendents of the 5,000 or so English longbow-men who played a crucial role in defeating a vastly superior force of more than 100,000 at Crecy in 1346 are alive today. Most of them probably do not realize that for the power of the longbows held in the hands of their ancestors, they would not be here. I'm certain they'd take a renewed interest in traditional archery — if only they knew.

Trouble is, the longbow — and the recurved bow also — have been forgotten by most modern archers. These trusty, dependable weapons are now relegated to second-class status and are degraded by being referred to as "stick bows." The weapons which were good enough to build nations — the weapons which were capable of sending bodkin-tipped arrows through body armour — are now considered unfit to hunt with.

Such views of the traditional bow are surprisingly common even among the American archery establishment. The archery "industry" — as a group of lead-ing modern archery tackle manufacturers is wont to call itself — has shown little interest in traditional archery, even though increasing numbers of archers are switching back to traditional gear. Some remarks coming from the archery industry and its spokesmen have even gone so far as to suggest that conscien-tious hunting archers should not use "stickbows." A thinking bowhunter, they suggest slyly, should use only the "best" equipment he can afford. By "best," they usually mean the latest in high-tech gear.

Such remarks by the "industry" are, in my estimation, purely self-serving. My experience in more than a dozen years of outfitting and guiding archery hunters in Alaska has taught me to expect precisely the opposite. In other words, the higher percentage of the hit-and-unrecovered big game connected with my hunting operation has been at the hands of hunters who were using modern compound bows and aluminum arrows with high-tech modular broadheads. Perhaps that's because bowhunters who use traditional gear are generally more experienced, whereas the neophyte archer most often buys the flashy, high-tech gear he sees advertised in the archery publications. At any rate, I can cite several examples if anyone wants to pursue the subject.

Surely the recent surge of interest in traditional archery presents a threat to the American archery establishment. After all, if the tastes of the American consumer were to switch completely to the longbow and recurve, many of the big tackle manufacturers would be in financial trouble.

To be certain, there is less money to be made from building traditional archery gear. The making of traditional tackle is labor-intensive and time-consuming. Such bows cannot be cranked out by modern production methods, but must be crafted almost entirely by hand. There is little profit to be made in building the traditional English-style longbow of crooked yew, and virtually none in building an Asiatic composite bow of horn, wood, and sinew. These latter bows sometimes take months to complete. Building them is not cost-effective for the archery manufacturer who relies on modern production methods and capital intensive industries.

Modern archery manufacturers prefer to build and market the sort of bows which utilize metal handles, steel cables, eccentric magnesium pulleys and other machined parts. Such equipment can be cranked out and assembled quickly on the production line with a minimum of time and labor. Even though mass-produced, the flashy, modern equipment easily dazzles the beginning archer because it is so heavily promoted and advertised — often with photos and testimonials from paid hunters who have used the new products to rack up impressive numbers of big game kills.

The neophyte archer, who has been force-fed on this diet of advertising and promotion, sees the results and is made to believe that true success (as in terms of game kills or higher target scores) will come his way if only he purchases the new archery products.

We live in a fast-paced, competitive society. In it, success is measured mostly in materialistic terms — not in such values as personal growth and self-satisfaction. Satisfaction, most believe, is to be found sitting astraddle a buck deer, no matter what methods are used to get there — and certainly not from stalking through the woods with your handcrafted traditional bow. Many American archers have not been informed of the differences between quality bowhunting and taking the easy way out. And there are certainly easier ways to bowhunting success these days than by using the methods of Ishi and Pope and Young!

Greed and laziness, however, is not without its price. An unfortunate side-effect of the results-oriented philosophy of modern archery is that certain qualities which made it unique have been lost, thus cheapening the sport and causing it to lose much of its magic and its appeal. At the same time, there seems to be a growing backlash against archery hunting. Only a few short years ago the bowyer's art and the appeal of traditional archery had all but disappeared. Robin Hood and Ishi seemed to have been replaced by Rambo and bowhunting celebrities. The romance of archery and the spiritualism of the natural world had given way to high-tech efficiency and a "whack'em" mentality, with its emphasis on steaming gut piles.

There's an old Chinese saying that, "Where everyone sees beauty, there is already ugliness." This adage is just as true in America. Don't think for a minute that the American public does not recognize the ugliness which has crept into our sport.

Consider, for a moment, the public icons of bowhunting — that image, or images, which exist in the mind of the public. In the early days of archery hunting, the icons of our sport were strong and positive. In the early part of this century, Art Young and Saxton Pope were seen as heroes, for they represented the epitome of American self-reliance, hardihood, and sportsmanship. Not surprisingly, their adventures were frequently written up in such prestigious publications as Harpers. Howard Hill was a frequent guest on such television shows as Art Linkletter's. Fred Bear's hunting trips were glowingly written about in such national magazines as Time.

Are we getting this sort of favorable publicity today? Hardly!

The most recent coverage of bowhunting I saw on television showed a well-known bowhunting rock star shooting a domesticated/feral pig from an elevated tree stand. The graphic film sequence showed the pig as it was shot through the chest with an aluminum arrow from a high-powered compound device. The camera zoomed in as the pig ran around frantically and then fell on the ground, kicking and squealing as only a pig can squeal. The sequence was revolting, even to a hunter. And it was shown on prime-time national television.

Such negative publicity only reinforces the distorted public perception of bowhunters as a bunch of camo-clad, kill-crazy dilettantes armed with space-age shooting devices which operate with pin-point precision. The public at large never gets to hear about the traditional archer who stalks quietly and who truly loves the woods and its wild inhabitants.

We seem burdened down by our negative "Rambo" image. The word "bowhunting" has begun to convey such images as Space-age archery equipment, camo clothing, treestands, and bait stations — images which are not entirely positive in the mind of the public.

Fortunately, there is a growing cadre of tradition-oriented archers who not only recognize the ugliness which has crept into our sport, but are willing to put forth the sweat and hard work which go into true archery. They are learning that real satisfaction in archery doesn't always come by taking the easy way out.

Learning to shoot a traditional bow is not easy. You can't just pick up a longbow or an Indian-style flatbow and learn to shoot tight groups with it in a single afternoon. It takes perseverance and hard work. Making traditional bows and arrows isn't easy either. But both making traditional gear and becoming proficient with it are well within the reach of an individual who is truly dedicated to archery. And the results are well worth the effort!

My own experience in archery, which now has spanned close to 30 years, has come around full-circle. I started out in the mid-1960's by making self wood bows of Pacific yew and Osage orange and then graduated to laminated long-bows of yew and fiberglass. After that I began building heavy-handled laminated recurved bows of maple and fiberglass and experimented with such things as overdraw systems and even bow sights. My arrows evolved along with my bows, starting out with birch dowels and Port Orford cedar and then changing to fiberglass and, for a short time, even aluminum alloy.

As my archery gear grew more sophisticated my success rates on large and small game went up drastically. The bows I designed, built and used in hunting would cast a fiberglass or aluminum arrow with great speed and accuracy. I came to feel supreme confidence, to honestly think that any animal within 40 yards was as good as hanging on the meat pole. A few of my kills were a lot further than that.

I never switched to the compound device and so I never completely abandoned traditional archery. However, it was obvious that at the peak of my deviation from tradition, my equipment had slowly, inexorably, moved toward greater and greater sophistication. As it did, my archery tackle seemed to become more impersonal, more inanimate. Although highly efficient, the fiber-glass-laminated recurved bows were heavy in the hand and awkward to carry in the brush. The bow quivers I often used added even more weight to the heavy-handled bows, making them feel less a part of me. I began to feel as if my bow and arrows were a thing — no longer an extension of my body.

From time to time I'd get this little feeling of nostalgia as I recalled my first season of bowhunting. I'd remember the light-as-a-feather feel of a yew wood bow in my hand and the soft, musical hum of its bowstring as a cedar arrow leaped forward in flight. I could almost smell the aroma of the linseed oil I rubbed on my bows before heading out on a somber November morning. I could almost hear the soft rustle of a dozen broadhead-tipped wood arrows in my oiled leather back quiver.

Like many other American archers, I came to feel distress at the direction archery seemed to be headed. Something valuable was being lost here. I began to understand how the Plains Indian and the mountain man felt when they saw buffalo trails being plowed under and traversed by the steel tracks of the railroads.

As the rising tide of high-tech archery gear became a flood, I began to feel as though I were being swept further and further away from true archery. More and more I began to miss the type of archery I had seen practiced by the old-time archer/bowyers of Oregon — men like Gilman Keasey and Earl Ullrich. My nostalgic longing for the old archery was becoming stronger even while everyone else seemed happily engaged with the new high-tech toys.

One cold November day, while making an annual sojourn to the Oklahoma woods of my youth, I found myself wandering the plowed fields of a river bottom farm, looking for arrowheads. On my brother's land, near the confluence of two creeks, was an ancient Indian village site; the plowed ground was strewn with chert flakes and chips and broken points. Nearby, in the rich soil of the river bottom, were hundreds of bois d' arc, or Osage orange, trees growing straight and tall.

The discovery of the ancient artifacts provided fuel for my imagination; the Osage orange wood provided the natural raw material. Together, they would send me on a path away from modern archery. At first I was reluctant to abandon modern methods of bow-making; I cut down half a dozen Osage trees, had the wood ground into laminations and used the laminations to build several wood-fiberglass recurves and longbows, all of which had small, traditional-type handle risers. For reasons I didn't understand at the time, I could not bring myself to build a heavy-handled bow with these Osage laminations, which I considered special. I instinctively felt that whatever bows I made from this wood must at least have a traditional design, even though I would laminate them with fiberglass on the back and belly. So I designed a short recurve bow, 60-inches overall length, with a small, longbow-type handle. I used the bows to take several big game animals.

After turning the corner which would take me back to traditional archery it wasn't long before I began making sinew-backed Osage bows. Sinew is a remarkable material, and when combined with good bow wood will make a bow which will rival the best glass laminated bows built. I've made several sinew-backed bows in the 60-70 lb class which will send a 500-grain field arrow through the chronograph at well over 180 feet per second — every bit as good as most of my wood-glass laminated bows will do. Sinew-backed bows are dependable and have a long life, plus, working with sinew and hide glue is much better for your health than keeping your hands immersed in epoxy resins and breathing fiberglass dust into your lungs!

After having made and shot sinew-backed bows exclusively now for the past several years, I'm sold on them more than ever. They are fast and they are durable, for the sinew backing makes a good wooden bow almost unbreakable and greatly extends its life.

At the start of this transition period — which for me began about a decade ago — there was no existing network of archery traditionalists. But unbeknownst to me, there were plenty of other archers out there who also were dissatisfied with modern archery. Most of us had simply followed our instincts in returning to traditionalism, feeling that if archery stayed the present course, we would, in the words of old-time archer Glenn St. Charles, "re-invent the wheel." That is, we would continue to improve the efficiency of archery equipment until we ended up with a crossbow or a bow-gun.

Several years ago this back-to-the-basics movement really began building, and as things swung back toward the old archery, traditional archery shoots began springing up all across the U.S. and Canada. Traditional archery books and publications started rolling off the presses. These developments were a sure sign that thousands of American archers were equally fed up with the way archery had gone high-tech.

Now, midway through 1992, archery traditionalism is stronger than ever. This is a refreshing change, for it means, among other things, that the forms of archery practiced long ago on the Steppes of Mongolia, in the forests of North America, on the African veldt, and in the sunny glades of England will continue to live on. It means that such desirable qualities as woodsmanship, self-reliance, resourcefulness, and hardihood — important attributes in any society — will once again be appreciated. The traditional archery movement means that taking game with the bow and arrow will once again be a meaningful event.

I hope Volume II of *The Traditional Bowyer's Bible* will help archers everywhere recapture the romance and excitement of our rich archery past. And to the contributors and the readers of this book, I extend a hearty salute, for these people represent that which I most respect and admire in the world of archery. Things which are truly worthwhile do not usually come easily, and to strive toward them is to gain strength of character.

BOWS FROM BOARDS

Tim Baker

Consider this quote: "Kiln dried-wood is brittle and will NOT make a bow...[it] was responsible for many of my early bow failures."— *Bows and Arrows of the Native Americans,* by yes, our own Jim Hamm.

Many archery luminaries of past and present report similar experiences. The next several pages could easily be filled with sad accounts of failed lumber bows. Its easy to see why the you-can't-make-bows-from-boards rumor got started.

But bows made from kiln-dried lumberyard boards can be as efficient and durable as bows made from air-dried staves, and often more so. And on the face of it, why shouldn't they? After all, kiln-dried wood is *wood*! And in fact, kiln-dried wood *is* air dried!

But the final, definitive reason kiln-dried boards will make safe, efficient bows is this:

Even if a kiln-dried board suffered all the damage it is sometimes alleged to have suffered, this board would still have *some* strength, and *some* flexibility.

It would be weaker and less elastic wood, but this is no obstacle to us. We now know how to make safe, efficient bows from "inferior" wood. *Make the limbs wider!*

If a hypothetical kiln-degraded stave of heavier rock maple descended to the energy-storage capacity of lighter red oak, for example, what have we lost? Only this: we would have the same weight bow but about 15% more limb mass, resulting in about 3 fps slower cast. This reduction in cast, incidentally, would be canceled out by the superior performance of the rectangular cross-section.

But it's unlikely you will encounter this weaker-per-mass board. In practice, a stave is no more likely to be degraded during its pampered, controlled visit to a modern kiln than by typical air-drying.

A phone call or so ago Jim off-handedly mentioned the latest bow he'd made: a 70 lb maple longbow ... from a kiln-dried board. He now visibly winces when reminded of that anti-board passage, wishing he could reach back in time and hit the delete button.

In early editions of *The Bent Stick,* Paul Comstock presented "Ten Commandments For Your First Wooden Bow," commandment number four being, "Thou shalt not use Kiln-dried wood." Comstock apparently has taken another walk up the mountain, for later editions list "Nine Commandments."

Manuel Lizarralde shoots a maple workhorse which has cast thousands of arrows, enough to have worn out seven strings. Typical of other properly made board bows, it shows no more set or strain than when new. All evidence shows that bows made from any of the available kiln-dried hardwoods equal the performance and durability of tree-split counterparts.

Both Hamm and Comstock insisted their conversions be reported here. Like most post-fiberglass woodbow makers they want the straight dope to get out, deriving more satisfaction from the rough and tumble exchange of information and experience than the false safety of dogma. A very different attitude from that of close-to-the-vest pre-fiberglass bowmakers and archers. One possible reason for this is that today's woodbow makers are largely hunters and not target shooters. True hunting, after all, requires analytical, skeptical thinking, and being open to new directions.

We are currently part of a woodbow renaissance. Imperfect conventions are being exposed to fresh air and sunlight. But one still wonders how anti-kiln dried rumors survived so long. Here are some possible reasons:

- As with other archery misinformation, one writer honestly reports a prevailing belief, and subsequent writers use this first report as a reference.
- Cause and prevention of internal cell collapse during kiln-drying was not well understood in the past.
- Kiln-dried staves are most often used by beginners, and beginners break bows.
- Virtually all kiln-dried wood is in board form. Unlike unmilled trees, board surfaces seldom parallel growth rings. Internal wood fibers and the weak, porous early growth ring approaches the bow's back at some angle. When

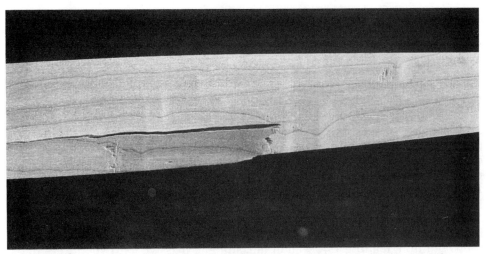

From an improperly selected, improperly prepared board, this limb was destined to fail. When making bows from tree-split staves, conforming to the peculiarities of the stave is half the skill. When making bows from boards, learning to read wood fiber is half the skill.

stressed, these porous rings and severed wood fibers are no longer being pulled longitudinally, the direction of wood's greatest strength. Instead they are literally peeled apart.

Over the last few years I have made approximately 350 bows from kiln-dried lumber. None of the last 250 broke, or even took a large set. And their performance is indistinguishable from same-design conventionally-cured staves. For reasons explained in detail farther on, I have come to prefer lumber staves.

Because of the momentum of dogma, many cannot easily accept the equality of board and tree-split staves. In the beginning I felt the same. Part of the motive for developing the Standard Wood Bending Test (p. 100, Vol. l) was to discover how inferior kiln-dried lumber was. When the tests instead began extolling boards staves, I doubted the test. Even after validating it with prediction-verifying lumber bows, I still felt uneasy.

Learning that other bowmakers have had good results with lumber staves relieved much of the unease. Professional bowyer Ron Hardcastle in Texas, Ben Walker in Canada, and others, have used lumber staves for years. In addition to his conventional staves and bows, Ron has begun supplying edge and bias-ringed staves and finished bows of hickory and maple. Due to their more rectangular cross-sections, both generally out-perform conventional staves.

BUT WHY USE BOARD STAVES?

Safe, efficient bows can be made from boards. But so what? Excellent bows have been made from split staves for millennia. Why change now?

There is no reason to *change*. Conventional staves will always likely be the best choice for most bowmakers. Board staves merely expand options.

For some, however, lumberyard staves can make the difference between having a bow and not having a bow.

Consider the following:

— You can have a bow *today!* If your bow breaks, or if one morning you suddenly get the impulse to make a bow, you can do so, and be hunting with it *that afternoon.*

— Even the less-expensive white-wood stave suppliers charge five to ten times the average price of a board stave. Board staves are an inexpensive way to learn the craft.

— If you live in a bowwood desert. Trees grow best in the summer. So when does it rain in California? In the winter! California is called the Golden State because of its rolling hills of dead summer grass. This state, especially my part of it, has endless vistas of no trees. Local oaks, with their drought-thin growth rings, could have been used, but straight staves of good length are rare. Bay Area Indians, it appears, largely acquired their bows by trade with Sierra Miwoks.

I was once bemoaning this local dearth of bowwood to Paul Comstock. His return letter enclosed a 3" by 5" photo of an Eastern country road. The road had been cut through a forest. A wall of tall, straight, massive hardwood trees filled the picture. On the back of the photo Comstock had written, "See any bow wood here?"

Most of the North American hardwoods have been planted locally, but they're in yards and parks. I won't say how many times I've acquired staves by acts resting between larceny and a bad pruning job. That is, before discovering lumber staves.

DIFFERENCES BETWEEN BOARD STAVES AND SPLIT STAVES

Because of controlled drying rates and conditions kiln-dried wood is often superior to air-dried wood.

Air drying is more likely to yield bacterial decay, insect damage, warped, and checked staves. Most competent wood bowmakers have evolved stave curing systems which work for their local woods and climate. But if you ever find yourself in the company of wood bowmakers, don't bring up the subject of purchased staves. Unless you want to hear grown men moan, swear, and tell competing horror stories. If tree-split staves are not very carefully seasoned they will be inferior to kiln-dried counterparts.

Kiln drying is more likely to cause internal cell collapse: High temperatures partially plasticize cellulose in wood cells. In extreme cases a surface which dries too fast will compress its wetter, weaker core, collapsing these plasticized cells. But unlike earlier times, the causes of such collapse are well understood now, and easily avoided.

Too-rapid air drying can collapse core cells also, especially with larger diameter stock. Direct sun, low humidity, and brisk winds cause surface wood to dry and shrink much faster than core-wood.

When done properly, both drying methods yield equally straight and strong bows.

When done improperly, both methods leave tell-tale clues: Sunken or rippled surfaces point to cell collapse. Avoid checked and warped wood, regardless of how it was dried.

Maybe one board in 25 shows some sign of drying damage, usually only mild

Arriving at the lumberyard at about 8.5% moisture content, two weeks of basement seasoning rehydrated this board. Now at 10% and ideal for my near-the-bay microclimate. Five miles east, just over the Berkeley Hills, 8.5% would be ideal.

checking. Inspecting for these signs of damage pays off. After making hundreds of bows from kiln-dried staves, I can't report a single example of failure due to kiln-damage.

One misconception concerning kiln-dried wood is that it is too dry. Force-drying wood with artificial heat is expensive. Taking moisture content lower than equilibrium is bad business. Hardwoods generally leave the kiln at about 8%, just right for moderately dry areas of the continent. Wood headed for moister areas often leaves the kiln at an appropriately higher moisture content — hardwoods shipped to Louisiana often being damper than if shipped to Arizona.

A lumberyard stave is more likely to be close to local equilibrium than a local air-dried stave. Unless reduced to near-tillered dimensions, wood takes a very long time to reach local equilibrium.

As with any stave acquired from outside your area, allow time for de- or re-hydration to local equilibrium. Once reduced to slightly-bending blanks, only a few days are usually needed. Here too, a moisture meter or a balance beam is helpful — balance the stave on one end of a fairly long, light rod, an equal weight on the other. Suspend the rod at its point of balance by a string. As the stave gains or loses moisture, it will rise or fall. Adjust the string to keep the rod parallel to the ground. When no change in balance has occurred for a few days, the stave has reached equilibrium.

Wood strength, or stiffness, rises about 6% per 1% change in moisture content. This means same draw-weight bows made of wetter wood will have more mass. Drier wood will have less mass, but be more brittle. 8% to 11% is a good range. Between 9% and 10% is ideal.

Another misconception is that kiln-drying damages wood due to overheating. This after centuries of successful steambending at 212-degrees. Kilns generally operate at about 170 degrees.

Steam bending weakens wood by up to 25%, depending on the severity of the bend. But safe bows nevertheless result because tillering compensates: weaker portions are automatically left thicker. The same tiller-induced strengthening should occur in staves with mild cell collapse; again, weaker areas are left thicker, and are therefore stronger.

THE ETHICS OF LUMBER BOWS

But is it right to make bows from boards? Isn't this cheating?

No!

Lumberyard boards are not some de-natured, synthetic material. Boards are *wood*! They came from *trees*!

Since the beginning of archery, staves have been traded from far away places. Since the beginning staves have been edge and bias-ringed. Since the beginning staves have been quickly heat-dried.

As for the indignity of being milled to unnatural, ungraceful, uniform dimensions … you have the opportunity to free them from this.

NAVIGATING THROUGH LUMBER

The "Design and Performance" chapter in Vol. 1 describes the superior performance of several lumber bows. Possibly a majority of readers were new to natural archery. They approached the subject of board staves without pre-conceptions. From the number of good results reported by Volume 1 readers, nearly as many board bows may be made this year as tree-stave bows the year before.

But there were some disasters. Robert Howard broke 14 lumber bows in a row. Showing even more determination, he drove several hundred miles for the shattered limbs to be autopsied. His tillering was excellent, especially the last several. Limb width was proper. Cross-sections were good. But there were two problems, neither of which would have caused certain failure alone: One, his staves, having been stored in an uninsulated barn in inland Southern California, had a moisture content of 5%. Two, rings ran from back to belly through the boards at an average angle of about 5 degrees. These staves had not been selected by culling, but had been given to him by a friend. He used them largely to avoid seeming ungrateful.

On his return home, he picked up a new, straight-ringed ash lumberyard board, and with the practice of 14 bows under his belt had it tillered and shooting the same day.

Yes, highest-quality bows can be made of lumber, but doing so is very much like walking through traffic. Send a convention of sleep walkers across the city during rush hour and maybe only one out of twenty will make it — but only because they didn't see the red lights and crosswalks. Make bows from boards

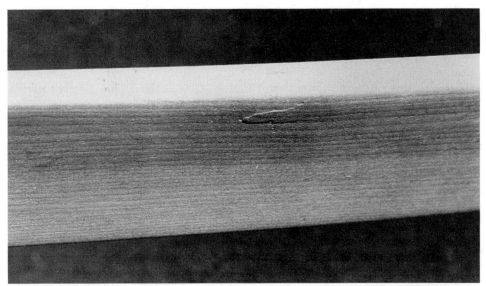

Back surface ring lines on this edge-ringed limb look straight, but wood fibers run through the limb from back to belly at about 5 degrees. If this had been the only problem, this two-inch wide limb, drawing 50 lb., would normally have held together, but with a moisture content of 5% wood becomes too brittle, at normal limb widths.

Robert Howard with bow number 15. Sixty-six inches from nock to nock, 2 1/16" wide from grip to mid-limb, then tapering to 1/2" nocks. These rectangular-section ash limbs draw 74# at 28". Bob tillered this bow from a $5 board stave.

selected at random, or donated, and maybe one out of twenty will make it also.

Making a durable bow from a tree-split stave is a midday taxi cab ride. Making a durable bow from lumber requires carefully reading the signs.

Board bows are considerably quicker and easier to make. And usually shoot faster.

Noticing this often superior performance of board bows led to **decrowned** tree-stave bows, and their usually faster and safer performance.

In other words it is often better *to convert tree staves into board staves!*

Here is worst-case proof of the advantage of "lumberizing" tree staves: My friend Bob Beene recently UPS'ed me a small log of willow. As per request, he had selected a straight, 3" diameter log, 68" long, Willow is about the worst possible stave choice, being weak in both compression and tension, as well as low in elasticity. Typically, Indian willow bows are longer than normal, and often intentionally deflexed to diminish limb strain. Despite these design accommodations such willow bows must be of low draw weight, or low draw length.

The goal with Bob's willow log was to see just how efficient a willow bow could be. A Standard Bend Test indicated that a 3" wide limb of this wood should make a 35 lb bow, giving moderate string follow. The test also showed that compared to stronger wood, this willow had more mass per unit of stored energy, enough to lower cast by a few fps. When tillered to 35 lb at 27" of draw, limbs took a 1 3/4 set. The bow shot a 500 grain arrow 124 fps, about 5 fps slower than if made from stronger, more mass/energy efficient wood using the same design. Decrowning raised willow's performance from extremely low up to the near-average range. In fact, this willow bow far out-performs many bows of "superior" wood, proving again that design is far more important than wood type.

At 50 lbs. of draw weight, willow bow limbs of this length must exceed 4" in width to be efficient. Given proper width and rectangular cross-sections, weak wood and strong wood limbs perform about equally. But the cumbersome size of weak wood bows limits their use.

Edge and bias ringed bows are not new. Prehistoric European bows were

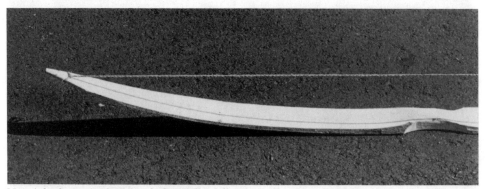

Ungainly, but quite functional, this 35 lb., full-draw willow bow illustrates the benefits of "lumberizing" staves from small and medium diameter trees (note bark on side of bow). If left with its natural crown intact, wedge-shaped edges would lower effective limb width to about 2", with the crowned center carrying an unfair, bowbreaking share of the load.

A decrowned Osage orange stave, shown actual size. Without decrowning, this small diameter piece of wood could only have made a low weight bow, or one excessively long and inefficient.

The back of the bow, after decrowning. The lines running the length of the bow are the early and late-wood rings which are cut through. As long as the lines run parallel with the limb, this design is virtually as durable and safe as a bow made from a regular stave. Wood with close yearly growth rings, as small pieces usually are, will show multiple lines on the back and be easier to read. What about the knots in a piece of Osage this small? By using a pocketknife or scraper to remove wood in the final stages and keep the lines straight, the knots are automatically compensated for and raised, very much like connecting the dots and just as easy.

Finished bow, 68" long, 60 lbs. at 28". Decrowning allowed a character-laden, durable, full-weight hunting weapon to be made from otherwise scrap wood.

often decrowned, or edge and bias ringed, as Paul Comstock explains elsewhere in this volume.

Logs generally follow the grain when split. The flat, open face of a split log therefore tends to present a surface of full-length, unbroken fibers, in perfect parallel with the tree. Such a split face invites itself to be a virtually-finished, board-like bow back or belly.

There is one occasional danger with backs taken from the middle or near-middle of trees. Should a small surface branch occur somewhere along the split the branch root can run straight across half the stave's exposed surface to the core. When placed under tension this seriously weakens the limb. If the center-split surface is worked down a half-inch or so, or if the log is cut or split just off-center, limb roots then run through the stave at an angle, reducing the percentage of limb width put in jeopardy. Another option is using the center-split face as belly. This requires decrowning, and results in back-side handle risers.

Quarter-split faces can also be used as backs or bellies. But a surface branch can now run across the face's full width.

Some species split cleaner than others, and are therefore better suited to this technique. Birch, mulberry, ash, and locust, for example, usually split cleanly. Osage, and elm on the other hand, leave deeply furrowed, coarse-splintered faces.

Half or quarter-split faces of clean-splitting woods make convenient back or belly surfaces. Note how branches occuring near the split disturb and endanger surface wood across the entire quarter-split face.

Board bows often out-perform tree-stave bows because they more often end up having rectangular cross-sections. Such sections can be wider without over-straining otherwise thicker central crowns. All portions of a rectangular section do equal work.

One caution with rectangular cross-sections: because all portions of rectangular sections do equal work, edges are more strained than on unevenly working, thin-edged, crowned limbs. Edge fibers are therefore more likely to begin lifting. This is especially true on steeply width-tapered limbs, since wood fibers are exposed at sharper angles. The back corners of rectangular limbs should be rounded slightly, to about the curvature of a small pea. The Grim Reaper of bows then has no place under which to get his fingernails.

Perfectly tillered limbs are far less likely to break or take a deep set. With a board-flat back, half of the potential for error in thickness tapering is eliminated. And thickness tapering is easier to judge. All parts of limb width and length end up carrying more equal load. This results in less set, less mass, and more safety.

The extra hour, and effort, spent selecting superior boards is like the extra hours spent moving through a forest. Selecting the one perfect board in the stack is like selecting the one best tree in the woods.

The "pyramid" limb design, discussed on page 67 of Volume 1, may be the most efficient straight-stave bow possible. But its wide, flat, near-handle limbs require far more time and effort to make than traditional designs. Flat board staves solve much of this problem.

Given a straight-stave, and a given draw weight, the bow pictured might be the fastest individual wood bow made since archery began. The reason, of course, is its design.

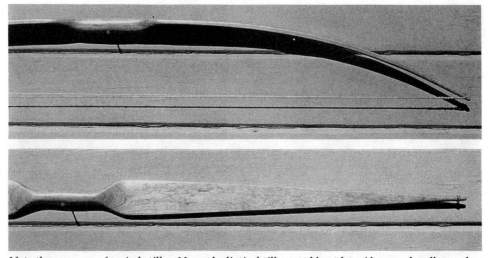

Note the more arc-of-a-circle tiller. Normal, eliptical tiller would not let wide, near-handle wood do its fair share of work, forcing too-narrow mid limbs to over-work. Back rings of this black cherry bow were violated fairly seriously here, but the large total square-inches of working surface lowered stress sufficiently at any one point.

A bow of this design is not just faster. Its wide limbs make it safer, and permit very little performance-robbing set. Its length and tiller yield a sweet, low-stack draw, and high energy storage. Its narrow, low mass outer limbs and tips yield a virtually shock-less release. Although fairly long, its light tips do not appreciably slow cast. It could also be designed somewhat shorter. Shorter bows stack more severely than longer bows, causing less energy to be stored. But this bow needs less energy because its low-mass tips return more quickly. And with its bend-more-near-the-grip design limbs do not shorten as much at full draw. As a result this design does not stack as badly as normally tillered limbs of equal length.

This bow is a ringer, and easily used for hustling out-of-town archers stopping in at The Bowmakers' Bar, where the chronograph is always lit and waiting…

With a medium-weight string and 28" draw, this 53 lb bow shoots a 500-grain arrow 164 fps. This equals the cast of "straight-stave" fiberglass laminate long-bows.

Limbs are 3" wide at the grip, tapering in straight lines to just over 1/4" nocks. Too narrow to accept conventional string grooves, a shoulder of fiber is wrapped and glued on instead. These wide limbs take just 3/4" set when first unstrung.

Grip length is 6". Two inches longer than needed, but this extra length offers several advantages. It's long enough to allow the arrow to pass slightly above grip center. Each limb is of equal length. The bow can therefore be tillered symmetrically. Both limbs are strained equally, and tiller is easier to judge. Obviously, either end of this bow can be the top end. This is a nice option because most wooden bows shoot better from one side than the other.

For those with an artistic sense (no such claim is made here), such wide limbs are a canvas, inviting the painting of natural or geometric designs, as for example, on Western Indian bows.

Idaho bowyer Rob Young, with a 56", 57 lb. Modoc style bow. Its near-pyramid design, and more circular tiller, gives this shorter bow the low-stack energy storage of a longer design (photo Al Young).

With pressure from the bow hand resting almost at center, and the arrow passing just above center, drawing forces are about as balanced as can be reasonably attained. This no doubt partly accounts for some of the reduced handshock in bows of this design.

The extra two inches of grip length must, of course, be added to limb length, maintaining an equal length of working wood. This extra bow length does not alter efficiency: the amount and length of moving wood is virtually the same as on a bow two inches shorter but having a 4" grip.

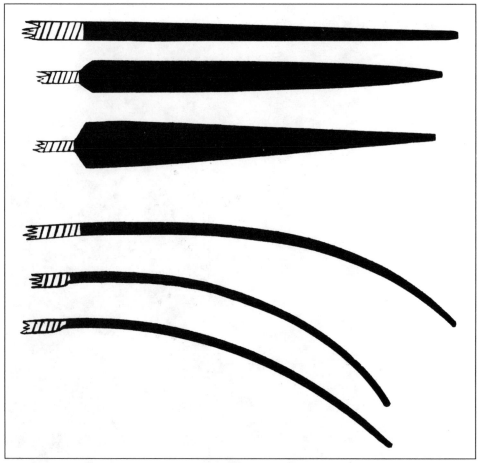

Thicker wood will not bend as far, or accept as much set, as thin wood. A 4" by 6" timber accepts little of either before breaking. On the other hand, a thin wood shaving exhibits both in the extreme. Pyramid limbs are tillered by width tapering, not thickness tapering. Near-grip wood is therefore thinner than on thickness-tapered, more parallel-width limbs, and capable of more bend near the handle. As front-view limb shape moves from pyramid to parallel, side-view shape moves from circular to elliptical.

To get the most from this pyramid design tillering must be more circular than elliptical.

Conventional bow limbs taper not just in width, but thickness. Thicker, gripward portions of a limb can not bend or take as much set as thinner tipward portions. For this reason properly tillered, evenly strained limbs take on elliptical tiller.

But the more pyramid-like a limb is designed, the more it tapers in width, and the less it tapers in thickness. *As front-view limb shape progresses from parallel to pyramid, tiller shape will progress from elliptical to circular.* Perfectly pyramid-shaped limbs, as geometry will have it, are perfectly uniform in limb thickness from tip to grip. Therefore they can accept equal bend, or arc of a circle tillering. With this slight modification:

Small degrees of set taken near the grip will project out to large tip deflex. To avoid such cast-robbing string follow, tiller pyramid limbs to bend s-l-i-g-h-t-l-y less than circular near the grip, just enough less to take no set.

SELECTING A BOARD STAVE

The potential weakness of board staves over tree-split staves lies in the fact that surface **fibers** are more likely to be violated on the bow's back. When selecting board staves this is the main concern.

On conventional flat-ringed staves and on edge or bias-ringed staves, longitudinal wood fibers on the bow's back perform all the tension work. If these fibers are parallel and unsevered for their entire length, the back will have maximum strength. If back fibers are not parallel to either side or top views, fibers are necessarily severed. When board bows break it is generally because of such severed back fibers, not weakened bellies. Tapered belly surfaces seldom follow rings or fibers, anyway — on board staves or tree-split staves.

When selecting board staves choose those whose back surfaces are, or can be, trimmed so that surface fibers parallel the bow limb from both top and side view. This emphasis of fibers over rings or grain is new to bowmaking, and needs explanation:

Imagine that a tree grows by adding annual rings composed of parallel

Conventional, decrowned, bias,
and edge-ringed cross-sections.

strands of fairly coarse string, weakly glued together. If a conventional stave is taken from this tree the untouched, under-the-bark, outside of the tree will be the bow's back. Full-length, parallel, unbroken strings will be visible on such a back.

Now imagine the outer layer of strings was damaged when the bark was removed. Discard the damaged strings, working down into the log, staying parallel with the original tree surface as you go down, until you arrive at an unmarred surface of uncut, full-length strings.

If, when preparing a bow's back, you do not stay parallel with the tree's surface, back strings are no longer full-length. They are "stepped." And when the bow is bent, when the back is strained in tension, *fibers attempt to peel apart.* And the limbs soon shatter.

Now imagine removing a bias-ringed stave from this string-and-glue tree. Keep the stave parallel with the tree's longitudinal surface so that full-length, uncut fibers continue to make up its back. Since the same number of full-length fibers comprise the backs of both flat and bias-ringed bows both backs will have equal strength in tension. If this bias-ringed stave was not kept parallel with the tree's surface its fibers would not run full length. They would be stepped, as with the angled-stave, above, and would be equally weakened.

An individual tree fiber does not care if it is being strained in a flat, edge, or bias ringed limb. It feels the same forces in each case. Fibers in a living tree may bend to an easterly wind one day, a northerly wind the next.

If an edge or bias-ringed bow's back is comprised of full-length, parallel, unsevered wood fibers, it will be as strong as a pristine tree-split stave (with two exceptions, explained later).

The reason we have been told to keep a bow's back within one growth ring is that by doing so we automatically remain fairly parallel with the tree's longitudinal fibers. To use Bill Vonderhey's term, a growth ring is merely a visual aid.

The **angle of violation** of wood fibers determines limb safety. This insight can be applied to conventional, flat-ringed, tree-split staves as well: For highest back

Whether flat, edge, or bias ringed, if a stave is milled out of side-view parallel with its original tree surface, its back fibers are "stepped through" and severed.

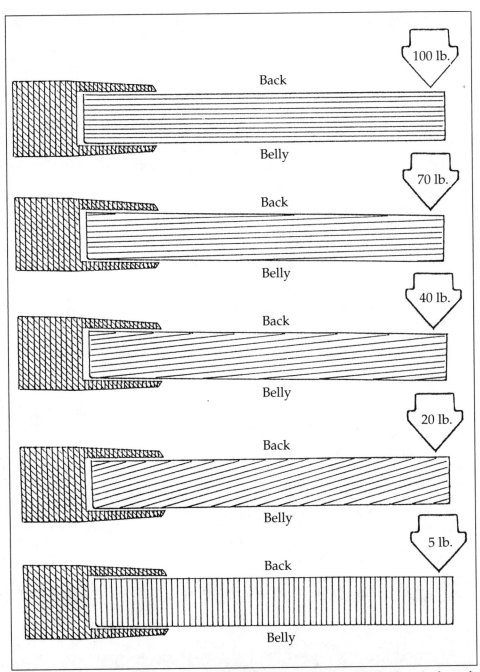

The angle at which fibers intersect a bow's back, determines back strength and safety. As the angle of violation increases less tension work is done by fibers, more by inter-fiber "glue." But wood's "glue" strength when under tension is insignificant compared to that of wood fiber.

Although made from a board, these bows look as if made from a tree-split stave. The board's back was square, or flat to the tree's original surface. Each bow's back was the crowned, under-bark surface of the tree some years back. Maybe one in 50 boards will yield such a waste-free, ready-to-tiller, conventionally-orientated stave. If willing to accept moderate trimming waste one in 25 might qualify.

strength and safety stay not just within an annual ring, but within a "monthly" ring as well. Preferably within a Fall, not early Summer "ring."

The simplest, most thought-free way of getting a bow from a board stave is to work down to one whole, flat growth ring, as if the board was merely a damaged tree-split stave.

Each growth ring in a board was the tree's outer ring some year in the past. Use your spokeshave as a time machine. Scrape back through the board's summers and winters, down to the first ring which covers a bow-sized area. On some boards this may only involve rounding edges to re-establish the tree's natural curvature.

This time-machine method of extracting bows from boards requires care, but not much thought. Following the natural surface of one growth ring, as on a conventional stave, is like navigating by following the coast line. There is no way to get lost. But when using boards whose faces are not flat-ringed we easily loose sight of land. To navigate we now need instruments. Rings are still used as landmarks, but indirectly.

Having been laid down on the surface of a tree as it grew, fibers are perfectly parallel with the tree's rings. Once you know how to read them, ring lines on edge and bias-ringed boards are perfect navigating instruments. They tell us precisely how to position the bow's back so it will be made up of parallel, unsevered, full-length fibers.

A perfect bias-ringed board. Ring lines are parallel to the bark from both side and edge views. The back of a bow made from this board is finished before starting.

The rare perfect, or near perfect, board, if 2" by 6" for example, might yield three self-riser bows. But if reduced to 3/4" thick staves, with glue-on risers, the same board will yield eight staves. At less than $3.50 per, at maple prices.

A board milled from a perfectly straight tree will have perfectly straight ring lines on both faces and sides. That is, if the board was milled parallel with both side-view and front-view planes of tree.

Ninety-degree edge-ringed boards are the most difficult to read because no ring lines occur on the board's edge. But a close look at the edge will reveal the board's string-like fiber structure itself. Whether these fibers are parallel or not

If a board is milled at some angle to the tree's front-view vertical plane, its surface ring lines will still be straight, but not parallel to the board. Note edge-view ring lines seem to be angling through the board, although fibers are perfectly parallel with the board's surface. Edge-view ring lines indicate fiber orientation only when surface ring lines perfectly parallel the board's edge.

To extract perfect staves from such a board only requires trueing the board to the tree's front-view vertical plane, with the only cost being some loss of wood. Note that once the board has been cut parallel with surface ring lines, edge-view ring lines become parallel also.

The pencil line shows this board's true fiber path. If a pure edge-ringed board was milled at some angle to the tree's side-view plane, or if the tree was wavy from its side-view, its surface fibers cannot be parallel to the board. They are stepped, and severed, although the board's edge-ringed face may look perfectly normal, as in this example.

can now be judged directly. A low-power magnifying glass is helpful here. As illustrated in the above photo, a sharp-pointed object used to score the wood will usually follow the fiber path also.

If a board was milled at some angle to both tree planes perfect staves require trueing to both planes. The only loss being even more waste of wood.

Often boards are milled at fairly severe angles to the tree. When trueing such boards fibers may run through the board at too great an angle, actually running through the board from front to back before yielding full stave length. Here are two solutions:

This is an unorthodox move, and looks a bit peculiar, but is sometimes the only way. Stepping up at the grip is sometimes needed with damaged tree-split staves also. (Refer to drawing, opposite.)

If the run-through angle is extreme, even stepping-up at the grip will not yield a full-length stave. The only solution in such cases, assuming the board is two-limbs wide, is to cut out two side-by-side billets, splicing them together at the handle. See "Splices," Volume 1.

Ring islands can be worked down to proper original-tree-surface contour, creating a snaked, wavy, or kinked limb when viewed in profile. Unless the wave is minor, it's usually better to move on to a straighter-ringed board. But if the angle of violation is small it might be best to ignore the problem, thereby keeping the stave back perfectly flat. Snaked-profile limbs are harder to tiller perfectly. Snake limbs will therefore be slightly weaker, more massive, and take more set. The safety of straight, flat backs can compensate for the dangers of low-angle fiber violation. This is especially true for diffuse-porous staves, but less so on ring-porous wood. Ring-porous wood having moderately thin, fairly

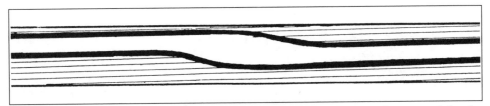

Begin trueing the board as usual, but only to the grip. Then rise up as many rings as needed and continue on to the other tip. This will only work with thick, non-bending grips.

Ring lines on the edge of an almost-90-degree, almost edge-ringed board are not accurate guides to fiber orientation. The smallest variation from parallel on the part of surface rings will cause edge-viewed ring lines to meander drunkenly.

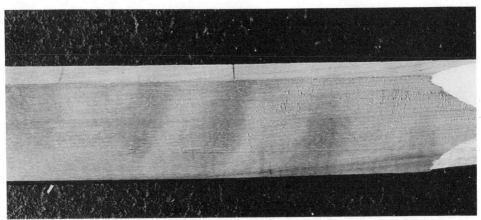

When held at certain angles to the light, boards from wavy-side-view trees reflect light where the board surface is parallel to a wave's crest and trough, but look dark at mid wave where fibers ends are severed and exposed. Spokeshaves, and other angle-bladed tools, tend to catch and tear at these open-ended fibers, a sure clue that fibers are not parallel to back surfaces.

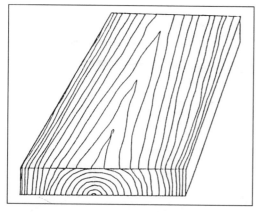

A near-center, vertical slice of a tree. Each edge is 90-degree edge-ringed, progressing through all angles of bias, becoming flat-ringed at center. This board was cut at some side-view angle to the tree. As a result, central ring lines display cone-like convergence. The more out of plane a board is cut, the sharper and shorter the cones. The entire board is out of plane, but note there is progressively less visible evidence of this moving from the flat-ringed center to the edge-ringed exterior.

strong early growth, like hickory, will tolerate greater angles of violation than wider, weak early-growth wood, like ash. Sometimes it's best to split the difference between staying board-flat and following natural contours.

But then there's this: It's as satisfying a challenge making "character" bows from board staves as from tree staves.

If one out of 25 boards will yield a stave — given moderate trimming waste, that number might fall to one in ten if the bow is backed. A less-perfect, to-be-backed, stave may display an oddly-ringed belly, but not so odd it won't do its job. Bellies are almost always violated anyway.

The strength and elasticity of backing materials should be matched to those of the wood to be backed.

Back a pine bow with a steel band. The bow will never break in tension, but it will take more set than if unbacked. The steel band is enormously stronger in tension, or resistant to stretch, than pine. As the bow is drawn the steel band

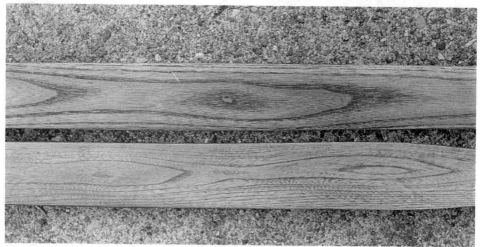

Islands, bowlegs, or knock-knees indicate hills or valleys in the original tree surface.

If you're having trouble determining fiber angles in a board here's a shortcut: Inspect all four corners; one will show converging "V's". Mentally peeling off one such "V" will expose original tree surface. You now have a zero-fiber-angle starting point as reference.

does not stretch. It therefore stores no energy. The pine is forced to store 100% of the bow's energy in compression alone! The result is greater than usual string follow.

This is an extreme example, but illustrates the point: Backings should have equal or lower stretch resistance than bellies have compression resistance.

Strong woods can have high stretch-resistant backs.

Weaker woods will take less set if backed with less stretch-resistant material.

Lighter woods will suffer unnecessary set if backed with hickory, bamboo, or linen, and will suffer again due to hickory's high mass. If light-woods are backed with hickory, the backing should be much thinner than usual. Ten percent of limb thickness is completely adequate. Hickory, and other strong-wood veneers, make adequate light-wood backing (see also Laminated All-Wood Bows, Vol. III).

For raw back protection plant fibers are unbeatable. Linen, for example, stretches 3% before breaking, compared to just over 1% for most woods. In addition, its breaking strength in tension is very high. One as-is board surface in ten might make a durable, serviceable bow if linen-backed.

Unless very gently twisted, reject boards from twisted trees. A flat stave from a twisted tree necessarily violates back fibers.

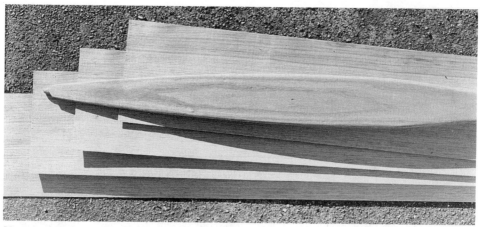

Veneers thick enough for backing can be purchased at better hardwood lumberyards. Selection ranges from hickory to pine, permitting low bend-strength woods to be backed with veneers having matching physical properties. Unlike rawhide, sinew, or other traditional natural-material backings, such veneer backed bows cannot be considered strictly primitive, although they are made from all natural materials.

Lighter wood can be efficiently backed with rawhide, gut, skin, silk, fiber, sinew, or cotton fibers. These backings are excellent heavy-wood backings also.

Elm is light weight, has high breaking strength in tension, and has lower stretch resistance than hickory. When backing light-wood limbs, elm performs better than hickory.

Traditionally-made flat-ringed bow limbs have a full, strong, summer-growth back surface. Edge and bias-ringed ring-porous back surfaces display a certain

Because of even large bamboo's relatively small diameter, bamboo backings are usually crowned. Wide, crowned limbs are less efficient. But even small diameter bamboo can be cut to narrow, parallel strips before applying, creating a flat backing. Split-bamboo window shades are an inexpensive source of pre-cut bamboo strips. Some shades are made of surface bamboo, others of interior splits. Bamboo's outer surface is stronger, tougher, more moisture resistant, and better looking.

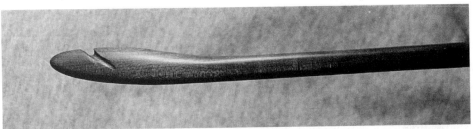

If you have to go down into a board to reach a useable growth ring you might leave grip and tips high, for grip comfort and slight recurve effect.

percentage of balsa-like early growth. Woods especially strong in tension such as hickory and elm do well. Neolithic European elm bows are commonly edge and bias-ringed, as are unbacked Pacific Coast bows.

LUMBERYARD WOODS

Hardwood suppliers are listed under "lumber" in the yellow pages. Often named So-and-So Hardwoods, Imported Woods, or Tropical Woods. If you see no such listing call the standard yard and ask what, if any, hardwoods they sell, or where else you might call.

Standard lumberyards will often have a small display of red oak and ash one-by. Larger hardware stores are also worth a try.

Superior bows can be made from hundreds of North American wood species, but only a dozen or so are available as lumber. In no particular order of preference, these are the most common:

Hickory	Red oak
Pecan	Black cherry
Rock or sugar maple	Redcedar
White ash	Birch
White oak	Black walnut

Other woods, even Osage, locust, or elm will sometimes appear in the stacks, but only rarely.

But don't forget the conifers: Fir, pine, and others. Heartwood from these species, when it contains a high percentage of late wood (the dark rings), makes fine bows. Occasionally old-growth fir heartwood boards with up to 40% or higher late wood can be found. Such fir will typically make bows equal in limb width, limb mass, and performance to low-medium weight hardwoods.

Many more tropical hardwoods are commercially available than North American hardwoods. Any of the heavier tropical woods will make serviceable bows. The following are more commonly available. When designed to proper width and cross-section each of these have made excellent bows.

Zebrawood	Bocote	Teak	Tulipwood
Goncalo alves	Kingwood	Satinwood	Greenheart
Lemonwood (degame)	Purpleheart	Cocobolo	Lancewood
Ebony	Padauk	Palm	Snakewood
Wenge	Rosewood	Pernambuco	Ipe
Bubinga			

Purpleheart frets sooner than its mass would have you expect, and teak fails sooner in tension, but if limbs are made slightly wider than normal each is perfectly safe.

Tropical woods are expensive, often selling by the pound instead of the board foot. They shoot no faster, smoother, quieter, or safer than our native hardwoods. Their appeal is in their color, and availability.

Even if a member of a save-the-rainforest organization you can buy these woods with clear conscience. The rainforests, and our primitive-archery kin who inhabit them, are being leveled primarily for cattle grazing and agriculture. Following far distant are furniture, veneer, tool handles, dowels, etc. The percentage of rain-forest wood converted to self bows would require too many zeros to express here. Substituting a few pounds of venison for beef will more than even the score.

One problem with lumber staves is that unless willing to accept a high percentage of trimming waste — therefore higher cost per stave — 50 boards must be culled through per stave. In many yards this will be frowned upon. So try this ploy: Say that you make wood bows, that the grain has to be just so, and that you need to look at fifty boards to find just the right one. It's likely that the guy you tell this to built a bow when he was eight years old, too. There is a very good chance he will allow you all the latitude possible within his job description. Don't be surprised if he sets choice new stock aside for you next time you come by.

"Straight lumber comes from straight stacks," reads a sign at MacBeath Hardwood here in Berkeley, a reminder of the bowmakers' lumberyard creed: Leave the stacks neater than you found them.

Short of doing a "standard bend test," here is a "ballpark" method of determining low-set, safe limb widths for staves of unknown strength/elasticity. For reference, this scale is based on 66" stiff handled bows drawing 50 lb at 28", with flat bellies and fairly rectangular cross-sections.

Wood weight per cubic foot	Limb width
30 lb	3"
35 lb	2 1/4"
43 lb	1 3/4"
55 lb	1 1/4"

Mid-weight hardwoods, like sugar maple, for example, weigh about 43 lb per cubic foot.

Wood must be cured when weighed. Measurement of volume and weight must be accurate. The larger the sample measured the more accurate the measurement. As for weight, a 4 lb sample weighed on a 25 lb scale will not give nearly as precise a reading as on a 5 lb scale. On average, below-35 lb wood is weaker per mass than heavier wood, therefore requiring wider-per-draw weight limbs. When in doubt of a stave's safety, make the limbs wider. If already wide, make them longer. In very rough terms, every 1% increase in total working limb length increases limb safety by about 5%.

At equal angles of violation some woods make more durable bow backs than others. Here listed in order of preference is a most tentative and preliminary rating of the ten common commercial hardwoods.

Hickory	Red oak
Pecan	Birch
Sugar maple	Black cherry
Black walnut	White ash
White oak	Redcedar

MAKING BOWS FROM BOARDS — WHAT'S DIFFERENT

The principal difference between making board and tree-stave bows is that tree-stave backs are already perfectly parallel with the tree's longitudinal surface. Boards must be selected, or modified, in order for back fibers to be parallel.

Mull the board over. Visualize how it originally rested inside its tree. Do what trimming is needed to bring its back parallel.

Once this is done, proceed as with a conventional stave, except for two small differences. One concerns ring-porous woods: Edge and bias-ringed limbs, and limbs which have been decrowned: The backs of such limbs display a certain percentage of porous, weak, early growth. Such backs are inevitably weaker. But they can be raised to normal strength by making them wider, adding more strong summer-wood to the back.

Early-growth, on average, occupies a much wider percentage of the annual ring in some species than others. Hickory has little early growth, oak has much more. When early wood occurs on bow backs, as with edge and bias-ringed staves, tension strength and safety is reduced in proportion to displaced surface summer-grown fibers. Replace these late-wood fibers by making the limb wider. In the particular case of hickory, no widening would be needed; hickory is unusually strong in tension to begin with.

For each inch of exposed early wood, widen limbs by about one-half inch. Not a full inch because one, even on pristine conventional backs some of the tension work is being done by just-under-the-surface early wood. And two, conventional backs are hardly ever pristine.

The champ! What other wood but hickory would tolerate such step-down on the back? Ash's high-percentage, balsa-like early-growth rings fail early when so abused.

To a smaller degree this same problem and solution applies to semi-diffuse woods, such as black walnut. Rings become denser and stronger as the growing season progresses, later summer wood being measurably stronger than spring wood. Diffuse porous woods, such as maple, are uniformly dense, exposed early wood being as strong as late wood.

A LUMBERYARD STARTER BOW

If you're reading this in the morning you can be shooting a fine, new, self-made bow by evening. Even if it's your first try. Complete this chapter, read "Tillering," in Volume 1, then proceed to your local lumberyard.

Buy a 1" by 2" by 72" board (actually just over 1 1/2" by just over 3/4") of the heaviest wood they carry. Choose the board whose ring lines most parallel its back to-be. You may have to take a 1" by 6", or a 2" by something. If so, saw off a stave of the above dimensions.

The aim here is to get a durable bow in your hands. If you're new to tillering stick to these safe, first-time draw weights: If hickory, up to 55 lb If mid-weight wood like ash or sugar maple, up to 50 lb If lighter wood, like cherry, up to 45 lb unless backed.

If conifer wood, select only close-ringed, high-percentage late-growth heart wood. Limit draw weight to 45 lb.

These weights can be raised by about 15%, or limbs shortened a few inches, once tillering skills are developed.

These dimensions for this lumber starter bow are essentially those of "The Perfect Bow," described on page 92 in Volume 1. Or the cherry longbow of "Some Favorite Bows," below. As with the cherry bow, let limbs remain full width from mid-limb to mid-limb, the center three feet of the bow.

If you're new to bowmaking you may not yet have proper tools. But if you simply *have* to get started on a bow (welcome to the club) remove bulk wood with a hatchet, Skilsaw, hand plane, heavy kitchen knife, chisel, or etc. Once the stave is bending use a coarse, then finer, rasp.

If you want to finish your bow today, don't dally. Let the chips fly. Conservatively decide where and how much wood needs to come off, then plow into it. Within an hour have the bow bending enough to begin true tillering. If you're going to ruin a stave, ruin it quickly. No need wasting wood *and* time.

Bows are not ruined by taking wood off too quickly, only by being unclear where and how much wood to take off.

Once you have proper tools, and a few bows under your belt, you can complete an unsanded but perfectly functional bow from a 1" by 2" board stave in between two and four hours. One to two hours if roughed out on a bandsaw.

These are average times. Many first-timers, and tenth-timers, take days. After making a number of bows unsanded construction time can fall to as low as one-half hour. This is not an exaggeration. Add 45 minutes if only hand tools are used. If starting from tree-split staves a bandsaw will save about one and one-half hours, eliminating the hatchet and drawknife work.

Tillering is the heart of bowmaking. When giving bowmaking demonstrations and classes I always bring several 1" by 2" full-length staves, already roughed out. These blanks let the principles and practices of tillering be demonstrated in just a few minutes. As a result, over the period of a day, many more individuals and groups get to see the entire tillering procedure.

Tillering these blanks takes so little time because after leaving the bandsaw they could just about be strung and shot. Such roughing-out takes about ten minutes each, including penciling in bow dimensions.

Once, at a traditional meet, a fiberglass bow man came up to our bowmaking class. He said someone had told him bows were being made in twenty minutes. He said this in a friendly but skeptical tone.

I apologized for having to disappoint him, saying I had no idea how such a story could have gotten around.

He seemed relieved.

Then I added that even with the dull tools at hand I didn't see how it could possibly take more than ten minutes to make a bow. "A first-class, really durable bow, that is," I clarified, "no need making one of those six-minute bows that only last a few years."

The fiberglass man expressed the gravest sort of doubts.

So a bet was made — for a case of soda pop.

One of the roughed out 1" by 2" staves was put in the vice. Tools were laid out at easy reach. Someone held a watch up and said, "start."

The bow was ready to shoot in nine minutes, thirty-seven seconds. It was unsanded, of course, but was a durable, well-tillered weapon, with very nice lines. And with properly matched arrows, capable of killing any animal on the continent.

Rushing a bow into existence by such unsubtle means might seem disrespect-ful. But a bow is not such a temperamental creature.

Bows are not made. They cannot be made. They are tillered. An emerging bow will not permit itself to be disrespected. Regardless of the bowyer's tools or mood, the act of tillering soon has his full mind and heart. Without this commu-nion proper tillering cannot proceed. The bow will not emerge. So make your bows as quickly or as slowly as you please.

SOME FAVORITE BOWS

Uncovering the information reported in this chapter, and "Design and Perfor-mance" in Vol. l, involved the making of over 600 bows. Many of these were broken, by accident or on purpose, many were given away, a few were sold. Just over 250 remain, all leaning against various walls in my house. Bows made of yew grown in the high Cascades, air dried for four years. Bows made of Osage grown in wind-free creek beds of east Texas. Bows of Cuba-grown lemonwood. Bows of ebony, teak, rosewood, goncollo, hickory, plum, sassafras, willow, Scotch broom, and dozens more. They are gull-winged plains bows; retroflexed cable-backed bows; short, sinew-backed, recurved bows; round-bellied English longbows ... in short, bows of virtually every design and wood species. They all have strings and are ready to shoot. But when it's time to choose just one of these, when it's time to pick the bow most likely to hit the mark, without hesitation I reach for just one particular bow:

It is a 73" bias-ringed, black cherry, flat-bellied, English-tillered longbow — 53 lb at 28". When just unbraced it follows the string by 1 1/8". For its mass, black cherry is strong and elastic in compression, taking less set-per-mass than about

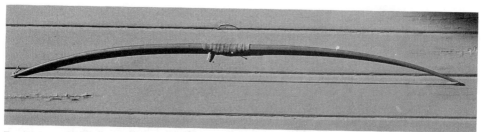

For its mass, black cherry is stronger and more elastic in compression than most other woods. But it is slightly weaker in tension. A bow designed to take advantage of cherry's compression properties will more likely break in tension. A moderately strong and elastic backing brings tension strength safety up to normal, resulting in a limb of exceptional energy storage-per-mass. Deer rawhide supples the tension safety here.

any other wood. It also has the lowest hysterisis tested so far. Hysterisis has little effect on bow performance; in this case it contributed one additional fps or so of cast. Cherry is slightly less strong in tension, and this particular board was slightly wavy-grained on its back. But a medium-thick rawhide backing made this bow tension-safe.

About 66" is usually the most efficient length for a 28" draw bow. But at only .50 specific gravity, and with its narrow outer limbs, this cherry bow's length does not appreciably slow cast. It does, however, yield a very low string angle, storing more energy, and permitting a sweet, stackless draw. All working areas of its limbs are perfectly rectangular, and 1.5" wide from mid limb to mid limb, tapering gently to 1/2" nocks. Tillering is elliptical, b-a-r-e-l-y bending at the grip. A built-up riser of tangled vegetable fiber is held in place by a thin leather handle wrap. This riser quickly adjusts to the hand, like an old familiar easy chair. Wrap pressure maintains the riser's slight crown. Using a loose grip, this-fiber/leather crown keeps the bow hand from bearing on belly corners, thereby avoiding grip torque.

With pronounced elliptical tiller and low-mass tips, this bow is extremely sweet on release. Its low set, narrow tips, and low limb mass account for this bow's high arrow speed, about 5 fps above average. Its stabilizing length, non-stacking draw, and no-torque grip insure an exceptionally consistent arrow path, shot after shot.

Except for length, another favorite bow is identical in design to the pyramid-limb cherry bow discussed earlier. On release it has absolutely no handshock. This is not an exaggeration. Instead there is a comfortable momentary sense of pressure against the bow hand; an unusual, mild, elastic push. Then the arrow is off in strangely flat and fast flight. The energy normally diverted to shocking the hand obviously goes into the arrow instead.

Shorter for mobility, made of hickory for indestructibility, pyramid shaped for speed...this is a first-class hunting bow. And to accustomed eyes, a beautiful design.

A third bow, from redoak, is not a favorite bow because of any functional qualities; it shoots with only average speed and comfort. It's a favorite because it became a good, durable bow against all conventional odds.

No experienced archer has failed to express surprise after shooting this hickory bow. It draws easily and releases softly. Experience expects an arrow flight of moderate speed and arc, but sees a startlingly flat, long trajectory. This bow is 61" long and draws 28". Two and one-half inches wide near the grip, its limbs taper in straight lines to 1/2" nocks. Mid-limb width is 1 7/8".

From a 1" by 2" reject redoak board. Rings run off and through this bow at dangerous angles. Appropriate backings, such as raw flax in this case, make such staves tension-safe, elevating them to wood's highest state: a working bow.

Unbacked, this stave would have separated along angled early-growth lines when only moderately strained. Raw, just-pulled-from-the-stalk flax fiber was glued to its back, taking on roughly 50% of the tension load. It is now a strong, dependable weapon, and less likely to fail than superior, unbacked, parallel-fiber staves. Board bows milled from twisted trees tend to twist when drawn. With so much of the tension strain carried by flax fibers limb twist is reduced to insignificance. Its strong backing permits, and to some small degree induces higher compression strain than normal, causing more set than normal. But mild recurving easily compensates.

Destined to live out its life as a waterbed frame, or worse, this bow now roves the sunny, blue-skied California hills.

ROOTS

An orphaned infant sea otter was rescued and raised to adolescence in a board-flat indoor pool. Finally the day came for his return to a natural kelp and sea urchin domain. Teary-eyed guardians lowered his container level with the ocean surface. The otter looked out at the vast, majestic, wave-torn Pacific. His eyes suddenly widened, then he began thrashing the water, clawing his way back into the box, screaming bloody murder not to be put in that terrible splashy ocean.

Dozens of callers to my Primitive Archery Switchboard have been advised on board selection and preparation. They often call back in a day or two, elated with the beauty and performance of their new bow. After some time has passed they often call again, having purchased or prepared a tree-split stave, quick-dried it, and made a "natural" bow. Some take to the challenge of a wild, character-laden stave. But others retreat to placid waters.

The irony here is that kiln-dried board staves, which just yesterday were so universally reviled, are now used exclusively by a growing number of new bowmakers.

Board bows are cheaper, easier, safer, and faster to make ... but except for "cheaper," this describes fiberglass bows as well. Board staves should be an option, not a refuge.

EASTERN WOODLAND BOWS

Al Herrin

The details of the daily lives of the Eastern Woodland Indians, before the arrival of Columbus, are lost in the mists of the past. Here and there a bit of information seems to stand out clearly for an instant, like a tree in the forest suddenly lit by the rays of the sun, only to fade again as the clouds thicken. Archaeologists and others interested in precise knowledge of pre-Columbian Eastern Woodlands bows and arrows find their knowledge is likewise clouded by mystery. There seem to be more questions than answers.

My purpose in this chapter is to collect what is known about the Eastern Woodland bow, examine some of the unanswered questions and show that, through a unique contribution of the Cherokee Indians, we can roll back some of the clouds and propose reasonable answers to some of the questions.

Before beginning our discussion, perhaps we should define what we mean by "Eastern Woodland" Indians. That area of the United States east of the Great Plains was, before the arrival of Columbus, a vast, almost unbroken forest. Hardwood trees such as oak, hickory, maple, and beech and, in some areas, evergreens such as pine and cedar dominated. Much of the hilly or mountainous land was carved with hollows and valleys which contained countless lakes and streams of pure water fed by abundant precipitation and spring water from deep in the earth. The forests and savannahs teemed with game such as white-tail deer, elk, woods bison, caribou, moose, grizzly and black bear, timber wolves, bald eagles, flocks of passenger pigeons that darkened the sun, turkeys in flocks of hundreds and smaller game too abundant to list. The streams, lakes, and marshes teemed with fish, mammals, and waterfowl by the countless millions.

The Eastern Woodland Indians were the people who called this paradise their home. They lived in harmony with nature, taking only what they needed for a simple, healthful life. They were divided into many tribes. Some of the more prominent tribes in the northern part of the region were the Sauk, Fox, Kickapoo, Potawatomi, Ottawa, Huron (Wyandot), Shawnee, Illinois, Miami, Iroquois, Algonkin, Abenaki, Malecite, Delaware, Ojibwa (Chippewa), and Mohican. The predominant tribes in the southern part of the region were the Cherokee, Choctaw, Chickasaw, Muskogee (Creek), Seminole, Catawba, Yuchi, Natchez, Timucua, Calusa, Tekesta, Caddo, Atakapa, and Chitimacha.

I use the Cherokee Indians as representative of the Eastern Woodland Indians

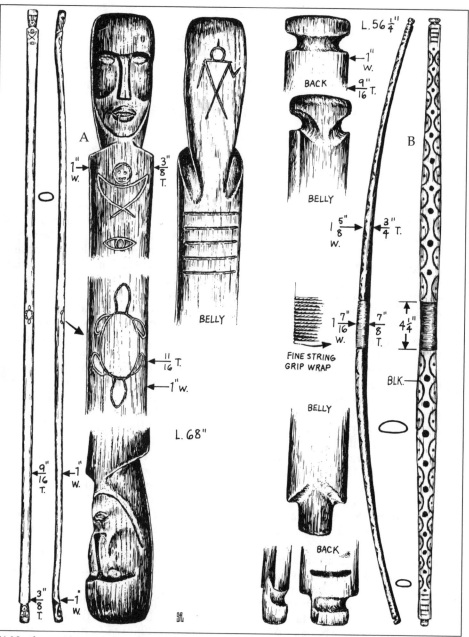

A) Northeast Algonquin — possibly Delaware, patinated hickory with slight recurves, dating from the 1700's. Note carved faces on each tip, possibly a "keeper of the game" spirit to ensure good hunting; other carved figures may be clan symbols (courtesy Ranley collection).
B) Choctaw — Mississippi and Alabama, Osage orange with black painted design on back, wrapped grip (courtesy Grayson collection).

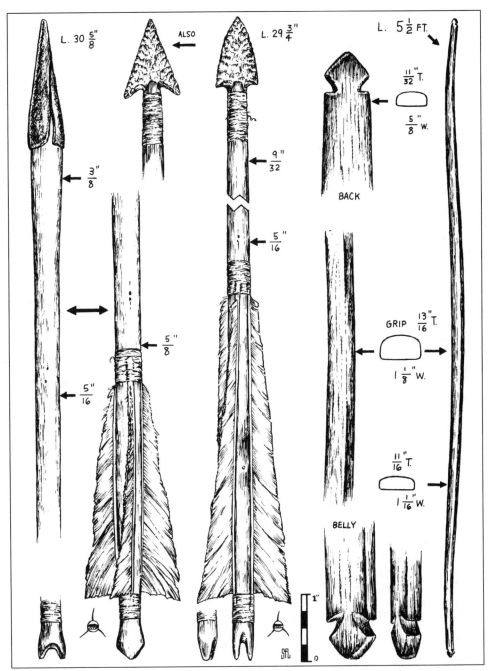

Creek — South Carolina and Georgia. Arrows fletched with white and black feathers, one arrow with glue, one without. Points (L-R), a thin piece of metal rolled into a cone around the sharpened tip, brown agate, and grey chert. Bow is hickory, dark with age. (courtesy Grayson Collection)

in this discussion. I have done so for two reasons. First, I am a member of the Cherokee Nation and, having been reared in the traditional way, have greater knowledge and insight into the culture and heritage of the Cherokee. Second, my people have made a unique contribution to the preservation of knowledge of the Eastern Woodland bow, which will be discussed a bit later.

My Cherokee ancestors occupied a vast area in the beautiful mountains they called Sa-go-ni-ge, "the place of the blue smoke," now called the Great Smoky Mountains. This homeland encompassed an area of approximately forty thousand square miles in what is now the states of Georgia, Alabama, Tennessee, South Carolina, North Carolina, and Virginia. They lived in permanent walled villages and towns, raised corn, beans, and squash in garden plots, caught fish from the streams, hunted game with bows and blowguns, and made war.

In fact, their favorite pastime was warfare with neighboring tribes including the Catawbas, Shawnees, and others. Every European observer of the colonial period remarked about the Cherokees' inordinate fondness for war. A great deal of daily life was taken up in preparing for and conducting raids on enemy towns as far away as Florida or defending their own towns from enemy raids. The object was not to wipe out your enemy because, if you did, whom would you fight then? Around 1730, English emissaries of the crown attempted to make peace between the Cherokees and the Tuscaroras, a neighboring tribe with whom they had warred for generations. But the Cherokee chiefs said, "Should we make peace with the Tuscaroras ... we must immediately look for some others with whom we can be engaged in our beloved occupation."

In the middle of the eighteenth century, the Cherokees boasted they could, on short notice, field six thousand warriors. The warlike lifestyle of the Cherokees affected every facet of their daily lives to the point that, even today, some families still use their military titles as family names such as Mankiller, Whitekiller, Fourkiller, Sixkiller, and Tenkiller.

The walled towns of the Cherokees were stoutly defended against enemy raids. James Needham, a Virginia trader, recorded the following details of the Cherokee town of Chota on the Little Tennessee River in 1673:

> "The town of Chote is seated on ye river side, having ye clifts on ye river side on ye one side being very high for itts defence, the other three sides trees of two foot or over, pitched on end, twelve foot high, and on ye topps scaffolds placed with parrapets to which men stand on to fight, many nations of Indians inhabit downe this river ... which they the Cherokees are at warre with and to that end keepe one hundred and fifty canoes under ye command of their forts. Ye leasts of them will carry twenty men, and made sharp at both ends like a wherry for swiftness, this forte is four square; 300: paces over and ye houses sett in streets."

Second to war, the Cherokees' next beloved occupation was the hunt. According to eighteenth-century white observers, both sexes enjoyed hunting. Other occupations of Cherokee men, less favored but deemed necessary, were the making of bows, tomahawks, war clubs, canoes, and earthenware. Women and "useless fellows" were relegated such work as gardening, tending poultry and hogs, tanning hides, smoking meat, making clothing, and the care of children.

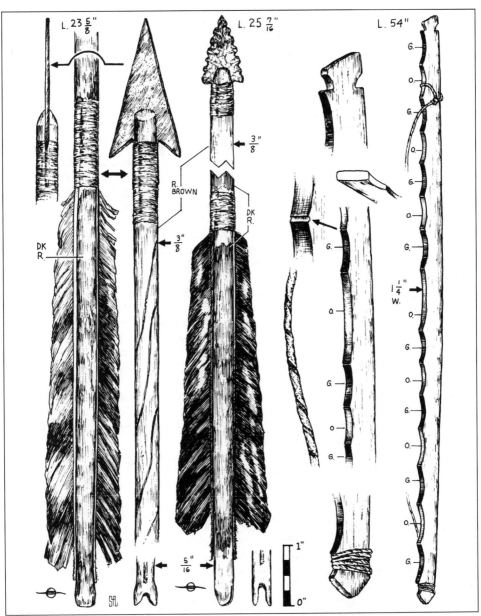

Potowotomi — western Michigan, northern Indiana, and northern Illinois. Arrows fletched with two hawk tail feathers, tied with sinew at front of quill only and glued. Shallow shaft grooves spiral around arrow. Back halves of arrows stained vermillion after fletching complete, front halves stained brown. Points of chert and iron with an unsharpened square edge (Mills County Museum, Glenwood, IA.). White wood bow showing the back, with scallops alternately painted dark orange, or red, and dark green. String is single-ply rawhide (National Museum of the American Indian).

For a Cherokee warrior, those truly were the "good old days".

In the following sections, what is known about the Eastern Woodland bow will be presented from archaeological and historical records and from other sources. Hopefully, our examination will reveal a clearer picture of the pre-Columbian Eastern Woodland bow and its use by the Native Americans of that area.

WHY WAS THE EASTERN WOODLAND BOW
NOT AS WELL KNOWN AS THE PLAINS BOW?

During the twentieth century, there has been a lingering interest in the "primitive" archery of pre-Columbian Native Americans, stimulated first by the appearance, in 1911, of Ishi, the last "wild" Indian. Saxton Pope (who was Ishi's physician), Art Young, and a few others became interested in traditional archery. The interest kindled by these men lasts until the present day.

During most of the twentieth century, the little sinew-backed "horse bow" of the Plains Indians enjoyed a highly inflated reputation, while the self bow of the Eastern Woodland Indians remained practically unknown. In researching the information available on pre-Columbian Indian archery for my 1989 book, *Cherokee Bows and Arrows*, I found there was almost no information available on Eastern self bows. I could locate no one, outside the Cherokee Nation, who were making bows of this type. The two books which had been written at that time, *American Indian Archery* by Laubin and *Native American Bows* by Hamilton, gave most of their coverage to composite bows and especially the sinew-backed horse bow of the Plains, while giving only brief mention of the Eastern self bows. Of course, this was an inaccurate representation because the horse bow was a relatively recent development, coming after the voyages of Columbus, and was used by only a few tribes in a very limited area. Even among the Plains Indians themselves, fewer than half of their bows were sinew-backed; most were self bows. The short sinew-backed bow was simply not representative of the vast majority of pre-Columbian American Indian bows.

The horse bow gained its disproportionate fame because of the time that elapsed between the first significant European contact with what is now North America in the sixteenth century and the migration of settlers across the continent in the eighteenth and nineteenth centuries. As a result, the Eastern Woodland Indians came in contact with the white man about two hundred years earlier than did the Plains Indian.

For example, the first contact between the Cherokees and the white man was with the Spanish DeSoto expedition in 1540. During the seventeenth century, the Eastern Woodland Indians came into increasing contact with colonists from France and England. Most of the Indians west of the Mississippi River, on the other hand, saw their first white trappers and hunters during the eighteenth century followed by the intrusion of large numbers of white settlers during the nineteenth century.

Many of the Eastern Woodland Indians obtained firearms and abandoned the bow and arrow during the seventeenth century. Few white people bothered to record any details concerning the design, materials, methods of manufacture, or use of the bow and arrows of the Eastern Woodland tribes. Among the Indians,

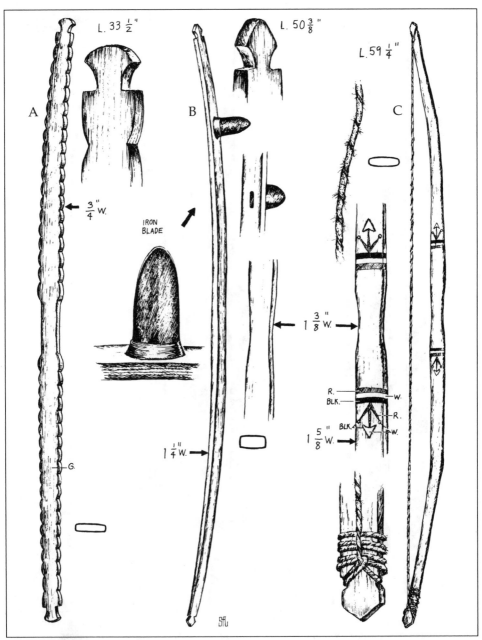

Fox — eastern Michigan. A) Boy's bow made from white wood. B) Possibly hickory or elm, slightly narrowed at the grip. Iron blade inserted into hole in upper limb and held in place with a wedge. Base of blade tang flush with belly of bow. C) White wood with slightly narrowed handle and painted design on belly. Single strip of rawhide with hair still attached twisted into string. (National Museum of the American Indian)

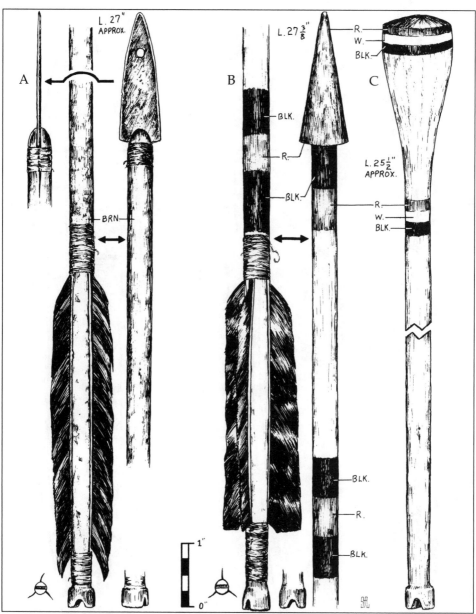

Fox Arrows A) Bulbous nock with small string groove, fletched with glued feathers of either mature golden eagle or buzzard. Shafts darkened from the feathers forward, perhaps for camouflage. Steel point with drilled hole. Keith Wilbur, in Indian Handcrafts, makes the observation that perhaps steel or brass points sometimes had holes so they could be strung on a thong in lots by traders. B) Blunt carved from a single piece of wood, fletched with glued mature golden eagle feathers. C) Large blunt carved from a single piece of wood (National Museum of the American Indian).

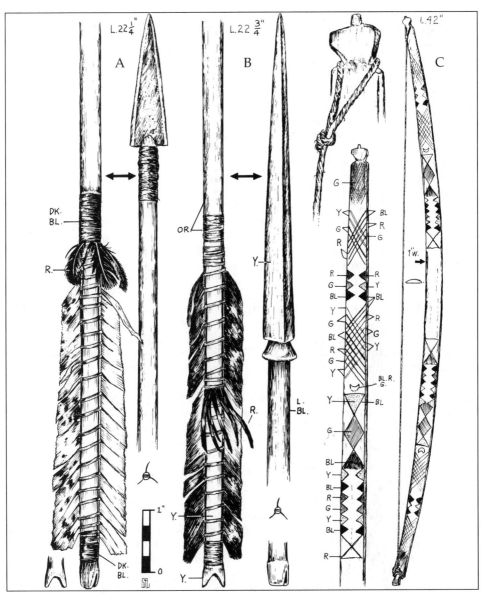

Caddo — *southeastern Oklahoma, northeastern Texas, northern Louisiana, and southern Arkansas. A) Dogwood arrow fletched with immature bald eagle tail feathers. Each feather sinew wrapped at each end, then a long piece of sinew "barber-poled" around the shaft through the vanes of the feathers, no glue. Steel point. (Museum of the Southern Plains). B) Wooden-tipped arrow carved from single piece of hardwood, fletched with turkey tail feathers. Feather attachment is very similar to "A". (National Museum of the American Indian). C) White wood bow with a protrusion at upper tip for attachment of horsehair decoration, an influence from the Plains (see Plains and Southwest Bows, Vol. III). Rounded back and flat belly with incised and painted designs (National Museum of the American Indian).*

this knowledge had been passed through the generations from bowyer to apprentice and was not written down. So, the knowledge died with the old bowyers, and the bows and arrows decayed with time.

The Plains Indians, on the other hand, were still using bows and arrows well into the nineteenth century. They had adapted the lifestyle to the horse and developed the short horse bow for shooting buffalo from horseback. Even after the introduction of muzzleloading firearms, the bow remained the more effective weapon for buffalo hunting from horseback because an Indian archer could shoot a quiver full of arrows while a rifleman was trying to reload after a single shot. Only after the introduction of repeating firearms was the bow abandoned by most of the Plains Indians.

During the nineteenth century, some white people became aware that the way of life of the American Indian was rapidly disappearing and began efforts to record some details of their lifestyle. Artists such as George Catlin and Carl Bodmer toured the West painting the Indians and detailing their lifestyle and implements. These paintings and descriptions gained worldwide interest. Although the little horse bows and arrows were not representative of the vast majority of Indian bows and arrows used in North America, they became imprinted on people's minds as typical.

In the last decade, we have witnessed a surge of interest in primitive Indian bows and arrows. Many archers are discovering the challenge and joy of making all wood self bows. Since *Cherokee Bows and Arrows* appeared in 1989, several other books on Native American bows have been published, "undiscovered" examples of Eastern Woodlands bows are being found in museums and private collections, suppliers have emerged to satisfy the demand for bow wood, schools for primitive bowmakers are available, and the oldest form of archery has become a whole new experience that is sweeping the archery world. The all wood self bow of the Eastern Woodland Indians are an important part of my heritage as a Cherokee and the heritage of all of us as Americans, and it has finally taken its rightful place among the great bow designs of the world.

WHAT ARE THE SOURCES OF INFORMATION ABOUT PRE-COLUMBIAN BOWS?

Archaeologists generally consider the evidence concerning the nature of the pre-Columbian Eastern Woodland bow to be limited to the following sources: archaeological evidence unearthed from scientific excavations, specimens collected and preserved while the bow was still in widespread use, and the descriptions and drawing of bows by contemporary observers.

Ethnologists, on the other hand, study the equipment and methods of living cultural groups. Since cultural traits tend to be relatively stable over time, some inferences can be made about equipment and methods that were used by a group in prehistoric times. During the nineteenth century, ethnological studies of the Native Americans were reported to the Bureau of Ethnology of the Smithsonian Institution. These studies preserved many cultural practices of the Native Americans that otherwise would have been lost. For example, ethnological observations of Native American flintknappers has prevented that art from becoming lost and has provided the information upon which the recent revival of flintknapping is largely based.

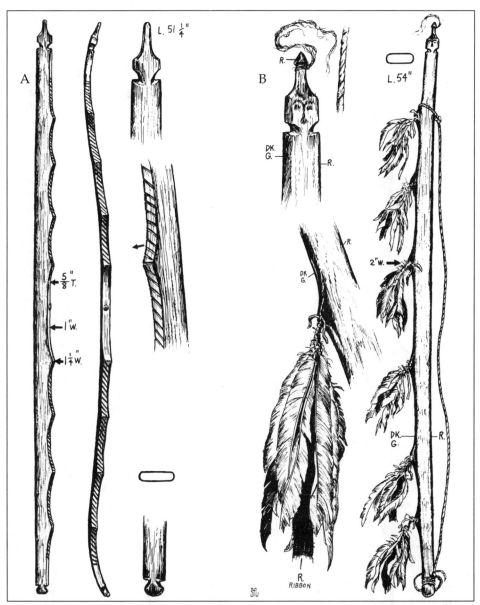

Seneca — western New York. A) Hickory recurve with grooves cut into sides of scallops. Note brass tack driven into right side of grip. Steve Allely, the artist who produced these drawings and who also wrote and illustrated the Western Indian Bows chapter in Volume 1, theorizes that the tack may have been used to ensure consistent hand placement on the bow. B) Scalloped edge painted dark blue or green, smooth edge painted red. Tips of scallops have drilled holes with thongs of buckskin holding bundles of split feathers (6 to 10 per bundle with 1" wide red ribbon). Tip of bow on top limb painted red, with small painted face. String is finely twisted two-ply rawhide. (National Museum of the American Indian)

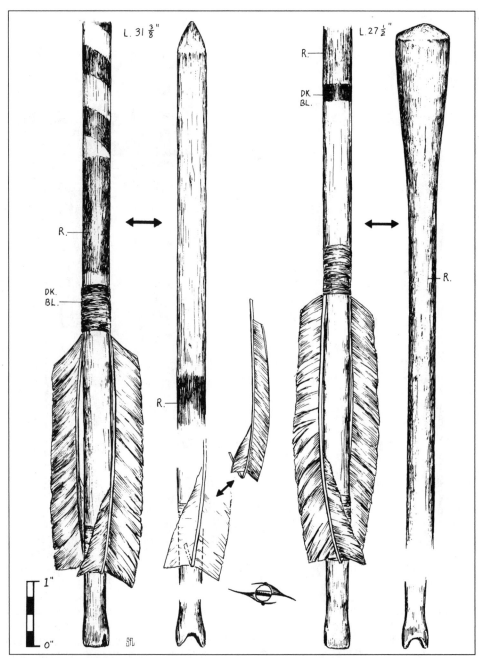

Seneca arrows with painted hardwood shaft and short hawk tail feathers. Two feather fletch with whole feather at back, stripped down to single side of feather at front. Tied inverted at back of shaft, then bent forward and front tied. Feathers put on with pronounced twist, sinew wrap, no glue. (National Museum of the American Indian).

Alex England,
Master Cherokee Bowyer

However, an examination of the nineteenth century *Reports to the Bureau of Ethnology* shows that ethnologists were evidently unaware that any Eastern Woodland tribes were still making and using bows and arrows. For example, T. M. Hamilton, who is well known and respected for his research in archaeology, wrote in his book, *Native American Bows,* "Since this area (east of the Mississippi) was the first to be settled, or, at least, invaded by the white trader, the bow, as a serious weapon, has long since disappeared." Most ethnologists concurred, and there is little mention of bows and arrows in their reports.

But the ethnologists were mistaken in believing the bow was extinct as a practical weapon! Unknown to them, the Cherokees continued to make and use their traditional bows and arrows and the knowledge of bowmaking continued to be handed down through the generations to the present day. This is the manner in which I learned to make traditional bows and arrows.

There are only a small handful of bowyers left among the Cherokee who learned to make bows from their elders. Their numbers decrease as the years pass; one day there will be no more. Fortunately, we do not have to let this valuable source of information be lost. By studying the methods and materials used by the present day Cherokee bowyers, the characteristics of the bows and arrows and the shooting methods used, we can gain important information concerning the Eastern Woodland bow and its use. More details about this later, but first we should examine the information on bows provided by archaeologists.

SURVIVING EASTERN WOODLAND BOWS
AND OBSERVATIONS OF CONTEMPORARY OBSERVERS

Archaeologists have found few Eastern Woodland bows and arrows in excavations. Usually all that remains are the stone arrowheads because the wood, skin, feathers, sinew, and other organic materials from which bows and arrows were made decayed rapidly in this region.

In 1963, a self bow, classified as early Caddoan, was recovered from a burial site in Louisiana which dated to the eleventh century. The bow was made from Osage orange wood with an overall length of 66 inches and a grip diameter of 1 1/4 inches. The bow's cross-section was circular, and it appeared to be a simple "D" bow with slightly recurved tips. A sixteenth century engraving of a war council of Southeastern Indians by De Bry shows some of the warriors with bows that appear identical to the bow recovered in Louisiana.

In 1956, a cane arrowshaft unearthed in Tennessee was dated as being over 2000 years old. The Cherokees and some of the other southeastern tribes were still using arrows of cane when first contacted by Spanish explorers in the sixteenth century.

Numerous Eastern Woodland bows are housed in museums, but archaeologists generally consider one of the best authenticated bows from colonial times to be the "Sudbury" bow, which is in the Peabody Museum at Harvard University. The faded inscription on the bow reads, "This bow was taken from an Indian in Sudbury, Mass., A.D. 1660 by William Goodnough who shot the Indian while he was ransacking the Goodnough house for plunder..."The bow is made of hickory and is 65 inches long, nock to nock. The limbs are basically flat in cross-section, about 1 3/4 inches wide and 9/16 inches thick at mid-limb and 3/4 inches wide at the tips. The grip or handle section is narrowed to about 1 inch in width with a corresponding increase in thickness to 1 3/16 inches. Museum officials list the bow as Wampanoag, who were the people who greeted the Pilgrims (a survey conducted in 1950 showed that only about 1000 descendants of the Wampanoag remained, while the non-Indian population of North America had grown to over 200 million. Look who came to dinner and stayed!).

Several drawings of bows and arrows from Eastern Woodland Tribes, including the Sudbury bow, illustrate this chapter. The Cherokee bows and arrows are from my own collection and were made by Cherokees within the past two hundred years. The other weapons are housed in museums and private collections around the country. I have not examined these latter bows and arrows personally, and so have depended upon their caretakers to authenticate their origins and ages.

In addition to surviving examples, there are some descriptions and drawings of Eastern Woodland bows which were made by observers during the sixteenth and seventeenth centuries. The first Spanish explorers who entered what is now Mexico, South America, and the Southeastern and Southwestern parts of the United States were more interested in finding gold and converting the natives to Christianity than in recording ethnographic details concerning the implements or lifestyles of the Indians. Even so, some information about bows and arrows was recorded because it was relevant to the military goals of the invaders. The English colonists likewise had more pressing interests than recording details

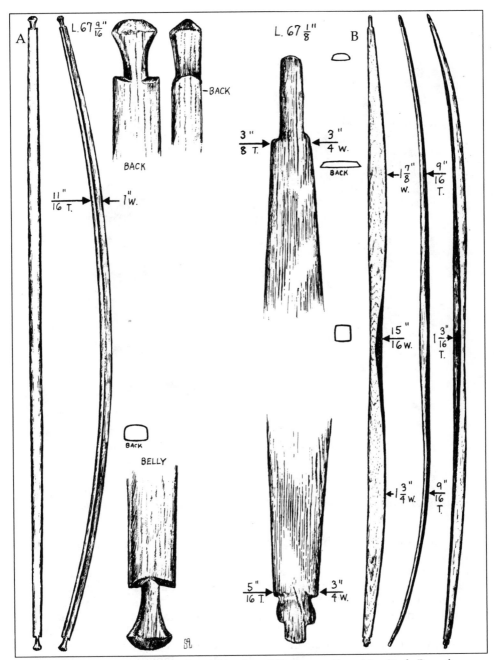

A) Algonkian (Kitchawank) — southern Ontario and Quebec, northern New York. Bow of hickory, collected in 1728 by Pierre van Courtland, a future Lt. Governor of New York (National Museum of the American Indian). B) Wampanoag hickory bow collected in 1660 in Sudbury, Massachusetts (Peabody Museum).

The Manner of Their Attire, a watercolor by John White, 17th century (National Anthropological Archives, Smithsonian Institution).

A Warrior of Florida, a watercolor by John White, 17th century (National Anthropological Archives, Smithsonian Institution).

about their Indian neighbors except those things which related to military matters.

John White, governor of the Virginia colony in the seventeenth century, made water color paintings of Southeastern Woodland Indians. Two of his paintings, "The Manner of Their Attire" and "A Warrior of Florida", showed well proportioned Indians holding bows which appeared to be taller than the Indians and were probably close to six feet in length. The limbs of the bow carried by the men seemed to be rectangular in cross-section. The warrior from Florida holds an arrow which appears to be close to three feet in length and may have been made of cane with a wood foreshaft. The Cherokees lived near the Virginia colony, and the traditional bows made by Cherokee bowyers today are very similar to those shown in the White paintings.

Le Moyne painted a gathering of Southeastern Woodland warriors called "Saturiona Goes to War". Although his original paintings were lost, De Bry made the engraving which was referred to earlier while discussing the bow found in Louisiana. I have reason to suspect the accuracy of the De Bry engravings. Having examined his engravings of the White watercolors, it is clear he tended to add things to the originals, such as horn tips on bows thick enough to pass for clubs. Also, his "Indians" look suspiciously like Greek gods.

However, shown in the De Bry engravings are two types of bows; straight bows which appear to be more than five feet in length and double-curved bows of about five feet with recurved tips. The limbs of both types of bows show to be round in cross-section, an observation supported by the bow found in the Louisiana burial. The double-curved self bow was found only in North America, so De Bry was apparently accurate in depicting this feature.

In addition to drawings, written descriptions by early observers provide information about the early Eastern Woodland bows and their performance.

James Adair wrote about the Cherokees in 1775, "They make perhaps the finest bows, and the smoothest barbed arrows, of all mankind." Timberlake, in 1776, wrote that the Cherokees used oak, ash, and hickory for their bows. Based on my own knowledge of Cherokee tradition and my experience with making bows, black locust was the preferred wood of the Cherokees in our original

Saturiona Goes to War, a De Bry engraving from 1591 (National Anthropological Archives, Smithsonian Institution).

homeland and is a greatly superior bow wood to the three mentioned by Timberlake. He also mentioned that the bows were liberally coated with bear oil and warmed before a fire to increase the penetration of the oil. This practice is still preserved among Cherokees today, although hog lard is usually substituted for the bear oil.

The length of Eastern bows was recorded by several observers. Columbus reported that the Indians (Caribs) had bows as large as those in France and England. Six foot bows were also reported by the Narvaez expedition among Indians of the Gulf Coast. Some tribes around the Great Lakes, such as the Chippewa, Menomini, and Assiniboin used somewhat shorter bows, typically four to five feet in length, with arrows to match of 23 to 26 inches. Most Northeastern tribes, however, appear to have preferred bows of five feet or more in length, such as the 67 inch long Sudbury bow discussed earlier.

The effectiveness of the Eastern Woodlands self bow was recorded by numerous observers from the expeditions which faced these weapons in battle. The landing party of Columbus was greeted by showers of arrows which sent them scurrying back to their ships. Of the Narvaez expedition into the Gulf Coast area, only the famous Cabeza de Vaca, along with two others, survived to finally reach Mexico. He reported that ten soldiers were completely transfixed by arrows, this in spite of their armor.

A chronicler of the De Soto expedition through the Southeast and into Cherokee country wrote:

"(The Indians) never remain quiet, but are continually running, traversing from place to place, so that neither crossbow or arqubuse can be aimed at them. Before a Christian can make a single shot with either, an Indian will discharge three or four arrows: and he seldom misses of his object. Where the arrow meets with no armor, it pierces as deeply as the shaft from a crossbow. Their bows are very perfect; the arrows are made of a certain canes, like reeds, very heavy, and so stiff that one of them, when sharpened, will pass through a target. Some are pointed with a bone of a fish, sharp like a chisel; others with some stone like a point of diamond; of such the great number, when they strike upon armor, break at the place where the parts are put together; those of cane will split, and will enter a shirt of mail, doing more injury than when armed."

In the second volume of the narratives, it says, "The Indians, on two occasions, killed three soldiers of the Governor's guard and wounded others, and killed a horse; and all that through bad arrangements, since these Indians, although they are archers and have strong bows and are skillful and sure marksmen, yet their arrows have no poison, nor do they know what it is." Up to that point, the expedition had suffered 760 arrow wounds.

In the account of another battle with the Indians, we read that Don Carlo's horse was shot in the breast with an arrow. Carlo dismounted to pull it out and was immediately shot through the neck and killed almost instantly. Later, 22 of De Soto's Spaniards were killed and 148 others wounded. There were a total of 688 arrow wounds. Seven horses were killed, three shot completely through both shoulders, and twenty-nine wounded.

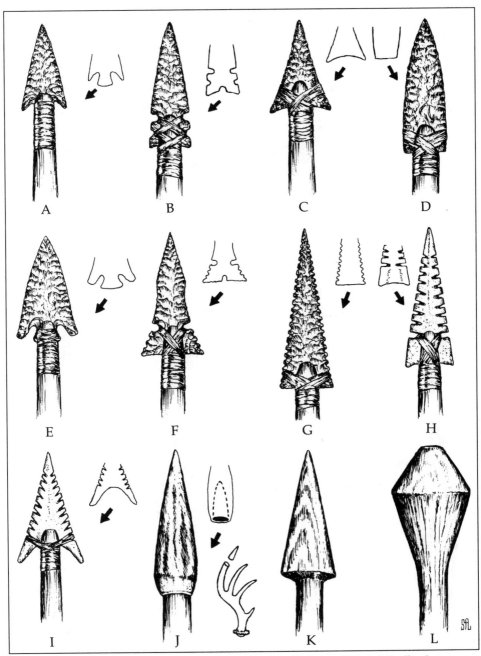

A) Potowotomi flint point, B) Late period "5 notch" point, SW Iowa, C) Late Woodland stone point, D) Historic 18th century Cherokee stone point, E, F, and G) Stone points from Cahokia Mound, Illinois, H and I) Bone points from Cahokia Mound, J) Seminole point made from antler, K) Sauk-Fox solid wooden point, L) Sauk-Fox solid bird blunt.

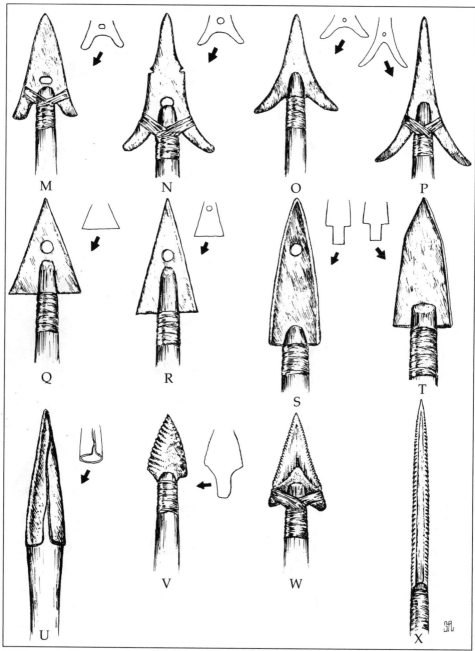

M) Copper point from Massachusetts, N, O, and P) Brass points from Ft. Shantok, CT, Q and R) Cherokee brass points cut from trade kettles, S) Fox iron point, T) Potowotomi iron point, U) Creek rolled iron point, V) Alligator gar scale point from the Texas coastal plain, W) Shark tooth point, East Coast, X) Stingray barb point, Gulf Coast region.

According to the chronicler's account, "The arrow shots were tremendous, and sent with such a will and force that the lance of one gentleman named Nuno de Tovar, made of two pieces of ash and very good, was pierced by an arrow in the middle, as by an auger, without being split, and the arrow made a cross with the lance."

De Soto captured an Indian and forced him to demonstrate his shooting of the bow. At 150 paces his arrow pierced a coat of chain mail. The Spaniards placed a second coat of mail on top of the first and the arrow pierced them both, but did not go completely through as it had with the single coat.

Armed with crossbows and primitive firearms, it is little wonder that the Spanish came to fear and dread the highly effective bows and arrows of the Woodland Indians.

CHEROKEE AND ENGLISH LONGBOWS

Several striking similarities emerge when we compare the pre-Colombian Cherokee longbow and the sixteenth century English longbow. There were, of course, some pronounced differences, such as the cross-sectional shape of the limbs and the wood from which they were made. But the similarities of design were certainly greater than the differences and a comparison of the two bows seems appropriate. We find that both were straight self bows with no sinew-backing. Their long length allowed them to shoot long, heavy arrows which resulted in greater accuracy, effective range, and penetration than is normal for a shorter bow.

It also seems appropriate to speculate that parallels in needs, lifestyles, and other factors led to the independent evolution of these similar bows in widely separated areas of the world. The climates of both England and the Southeastern part of North America have ample rainfall and humidity which would make it difficult to keep sinew on sinew-backed bows. Good bow wood was available in both areas so there was no functional need for a backing. Long, straight self bows were relatively easy to make and were stressed less than shorter bows, which made them longer lasting and trouble free. The archers of both areas used the bow on foot rather than from horseback, so the length of the bow was not a handicap.

The written records and legends of the English tell us that their longbow could be used as an effective hunting weapon, at least for Robin Hood and his men and the nobility, but the primary use, and the one which made this bow famous, was as a weapon of war. The accounts of battles in which the English longbowmen turned the tide with their long-range volleys of armor-piercing arrows, such as the Battle of Agincourt, leaves no doubt about the effectiveness of the English longbow as a weapon of war. Another recorded military use of the longbow was in long-range shooting from behind walled towns or castles at enemy soldiers besieging the fortress.

Records from sixteenth century England tell us that every able-bodied man was required, by the King's law, to possess a bow and arrows and to practice frequently at long range in preparation for war. The distances at which they practiced is indicated by the ancient shooting field at Finsbury, near the outskirts of London, where targets range from about 70 yards to over 250 yards, with most of the shots between 160 and 200 yards.

The early Cherokees probably used their bows and arrows in warfare in methods similar to those employed by the English. Every able-bodied Cherokee man and many women kept their bow and arrows nearby at all times. They were skilled at close range shooting at game, but there is evidence they also fired long-range volleys of arrows during battle. Part of that evidence comes from the Cherokee sport of cornstalk shooting which survives to the present day. The origins of cornstalk shooting are uncertain, but I believe this game came down from the pre-Columbian Cherokees who used it to practice long-range shooting for warfare just as the English archers practiced. In cornstalk shooting, the archers shoot at targets made from ricks of cornstalks from distances of 80 to 120 yards. The score in the game depends not only on hitting the target but also on the depth to which the arrow penetrates.

Modern Cherokee cornstalk shoot (courtesy Cherokee Nation).

Setting an Enemy's Town on Fire, a De Bry engraving from 1591 (National Anthropological Archives, Smithsonian Institute).

Further evidence that the Southeastern Woodland Indians used the bow as a long-range military weapon is provided by a sixteenth century painting by Le Moyne, depicting a group of warriors shooting fire arrows into a walled enemy town to set the houses on fire.

The walled defensive towns the Cherokees built allows us to speculate on another parallel use of the bow by Cherokee and English. The Cherokees, as did the English, cleared an area around the walls of their fortified towns. It is reasonable to assume that Cherokee warriors stood on the scaffolding behind the walls and shot arrows at oncoming enemy warriors while they were still at long range, just as English archers defended the walls of their towns.

Both bows shaped the history of the people who used them. It has been said that England was built on a base of iron arrowheads driven by the mighty English longbow. In even earlier times, Cherokee archers with their longbows established dominance over a mountainous area of about forty thousand square miles, an area almost as large as England.

CHARACTERISTICS OF THE EASTERN WOODLAND BOW

Among the many tribes living in Eastern North America, there were variations in the design of bows and the wood from which they were made, but there were some universal characteristics. In general, they were self bows, made

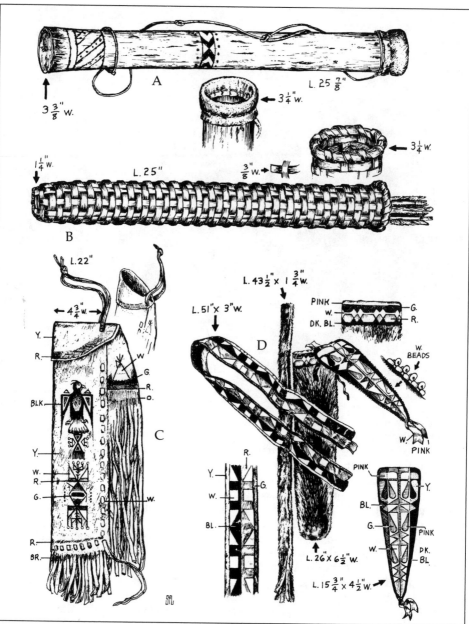

Quivers. A) Seneca — western New York. Hollowed branch with wooden plug at base and burned designs. B) Seneca. Woven basketry. (both from Museum of the American Indian). C) Potowotomi — western Michigan, northern Indiana, and northern Illinois. Buckskin belt quiver stained dark yellow overall, then painted with designs (Mills County Museum). D) Sauk — eastern Michigan. Tanned otter quiver and bowcase with appliqued silk ribbon on red cloth (National Museum of Denmark).

from a single piece of wood, five to six feet in length, with limbs of a flat or rectangular cross-section. Recurves were unusual but not unknown.

The woods from which bows were made included Osage orange, black locust, mulberry, sassafras, hickory, ash, cedar, elm, dogwood, birch, persimmon, iron-wood, black walnut, pecan, oak, sycamore, witch hazel, Florida snakewood, some palms, and others. Some bow woods were preferred over others, and prized wood, such as Osage orange, was distributed over a network of trade routes hundreds of miles from where it grew. The pre-Columbian Cherokees used several woods for bows but black locust was preferred.

I choose the Cherokee bow as representative of the Eastern Woodland bow but, before continuing our discussion in this section, I want to point out an observation concerning the length of Cherokee bows and a theory concerning the observation.

Among present day Cherokee bows, there appears to be two distinct lengths: a long bow of about six feet and shorter bow of about five feet. Today, the longer bow is preferred for the long-range sport of cornstalk shooting, and the shorter bow is preferred for hunting since it is easier to use in brush. The longer bows are often of heavier draw weight, 60 to 80 pounds or even more, while the shorter bows usually draw about 45 to 55 pounds.

I believe these two types of bows reflect aboriginal types which have been handed down from the pre-Columbians to the present day. The longer bows were used by the early Cherokees primarily for warfare while the shorter bows were used mainly for hunting. Even after the adoption of firearms and "civiliza-tion" by the white man in the seventeenth and eighteenth centuries, and down to the present day, a combination of factors led to the preservation of the bow and the art of bowmaking among the Cherokees while these arts were lost among the other Eastern Woodland tribes. These factors were: 1) A love of war-fare and the desire to preserve the bow as a token of their "beloved occupation", 2) The enjoyment of cornstalk shooting as a sport, and 3) The love of hunting with the bow and arrow, added to the fact that the bow was a silent weapon with which the hunter could evade detection by hostile white settlers, and, in more recent times, game wardens who take a dim view of the Indian's aboriginal rights to wildlife.

In any case, whether for these or other reasons, the Cherokee bow was pre-served, and we can accurately measure the dimensions and the performance of the bows presently in use among Cherokees in Oklahoma. I, and the other Cherokee bowyers of today, prefer Osage orange wood and metal hand tools, but I believe the basic design is the same as that used by Cherokee bowyers before Columbus.

The longer bow, which I refer to as the "war" bow, is usually close to six feet in length and rectangular in cross-section. There is no handle section, and the widest part of the bow is in the middle. The bow bends throughout its entire length in a smooth arc, like the letter "D", from which comes the name D bow. The dimensions of the bow illustrated are as follows: Length between nocks, 71 inches; width at widest point, 1 9/16 inches; thickness at handle, 5/8 inch; width of tip at nock, 1 1/16 inches; thickness of tip at nock, 7/16 inch, draw weight, 65 pounds at 28 inches.

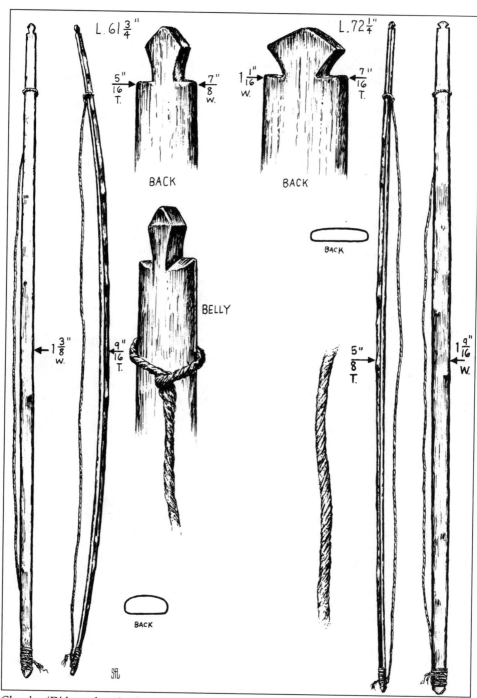

Cherokee 'D' bows, hunting bow (left) and war bow, both of Osage orange (author's collection).

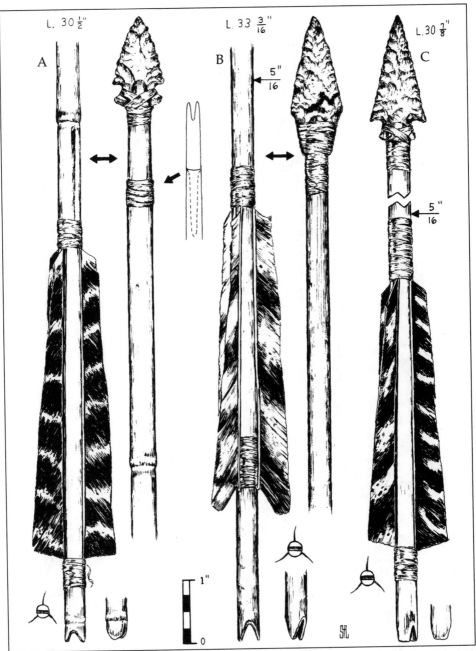

Cherokee arrows (author's collection), A) Cane war or hunting arrow, flint point in short foreshaft of Osage orange, turkey wing fletch glued in center, B) War or hunting arrow, Osage orange shaft, redtail hawk fletch glued in center, C) War or hunting arrow, dogwood shaft, stone point, turkey wing fletch.

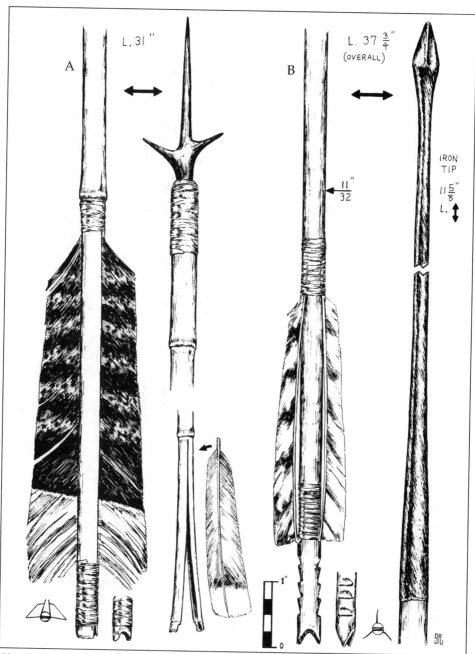

Cherokee arrows (author's collection), A) Two fletch child or quickie arrow, whole turkey tail feather inserted into split cane shaft, wrapped with sinew at ends, tip of thorn from honey locust tree, B) Old corn stalk shooting arrow, shaft of black locust, redtail hawk tail feather fletch, steel spike tip made from buggy spring. Note notches cut in rear of shaft to improve grip of fingers.

The shorter bow, which I refer to as the "hunting" bow, is generally about five feet in length. This illustrated bow is also a D bow with rectangular limbs and no handle section. The dimensions: length between nocks, 60 1/2 inches; width of limb at widest point (center of bow), 1 3/8 inches; thickness of limbs at handle, 9/16 inch; width of tip at nock, 7/8 inch; thickness at nock, 5/16 inch; draw weight, 50 pounds at 28 inches.

The Cherokees, and other Eastern Woodland tribes, also made another type of bow besides the D bow, which I refer to as a handle bow. These had a non-bending handle section a few inches long which was normally narrower and thicker than the maximum dimensions of the working limbs. The Sudbury bow, which we previously examined, falls into this category.

ARROWS

Historical records indicate that cane was used for arrows by the pre-Columbian Cherokees. Today, we still make arrows of River Cane with fore-shafts of hardwood. We also use Rough-leafed Dogwood for arrow shafts. For cornstalk shooting, we like a tough, heavy arrow, so we split the shafts from billets of Osage orange or black locust and whittle them to size.

The traditional Cherokee fletching for arrows was three feathers with their quills wrapped front and back with sinew and the remainder of the quill loose from the shaft. No glue was used. The feathers were tied on at an angle so that the arrow would spin in flight. Today, in preparing feathers for fletching, the quill is scraped very thin, and a short length of quill is left protruding at each end of the feather. In attaching it to the arrow, we first tie down the quill on the back end of the feather with the feather upside down and pointing backwards on the shaft. Then the feather is folded forward, over the sinew wrapping, and the front of the feather wrapped to the shaft with sinew.

There is a misconception held by some that Cherokee arrows were typically fletched with only two feathers. Occasionally, cane arrows were fletched by splitting the cane and inserting a whole tail feather into the split, resulting in a two-feather fletch. However, these arrows do not spin in flight and therefore do not shoot as accurately as three feathers and are generally only used as children's arrows or quick "emergency" arrows. A few people who have seen these two-feather fletched arrows concluded that all Cherokee arrows were fletched in this way, but such is not the case.

Many of the details of the design and usage of the Eastern Woodland bow will always remain clouded by the mists of time. In one sense, this is sad because the knowledge is lost forever. But there is also a good side; the feeling of mystery is one of the things which attract us to traditional archery. The mysterious is always more interesting than the familiar.

Every day, more archers are discovering the fascination of primitive archery. This renewed interest, including making and using the bows, is the best hope we have of rediscovering and preserving some of the secrets and magic known by the bowyers and hunters of old. I believe you will find, as I and many others have found, that as you discover new things about this oldest form of archery, you will also discover new things about yourself. You can venture back through the mists of the past and live, at least for a little while, in the unspoiled world of the pre-Columbian Indian hunter.

ANCIENT EUROPEAN BOWS

Paul Comstock

Picture a time before the invention of the wheel, before civilization, the written word, or the development of cloth or metal. On such an ancient day, skin-clad tribesmen wandered the primordial landscape of Europe, armed with cleverly engineered, highly effective bows and arrows. Skilled and resourceful archery technicians, these people found creative solutions to archery challenges.

We know today that many recent so-called innovations in natural archery were first used by European bowyers of the Stone Age, the Bronze Age, and the Iron Age. American archery publications of the past have covered in great detail bows and arrows of Native Americans. Archery of medieval Europe, in particular the English longbow, has also been the topic of many writings. The world of ancient European archery has drawn less attention. It deserves a close look. There are surprises and mysteries waiting for us. And opportunities. The modern craftsman can duplicate the design concepts of the ancient Europeans and return these weapons to their rightful place in the woods and fields.

This chapter is not intended to be the definitive catalog of prehistoric archery artifacts. Instead, we will discuss the basic bow types of ancient Europe with emphasis on how the modern bowyer can use these old designs to his advantage. We will also offer — here and there — a little speculation on why the ancient bowmakers did what they did.

Many of those interested in historical bows — particularly Native American bows — feel they need to duplicate the old weapons' precise length, width, and thickness. They feel that unless they can perfectly match the old bows' dimensions, their efforts are failures. This approach has its place, but for the amateur craftsman it is of limited use.

If the modern bowyer succeeds in duplicating the artifact precisely, the only thing he will have learned is what draw weight and draw length were used by the man who made the artifact. And this is a useless piece of information. If the bow pulled past 20 inches or so, an aborigine could have shot it well enough. And if it pulled 30 pounds or more, it would be powerful enough to kill people and deer-sized animals. So who cares how far it pulled and how strong it was?

If we examine a group of bows made by the same group of people, we find that dimensions are not consistent. There will be variations in bow length, width, and thickness. These variations were caused by bowyers using different pieces of wood, and building bows to pull different weights, possibly at different lengths. This is the case when examining ancient European bows. No two are exactly the same dimensions.

Instead of concentrating on precise measurements, we would be better served by studying the designs of ancient European bows. We need to ask ourselves: What was the fellow who made this bow trying to accomplish?

It is very important to remember that the requirements for a deadly, reliable, and accurate wooden bow are surprisingly low. The most crude, crooked, ghastly-looking, and inefficient stick imaginable will shoot an arrow as straight as a bullet and kill you dead. Making such a hideous bow long enough is all it takes to increase durability. And making it wide enough will go a long way toward increasing efficiency.

The point is this: People tend to stop experimenting when they have found something that works. And almost any wooden bow will work.

Was the bowyer most interested in economy — producing a bow quickly and easily? Was he most interested in cast per pound? Was he most interested in durability? These questions can best be answered by trying to decide what prompted the bowyer to select the design he used. And specific measurements down to the thousandth of an inch are going to be of very limited help.

What information we can obtain on ancient European bows comes from books written in Europe. Our sources on statistics and dates on ancient European bows are mainly:

• *Neolithic Bows from Somerset, England, and the prehistory of Archery in Northwestern Europe,* by J.G.D. Clark of the Department of Archaeology and Anthropology at the University of Cambridge in Great Britain. This was actually a paper published as part of the *Proceedings of the Prehistoric Society for 1963 — Vol. XXIX.* It is particularly valuable because it contains photographs of several ancient bows and arrows.

• *The Bow: Some Notes on its Origin and Development,* by Gad Rausing, published in Germany and Switzerland, no date listed. This work borrows from earlier academic works, including Clark. But it is quite comprehensive and contains many details. It is often lacking in specifics, particularly dates. But many of the artifacts have not been or cannot be dated.

Clark does some speculating on the origin of the bow. He says all available evidence points to the bow emerging from Africa about 15,000 years ago. Rausing believes the bow is at least 50,000 years old, but admits this date is speculation.

A writer for a mainstream archery magazine once made the preposterous statement that bows and arrows have been around 100,000 years. His point was political. He was attacking the so-called "traditional" anti-compound bow movement. Anything less than the 100,000-year old bow, he argued, isn't traditional. This 100,000-year-old bow exists only in his fertile imagination.

A big archery business used to distribute a lot of written material which often implied that the bow and arrow were a critical factor in primitive man's survival. This is another hoax. Plenty of primitive hunting-gathering people have gotten along just fine with no bows and arrows.

This raises an important question: Did primitive people really need archery at all?

There is not the tiniest shred of proof bows and arrows existed during the majestic Ice Age, when hunters brought down mammoths, mastodons, wooly rhinos, and other giants. Certain cave paintings show darts that appear to be feathered. Other artifacts look like arrowheads. But feathered darts and arrow-head-shaped points are also used with the atlatl.

It is accepted that for bringing down an animal like a mammoth, an atlatl would yield consistently better results than a bow and arrow. An atlatl dart weighs at least 1,000 or 1,500 grains — much heavier than the average weight for arrows of between 300 and 600 grains. Some Africans have gone after elephants with big, heavy bows and heavy arrows, but there is no evidence this was done in the Pleistocene.

Paleolithic spear-throwers may have been of a form not familiar to most primitive technology buffs. For example, the speed of a hand-thrown spear can be increased by using a cord, with one end held in the hand and the other twisted

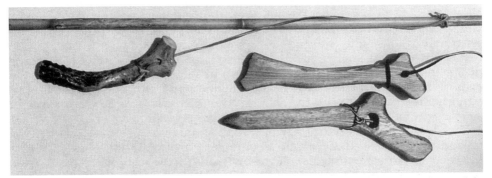

A spear-throwing cord and handle are shown at top, with the cord twisted around the center of the dart. The cord is held in place on the shaft by being twisted over a knot in the end of the cord. Below are two copies of Paleolithic baton de commandement artifacts, each of which can send a 1,500 grain dart over 65 yards.

around the spear to aid thrust and fall from the spear as it is released. Speed of the cord-assisted spear can be improved by using a handle tied to the cord, instead of holding the cord in the hand. It is well for this handle to have some fork or indentation to rest against the spear during the throw. It is also well to have the cord pass through a hole in the end of the handle, to assure straight flight. Such a handle will resemble the baton de commandement artifacts first created by Ice Age hunters 9,000 years before the atlatl was invented.

The advantages of archery increase when hunting smaller, deer-sized animals. With a bow, the hunter can shoot from concealment, and it is easier to carry a lot of arrows, compared to atlatl darts. But it is also important to remember primitive people have hunted deer-sized animals successfully with no bows. The Hopewell and Adena Indians of Ohio used atlatls. Atlatls were also widely used in Australia, where there is scant evidence bows were used at all. When Europeans found them, native Tasmanians did all their hunting with throwing spears.

We can only conclude that archery has proved quite valuable for those who have learned to use it. Those who have not have managed to cope in other ways.

Rausing and others speculate the earliest bow was a naturally tapered branch or sapling, strung to make an asymmetrical bow bending more on one end than the other. This type of bow would be held below center, similar to an asymmetrical Japanese bow. The slender section of the sapling would then be the limber upper limb. And the thicker section would be the stiffer lower limb.

To test this notion, I cut a six-foot length of a hackberry sapling. The small end was 3/4-inch in diameter, the large end 1 1/2-inch. I chopped off all the twigs and removed the bark. When the wood was thoroughly dry (about 9 percent moisture), I strung and shot it.

This bow pulled 32 pounds at 29 inches. It repeatedly shot a one-ounce (437 grain) arrow 95 yards at an elevation of 45 degrees. A regular 30-pound wooden bow can be expected to send the same arrow about 20 yards further. So this unworked sapling bow shot about 82 percent as hard as a wooden bow made the normal way. I would rate that as impressive considering the bow was made with no woodworking. This 32-pound bow is a small-game weapon. If it pulled 40 pounds, it would make a credible weapon for deer-sized animals. The bow was strung five inches high and followed the string about four inches when first unstrung.

When strung, the sapling had twisted in comparison to the way I had cut the nocks. To avoid this problem, the most obvious solution is to simply sharpen the ends of the sapling. In this manner, it could be braced with a tied-on string, or a string with small loops. Or the sharpened ends could also be wrapped with sinew to provide a shoulder for a string with larger loops.

Based on this experience, I would say some ancient pointed pieces of unworked wood have the potential to be archery artifacts. There is one catch. At the time such an unworked sapling bow would have been used, hardwoods were scarce. The oldest bows made the conventional way (ie., tapering in two directions) appeared even before hardwood trees spread to most of Europe.

European archery artifacts are important not because they are European, but because they exist. Archery was probably quite widespread when the ancient European bows were used. But ancient bows outside Europe are very rare. (We are speaking here of bows more than 4,000 years old.) The reason is that Europe contains bogs, into which a number of bows found their way. Immersed in water permanently, the European bows were protected from rot-causing bacteria and allowed to survive. We owe a debt to the European peat-digging industry, which uncovered many of the artifacts.

Which takes us from the realm of guesswork to the realm of evidence. It takes a bow stave or nocked arrow to provide conclusive proof of archery. About 10,000 years ago, this proof appears.

THE OLDEST ARTIFACTS

The oldest definite bow artifacts are the Stellmoor bows, the Holmegaard bows, and the Neolithic yew bows.

To the modern bowmaker, the most striking characteristic these bows share is they do not follow one ring on the back. This is an innovation that came later.

Knowing this, a modern bowmaker would next ask why these bows did not break. The answer is that the edges of the cut-through rings did not run from

This bow is one of many made of board staves by Tim Baker. It shows the rings as straight lines on the back, critical for success in a bow of this type and in the tradition of the Stellmoor bows.

one side of the limb to the other. Instead, the bows were made so the cut-through rings appear mainly as straight lines on the bow's back, parallel with the limbs. Also, the bowyers carefully followed the radial grain of the wood from one end of the bow to the other (see Cutting and Seasoning Wood in Vol. 1 for a complete discussion of growth rings and radial grain). These are the single most important requirements for successful duplication of the oldest bow designs. It is an issue Clark ignores completely, and Rausing hints at only vaguely. We know it is true by careful reading — particularly of Rausing — and examining photographs and detailed drawings of the artifacts. All available photos and drawings showing the grain and growth rings reveal this characteristic.

As amazing as it sounds, there is good reason to suspect the ancient bowyers did not know how to follow one ring on the back. If true, this may weaken the case for the ancient asymmetrical sapling bow. If the sapling bow was made with little or no woodworking, early bowyers would have known that following the surface ring would have made a good back.

It is also important to note that all evidence says the oldest bow artifacts (and lots of others since then) were as tall as the men who shot them. This is an important element in keeping string follow to a minimum. Unbacked shorter bows will show more string follow, on average. As string follow increases, cast per pound drops.

STELLMOOR

The Stellmoor bows were fragments found in the 1930's in northern Germany by archaeologist Alfred Rust. Some publications date the finds to 10,000 years ago. The fragments consisted of two pieces of the outer ends of the limbs, the longest being 9.8 inches. They were destroyed in a fire in Hamburg, Germany, during World War II.

All available evidence confirms they were bows, particularly considering Stellmoor arrows with string nocks were found. Clark concedes the Stellmoor arrows were arrows, but does not think the fragments were bows. Rausing accepts them as bows.

The Stellmoor bows were made from the best material available at the time and location, the heartwood of Scotch pine. Rausing says in late glacial times, yew and hardwoods such as maple and elm were not found in the area of the Stellmoor bowyers. Evidence suggests the bowyers cut the trees a good distance from the hunting grounds where the artifacts were discovered. Rausing also notes Siberians were using bows of Scotch pine well into the historical era. So the wood is proven bow material.

Rausing also says the rings in the Stellmoor bows were not "at right angles to a line parallel to the arrow." In other words, the rings' edges were not seen on the sides of the bow. This means the edges of the rings had to be seen on the back.

Keeping that in mind, consider what it takes to obtain bow wood from Scotch pine. The soft and weak white sapwood is quite thick. So, a large log has to be cut to yield a good piece of heartwood. Makers of Osage orange bows know what a job it is to remove white sapwood and work the back down to one ring. Again, Scotch pine sapwood is quite thick. If a bowyer was really interested in a faster approach, could he find one? Yes. He could take a stave that split cleanly down one side, and use this clean split as the back of an edge ringed stave. In this way, no work would be needed on the back other than smoothing and polishing. The back would follow the fibers, because the split followed the grain. The edges of the rings would appear on the bow's back and belly, just like the Stellmoor artifacts.

Rausing says the Stellmoor fragments were flat backed with a rounded belly, growing almost circular further from the end. This circular cross-section appears later in Africa, and on some of the English bows pulled from the Mary Rose ship. This design suggests a bow at least as tall as the archer, true of many African bows and all the Mary Rose bows. The length of the Stellmoor arrows also suggests the bows were man-sized.

It is doubtful if the Stellmoor bowyers could have used a sapling bow, which works well if it is hardwood. A pine sapling bow could be expected to perform very poorly.

There is good reason to suspect that economy is a big factor in this basic shape. Starting with a square stave and using a drawknife and spokeshave, a good bowyer can have a flat-backed round-bellied yew ready to try out on the tillering board as quick as 15 minutes. With a round belly, the woodworking tool is cutting only a narrow piece at a time, so there is less resistance to the tool and things go fairly quickly.

If we make a flat-bellied bow, the work slows down because the woodworking tool is resting on more wood, creating more resistance. By comparison, a wide-limbed bow with a narrow, deep handle slows the work even more.

HOLMEGAARD

The next oldest bow artifacts are the Holmegaards (named for the area in Denmark were the first specimen was found), which are dated to about 8,000 years ago. Many bows made in the Holmegaard style have been discovered, with 4,000 years separating the oldest from the youngest. The oldest come from the island of Zealand in Denmark, and are made of elm. Some later Holmegaard-style bows were made of yew, and were found in Germany. Like the Stellmoors, the Holmegaard artifacts have flat backs and round bellies.

Some of the Holmegaard artifacts are fairly narrow. But the two oldest elm Holmegaard bows deserve to be called wide-limbed. The largest of the two oldest Holmegaards was 64 inches long with limbs 2.36 inches wide. Modern American bowyers have learned the best way to get top cast-per-pound with a wood like elm is by "overbuilding" — to make the bow long and wide. At first glance, this step seems unnecessary and only serves to give the bow more bending capability than needed. But the real advantage of overbuilding is to reduce the strain on a bow made from marginally elastic wood. All else being equal, this will decrease string follow and increase bow efficiency. This Holmegaard artifact certainly qualifies as overbuilt.

Skilled modern bowyers have made elm bows 64 inches long and two inches wide. These bows show only a slight amount of string follow when pulling 60 pounds or more — for 27 or so inches of draw length. These bows shoot like demons and give nothing away to more so-called traditional narrow bows of yew and Osage. If this 8,000-year old elm bow was made out of dry wood and well-tillered, it could match the performance of the best wooden bows made today.

The second of the oldest Holmegaards was smaller — 60 inches long with limbs 1 3/4 inches wide. Compared to the larger bow, this one was probably lighter or used by a smaller person, or both.

Clark points out that what is man-sized today was not necessarily man-sized long ago. He says the average Neolithic man in Great Britain was five feet seven inches tall, while the average Neolithic man in Switzerland was five feet four inches tall. An ancient Dane was found who was about as tall as the ancient Swiss.

While the oldest Holmegaard elms suggest a high-performance emphasis, some of the later elms do not. Some of them are fairly narrow and deep, which would indicate they would show more string follow than the wider elms. Even so, no Stone Age Dane ever wanted to get shot with one. Since yew can stand higher levels of strain than elm, the narrower Holmegaard yews were no doubt quite efficient weapons.

Two such bows were found at Diepholz, Germany. At least one limb tip is missing from each bow. The maximum widths of these yew bows are 1.18 inches and 1.3 inches. Called the Ochsenmoor bows, they are dated 2,400 to 1,800 B.C. Elm Holmegaard bows have been found only in Denmark.

Holmegaard-style bows have also been pulled from a lake in Italy, and dated to the Bronze Age. Rausing cites a piece of pine pulled from a Swedish bog which one historian said was a Holmegaard-style bow. Rausing said this diagnosis is incorrect, but does not explain why.

Everything we have said so far about the Holmegaards has just been by way of introduction. Now comes the real meat of the Holmegaard style:

The bows were bent backward. That is, the side of the tree that formed the outer surface became the belly, and the inside wood became the back.

To my knowledge, Tim Baker was the first person to figure out that this could be done in almost the same way as the Holmegaards were built. The trick for such a backward bow is to use a fairly small piece of wood. Baker has shown that with this configuration, the cross-section of the bow limb is such that the rings form an arch. Because the rings are arched, both sides of each ring appear as straight lines on the bow's back. We could call such a back "double-edged ringed" because each ring appears twice as a straight line.

With such a backward bow, it is not 100 percent necessary for the parallel lines on the back to run the length of the entire limb. The limb can be tillered by cutting the taper only on the back. When this is done, the outer rings will continue as straight lines, while the rings in the middle of the limb will feather to a point.

As will be explained later, this does not damage durability if the bow is long enough, and if the limbs are about the same length and bend evenly.

Holmegaard style bows differ from pure backward bows in two respects. With a pure backward bow, all the tillering is done on the back. With the Holmegaards, tillering was done on the backs, sides and bellies. In addition, the Holmegaards had narrow, deep handles protruding from the back of the bow. (This makes handle "dips" an 8,000-year-old innovation.) This requires a larger

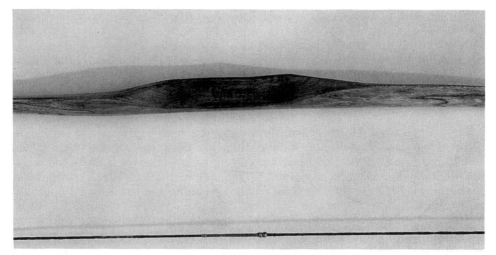

The handle protrudes from the back of a Holmegaard-style bow. This is accomplished by working down the back and leaving the handle high.

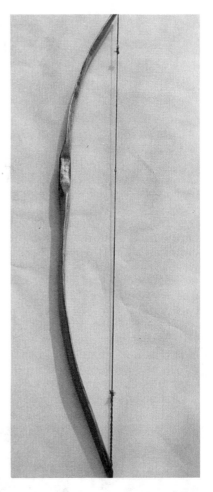

Full length view of the bow.

piece of wood than a backward bow using the same cross-section its entire length.

Rausing seems to suggest the Holmegaards were worked only on the belly. But the handle protruding from the back cannot be made without working the back down, and leaving the handle high.

Pure backward bows were made in the prehistoric era. Making a backward bow is economical. Woodworking is greatly reduced by starting with a small piece and only cutting on the back. But a Holmegaard requires a larger piece of wood to begin with, plus much more woodworking.

On top of that, the Holmegaard bowyers were starting out with a piece of wood big enough to let them use wide limbs and narrow, deep handles, with the backs following one ring. A later Iron Age bowyer would have followed a single ring along the back. Yet the Holmegaard bowyers didn't do it. Why?

I don't know. But if I had to bet a nickel, I'd say they didn't know how to follow one ring on the back. The only evidence I can submit for this theory is

The belly of an elm Holmegaard replica. The originals were worked on back, belly, and sides.

this: During the Bronze Age, bowyers started making their bows follow one ring on the back. And they never stopped once the innovation was introduced. The only exception is when a backward bow was made out of a small piece. There was a real benefit to this. It let them get a good bow out of a small piece of wood. But they only did it when there was an economic advantage. If there was no advantage, Bronze Age and Iron Age bowyers did not make the bow backward.

Yet the Holmegaard bowyers made the bow backward even when there was no clear benefit to doing so.

This is not intended to condemn the Holmegaard style as the product of a bunch of dummies. Far from it. The Holmegaard bowyers found an answer to their problem, and it worked. When a bow style survives for 4,000 years, it cannot be called anything but a success.

Wide flatbows were made in ancient Great Britain, Denmark, Holland, and Sweden. The bow at left is a Holmegaard replica. The bow at right is patterned after the Meare Heath bow. Although stylized, the bow in the center is the functional equal of the other two and follows the ancient European flatbow tradition.

NEOLITHIC YEW BOWS

The Stellmoor and Holmegaard bows are real Stone Age weapons. The Stellmoor is from the Mesolithic (middle Stone Age) and the Holmegaard is usually considered Mesolithic or early Neolithic (new Stone Age). The earliest beginnings of the Bronze Age are usually traced to 3,000 B.C. or 3,500 B.C., which is before most early yew bows. Even so, Clark and Rausing judge the oldest yew bows as Neolithic, under the assumption the Bronze Age had not yet spread to the bowyers.

Like the Holmegaard bowyers, the Neolithic yew bowyers had some ideas about grain that are a little removed from the modern mainstream. And the Neolithic yew bows also did not follow one ring on the back.

Rausing discusses 22 yew bows found at prehistoric lake-shore settlements in Switzerland. One of them was a backward bow. And all the rest have a

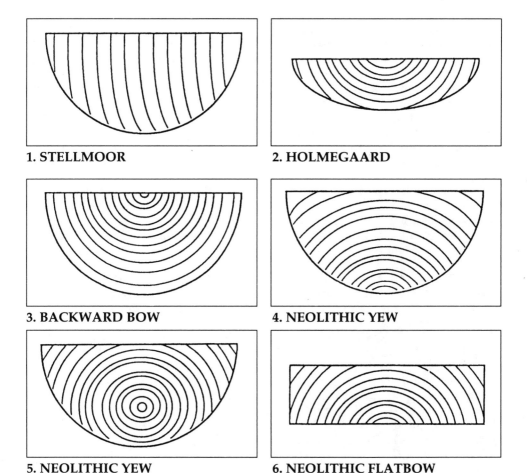

1. STELLMOOR **2. HOLMEGAARD**

3. BACKWARD BOW **4. NEOLITHIC YEW**

5. NEOLITHIC YEW **6. NEOLITHIC FLATBOW**

Cross-sections of prehistoric bows. Backs are towards top. Graphics by Tom Williams.

cross-section basically like Illustration No. 4 or No. 5. (One bow has a keel on the belly that makes the cross-section almost a triangle.) These are not backward-bending weapons like the Holmegaards. But they have a double edge-ringed cross-section, as do the Holmegaards.

Like the Holmegaards, the bows in Illustrations No. 4 or No. 5 have rings appearing on the back of the bow as straight lines parallel with the limbs. Wide-limbed bows also showed this characteristic, as seen in Illustration No. 6 (regardless of whether the cross-section was a rectangle). Clark shows photos of the Meare Heath artifact and one of the yew bows from the lake shore sites described by Rausing. Each photo clearly shows the cut-through rings on the back as straight lines parallel with the limbs. Rausing points out that a number of the Swiss bows show the very center ring of the log (as in Illustration No. 5). Rausing says the Swiss bows were made by using wood deep from the log. He assumes the log was pretty big to begin with. These bows could have also been made by using a fairly small piece of wood, and cutting the outside off. If you were to make such a bow with stone tools, what would you want: a big log or a smaller one? I'd pick the smaller one.

The Swiss bows and all other Neolithic yew bows are completely heartwood. Were these bowyers somehow influenced by the Stellmoor bows? Could they have assumed yew sapwood is as poor as Scotch pine sapwood? Or does their behavior indicate (like the Holmegaard bowyers) that they never thought of following one ring on the back? Remember, in the Bronze Age, the cross-sections of No. 4 and No. 5 disappeared for good.

We should stop here for a moment and address a separate issue. Certainly by now, some modern readers have said to themselves, "Shucks. Them old bows was sinewed."

There are no traces of a sinew back on any of these artifacts discussed so far. None of the bows shows back scuffing, which could be expected as an aid to the gluing process. But the best answer to the issue is this: These designs work with no backing at all. People tend to use sinew when they need it. Like on 40-inch horse bows or composite bows. The bows we have discussed so far did not need sinew then, and they don't need it now.

The D-cross section was perhaps the most common among the Neolithic yews. Some were what are now called D-bows. That is, the cross-section of the handle matched that of the limbs, and the bow bent along its entire length.

In September, 1991, headlines around the world proclaimed a 5,300-year-old corpse had appeared in a melting glacier at 10,500 feet in the Tyrolian Mountains on the Italian-Austrian border. The man's body was well-preserved, along with his property. This included a copper axe and a longbow. The January, 1992 *Discover* magazine published a photo of the corpse and its property. The bow appears to be a routine Neolithic-style yew, with a D cross-section along its length. The bow is wider than some of the other Neolithic yews. Yet Rausing notes that for use in cold climates, ancient bowyers often made the bow wider than normal. One end of the bow is missing, probably broken off under pressure of the glacier. The surviving limb tip shows a common Neolithic nock style. The limb tip is sharpened to a point. The bowstring was either tied on, or used small loops, or rested on a sinew wrap collar, or some combination of all three.

A scientist involved in the study of the corpse wrote a letter to Tim Baker. The letter suggested the bow was being built to replace one lost or broken in the field. This diagnosis was based on woodworking marks still on the bow.

One variation of this common style is the Ashcott Heath bow. Like the Meare Heath, the Ashcott was found at Somerset, England. The Ashcott is dated to 2,665 B.C., making it a few years younger than the Meare Heath.

The Ashcott may claim the distinction of being the oldest recurve. Only one limb survives. Its nock has more of a defined shoulder than most Neolithic yews. The nock (as photographed in Clark) shows a definite string wear groove. This groove is on the side of the limb tip that is gradually, but definitely, curved toward the bow's back.

The Ashcott also appears to have a thicker grip than the usual Neolithic yew. The flattened back gradually rises to a higher spot at the handle. The Ashcott Heath and Meare Heath artifacts are each one surviving limb. It seems the Meare Heath broke because of compression failure in the handle.

I lost a yew bow this way. The wood on the belly side of the handle popped off, and the bow broke at the handle in the next instant. The Meare Heath artifact shows identical damage. Veteran makers of yew bows blame such failure on the wood itself, not the bow design. My bow was a typical English yew, 68 inches long.

Clark shows a photo of the handle section of an extremely interesting yew from De Zilk, Noordwijkerjout, Zuid Holland, Netherlands. This bow was radio-carbon dated to 1,550 B.C., give or take 100 years. Rausing says the date cannot be trusted, because the circumstances of the bow's discovery are not documented. He also says the bow is Neolithic, not Bronze Age as claimed by Clark. This bow is completely heartwood. It appears to have the routine Neolithic yew back. It also looks almost exactly like a 1930's American flatbow. Its maker beat *Archery, The Technical Side* to the punch by about 3,500 years!

The bow has a narrow, deep handle. The sides of the limbs are squared off near the handle. The limbs are two inches wide. The entire bow is about 63 inches long, very close to the likely size of an ancient Dutchman. Rausing indicates the belly is slightly rounded. The Americans of the 1930's would have made the belly perfectly flat. Even with a slightly rounded belly, the Dutch yew is the functional equal of the American flatbow because of its two-inch limbs.

Rausing cites a neolithic yew bow from Bodman, Germany, that had a flat back, flat sides, and a belly only slightly convex.

Another yew bow, from the Swiss lake shore site of Burgaschisee, has a perfectly flattened back and belly. Rausing suggests this bow was never completely finished. If he is correct, the ancient bowyers may have left the belly slightly rounded on a wide-limbed bow because it was an easy way to finish the tiller and reduce the bow's weight. To be more specific, the woodworking would go quicker when compared to flattening the belly perfectly.

The Meare Heath bow had limbs 2.6 inches wide. Clark's photos show the back to be slightly crowned and the belly quite flat. Both Clark and Rausing seem flabbergasted by the size of the Meare Heath bow, which would have been about 74 inches long if limb length was equal. This length, about 190 centimeters, is only slightly more than the tallest Britons of that era (says Clark)

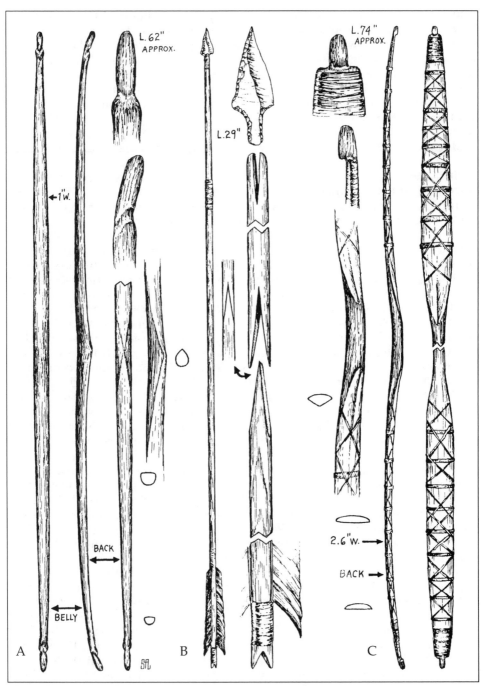

A) Ashcott bow, showing slight recurve, circa 2665 B.C. B) Stellmoor two piece spliced arrow, circa 8000 B.C. (fletch speculative). C) Meare Heath bow with distinctive wrapping, circa 2690 B.C.

who were about 180 centimeters tall. If a six-foot man shot the Meare Heath, the bow's dimensions are proportionately correct when compared to the largest ancient Holmegaard, which had limbs 2.36 inches wide, and was 64 inches long. The Meare Heath has a length to width ratio of 28.4:1, while the Holmegaard's is 27.1:1.

The Meare Heath is made of yew and it certainly could have been made narrower. But overbuilding the bow would have traded some efficiency for durability, by further reducing the strain in the limbs. Unfortunately for the bowyer, the wood in the Meare Heath handle turned traitor.

Clark and Rausing also have difficulty explaining why the Meare Heath bow was wrapped. It was wrapped with as many as 18 wide bands of rawhide or leather. A separate wrapping used much smaller strands. The smaller wrapping surrounded the limb in a series of X's. One small piece of this survives, and Clark says it is either sinew or gut. The bow also shows signs of being wrapped at the nocks.

Unlike most Neolithic yews, the Meare Heath had pin nocks with well-defined shoulders for the string. Modern bowmakers know a yew bow can split at the nocks. The Meare Heath's wrapped limb tips served a real function.

Clark's depictions of a reconstructed Meare Heath were apparently the first published. They show the pin of the nock to be thicker than the rest of the limb tip. The deep section extends on the belly side from the pin into the limb, creating a bump where it meets the limb's belly. The artifact is broken at the nock and there is scarcely enough wood left to confirm the deep section existed. Whether it would have resulted in improved durability is a good question. Yew nocks usually split where the string rests. With the Meare Heath, this would be the shoulder, not the pin.

The rest of the wrapping could have been an attempt to prevent fracture. Or it may have been cosmetic. If the Meare Heath's wrapping was cosmetic, we can hardly blame the bowyer. It must have been something to see. The belly side of the limb near the handle has a slightly raised crown that forms a straight line centered in the limb. This is a cosmetic feature rare for a European bow. Ridges of this type are more often found on Native American bows.

Rausing and Clark are also surprised that the back of the Meare Heath shows where the bowyer trimmed the wrap but allowed his blade to scratch the wood. Rausing notes bowyers are careful not to damage the fibers of a bow's back. When the back follows one ring, it is indeed risky to damage the wood. But the Meare Heath did not follow one ring. The later section on reconstructions will show the double edge-ringed structure is not so sensitive to such abuse.

Another oddity among Neolithic yews is the Edington Burtle bow. Clark says it is also from Somerset and dates to about 1,320 B.C. It has raised knots on the belly and may be the oldest example of this technique. The bow is only 4 feet 11 inches long and one limb is almost six inches shorter than the other. The limb tips do not match. The long limb has a routine pointed nock. The shorter limb ends with a semi-pin nock. It has slight shoulders and the pin is shaped like a knob. Even more surprising: the longer limb is straight and the shorter limb is recurved similar to the Ashcott Heath. Since 4 feet 11 inches is short for a Neolithic yew, I wonder if the archer didn't break the bow and then attempt to repair it. If so, he may have made a mistake by recurving the shorter end. It could have made the tiller more uneven by making the short limb even stronger. Because the one limb is so much longer than the other, he could not be criticized had he left both limbs alone, allowing the longer limb to bend more, similar to a Japanese bow. The asymmetry of the Edington Burtle is very unusual. A Holmegaard would probably break if given this treatment, as will be discussed later. The Edington Burtle is probably an aberration, or at the least a bold experiment.

Some Neolithic nock types were pointed with a gradual taper. Others were pointed, but the thickness of the limb swelled suddenly. This would have been an aid if the string was tied in place, or used small loops. Other bows had squared tips with faint string shoulders.

One of the prettiest nocks was found on a Neolithic yew bow at the Swiss Niederwil, Thurgau, settlement site. The limb tip was cut into a graceful spoon shape, and apparently wrapped with sinew beneath the spoon to hold the string.

The nock at top is typical for Neolithic European bows. The limb tips are pointed, then wrapped to form a shoulder to hold the string. The spoon-shaped nock at bottom is patterned after a Neolithic yew found at Niederwil Thurgau, Switzerland. The artifact had a shadow on the wood that suggested this type of wrapping was used.

THE NEOLITHIC BOW IN ACTION

There are apparently no Neolithic bows surviving from the Mediterranean area. But the use of these weapons is depicted in a number of rock paintings in eastern Spain.

Many books on early man show depictions of these paintings. Photographs, however, do them more justice. People in the drawings are somewhat stylized, but the proportions are good, particularly when animals are shown. It is fair to assume the Spanish bows were typical Neolithic yews. Quality yew grew in the high country of Spain and Italy. Centuries later this wood was exported to England to create an archery legend of a different sort.

Some bows in the drawings show a set-back in the handle even when drawn. Clark incorrectly says this can only be accomplished by artificially warping the wood, but as hundreds of modern bowyers know, it is easily accomplished by using a naturally reflexed stave.

Bow hunting is often shown as a dynamic team effort in the drawings. The most famous shows a line of bowmen shooting arrows into red deer, presumably being moved in a drive.

Another drawing shows a melee of archers shooting ibex. Curiously, most of the ibex are shot in the neck. This may have been done to prevent a fast kill that could send the ibex down a mountainside — a hazard faced by modern sheep hunters. Perhaps it was more effective to deliver a wound that would leave the ibex dead in his bed, where he could be retrieved the next day. Several red deer are also shown shot in the neck.

The Spanish archers had plenty of nerve. One painting shows an auroch bull, impaled with arrows like a pin cushion, thundering in a mad rage after a fleeing bowman. The result of such an encounter is left to our imagination.

The Spanish rock paintings also document early military use of archery. One shows a unit of about 10 men trading shots with a group of about 17. Most of the combatants are running, and they are shown only a few yards apart. The scene suggests a combination of military organization and blood lust.

Other paintings may depict such organization. In one, a group of men with bows raised over their heads walks single file behind a man wearing a headdress. Another painting shows a warrior wearing a headdress mortally wounded and falling in battle. Yet another shows a prone individual, filled with arrows, who has just been executed by a line of archers.

Other ancient European artwork shows bowhunters chasing game while accompanied by dogs.

THE BRONZE AGE

The Neolithic yew styles survived well past the beginning of the Bronze Age, but they were soon to disappear.

This happened when bowyers learned they could make a bow with a single ring forming the back. This yielded an economic benefit. If the wood immediately under the bark could be the bow's back, the woodworking required to finish a double edge-ringed back was eliminated. Backward bows would sometimes still be made of smaller pieces of wood. But if larger pieces were used, the back followed one ring.

In the Bronze Age, bow design and construction settled into a familiar routine that would last for centuries.

This new technique also made things much easier when using "character" wood with bumps and dips on the surface. Evidence suggests all the older bows were made of extremely straight-grained material. By making the back follow one ring, bowyers could now handily use more common pieces of wood with more flaws.

Rausing said the oldest example of a bow with a single ring on the back is the Margreteberg, Vasby bow from Sweden. One end of a limb was found but the wood type is undetermined. Rausing says the first composite bows appeared in the Bronze Age. He speculates the Margreteberg bow could be a wooden copy of a composite. He says this because the bow had a very deep section of wood left behind the nock, which was cut across the back. Cutting the outer ring for the nock, however, could require such reinforcement to prevent fracture.

The bow apparently began a decline as a military weapon during the Bronze Age. The Iron Age began about 1,000 B.C., hot on the heels of the Bronze Age. Rausing classifies succeeding bows as Iron Age types.

These small knots on the back of an elm Holmegaard replica are showing no signs of deterioration.

Longbow, by Robert Hardy, lists some finds not included by Rausing. They include the 1935 discovery of an oak longbow found in Denmark, and dated between 1,500 and 2,000 B.C. Hardy says wood was removed only from the belly side. If this bow follows one ring on the back, and the dating is accurate, this may be the oldest bow of the modern conventional type. Hardy also mentions an oak flatbow found in Scotland, dated to 1,300 B.C.

Other recent finds were described in an article published by the *Society of Archer Antiquaries.* A number of bows were described that were found in the Italian lake of Ledro between 1929 and 1967. The wood is not identified. The bows are dated to the Bronze Age. They include bows made in the Holmegaard and Neolithic yew styles.

They also include a surprise. One of the bows looks just like a deflex recurve, which — in laminated glass form — became so popular in the 1950's and 1960's in the United States. The longest of these artifacts is 144 centimeters (56.5 inches). This appears to be a deviation from the man-sized bows used further north. The article describing these bows depicts the artifacts, and they show an extreme level of string follow. Shorter unbacked bows drawn fairly long lengths tend to follow the string excessively. By comparison, strain on the wood is at a more acceptable level and string follow tends to be reduced in unbacked man-sized bows.

THE IRON AGE

When the Iron Age began, archery was apparently suffering a decline in Europe. By this time agriculture supported nearly every population; the bow no longer fed as many people as it once had. Advances in weapon technology produced swords and socketed spear heads. When archery reappeared in war, it was as long-range artillery. The close-range fighting was done by the man with the sword, who was relied on to close with and crush the enemy.

The bogs of Denmark and Northern Germany have yielded a number of Iron Age bows. They include discoveries at Vimose, Kragehule, Thorsbjerg, and Heechterp. Thirty-six bows were also found on a buried boat at Nydam. These bows date between 100 and 350 A.D., and are made like the English longbow. They follow one ring on the backs and have a basic D cross-section along their entire length. Some — like the Stellmoors and Mary Rose bows — also show a near-circular cross-section.

As a group, they are all not as wide or deep as the bows from the Mary Rose, which sank in 1545 A.D. Hardy says one of the Nydam bows was 1.1 inches wide and 1 inch deep at the thickest point. Rausing says these bows were yew, but Hardy said they were yew and fir.

The Vimose bows range from 66 to 77 1/2 inches in length. The strongest was 1.4 inches wide. The bowyers apparently left the yew sapwood as they found it on the tree. Some limb tips are almost entirely sapwood.

Rausing claims the Kragehul bows were ceremonially broken. Aside from that, they are identical to the Vimose bows. The Nydam bows' lengths range from 70 to 73.6 inches.

While these bows are virtually identical to the later English yew bows, they had their own peculiar features. Some had nocks cut into the wood, while others had two sets of nocks cut on each end. Presumably, this allowed the archer to use a heavier weight with the inner nocks, and a lighter weight with the outer nocks. Some nocks were cut as slots in the bow's back. Others had nocks cut in from both sides.

Jim Hamm has a theory about double-nocked bows that deserves consideration. A sinew or gut string will stretch in wet weather, dropping the bow's brace height. Under these circumstances, the archer could return brace height and bow weight to normal by simply slipping the string from the inner to outer nock.

Some of the bows are cut on the ends, as if they had been fitted with horn or metal nocks. A metal nock survives on a Nydam bow. Rausing describes it as 3.5-inch sharpened point, which could have been used as a lance in a fight.

A number of these bows also show signs of being wrapped. None of the wrappings survive, but marks are left on the wood, perhaps by resin used to attach the wraps. The wrapping were put on as ribbons about 4/10ths of an inch wide. Some wrappings circled the bow like stripes on a candy cane. Others crisscrossed on the back and belly. (Whatever urge the Meare Heath bowyer felt was obviously duplicated by these bowyers.)

If a modern observer was handed one of these Iron Age bows, he would certainly identify it as an English longbow. But just as Leif Erickson beat Columbus to the New World, other Scandinavians also beat the English to the English longbow.

This bow type may have survived until the English adopted it. Germanic tribes used the design to inflict losses on the Roman legions in several battles. The Germans' descendants later became the Saxons of England, but it has never been clearly demonstrated that the yew longbow went with them. Many later writers claim the English Saxons used short bows.

There is plenty of reason to think that mass production played a role in the development of the long yew design. The Danish, German, and English bows were all used for fighting. So the bowyers had the task of arming a number of men. Under these circumstances, there is a real advantage to producing as many weapons as possible from a single log. Make the bows narrow, and you will get more bows per log. Make each bow thick enough, and you will obtain the desired draw weight. Make the bow long enough and you will be assured of durability. The highly elastic yew will stand the strain of such a design. The Danish-German-English bow fulfilled all of these requisites.

In his 1926 book *Archery*, Robert Elmer argues that Scandinavians and Saxons spread the yew longbow to Great Britain before the Norman invasion of 1066. Elmer disputed claims that the Saxons were using short bows in 1066. He said this error stems from Saxon drawings not drawn to scale, and was given credence by an incompetent writer for Encyclopedia Britannica, who spread the information. Elmer also attacks the idea that the English longbow was copied from the Welsh bow. This claim deserves thought, since the Welsh bow was elm and the English bow was nearly a carbon copy of the Continental yew.

Rausing said the yew longbows appeared again in Germany in the 8th Century. Those we call Vikings, who came from Norway, Sweden, and Denmark, also used the same yew longbow. As evidence of Elmer's claim of Viking forays into the British Isles, Rausing said a Viking longbow and sword were found in an Irish crannog. In 870 A.D., the Danes defeated the Anglican King Edmund in Great Britain. Adding injury to insult, they tied him to a tree and skewered him with arrows. According to legend, this tree was torn apart in a storm in the early 1900's and metal arrowheads came falling out.

In case we agree too quickly with Elmer's arguments, Rausing said a Saxon grave on the Isle of Wight contained arrowheads and "traces" of a bow five feet long. A few such traces, however, are a poor substitute for an entire bow.

He also writes the Franks were using short flatbows in the 10th Century, and bases this conclusion solely on depictions of artwork, which are poor substitutes for actual artifacts. Elmer's criticism is a valid one: Much old artwork is so stylized that the dimensions are completely unreliable. As an example, Elmer cites Swedish rock carvings. One shows a man shooting a bow that looks about three feet long. But a nearby carving shows a man behind a plow being pulled by animals "that look more like Scotch terriers than anything else."

Even though the narrow, long yew was spreading near and far, the old concept of the wide-limbed Holmegaard and Meare Heath was still around.

In Asby, Stigtoma, Sweden, the ends of a spruce flatbow were found, dated between 400 and 700 A.D. Rausing shows a drawing of one of these pieces. The bow appears to follow one ring on the back in typical Iron Age style. But the end of the limb is extremely wide with very little width taper. If this bow was close to man-sized, it was just as overbuilt as the Meare Heath or the largest Holmegaard. This overbuilding would have been very valuable in a bow made of spruce, which is much less elastic than yew.

An early wood-backed bow appeared in Europe. A 1678 account describes the contemporary Lap bow of northern Scandinavia. The bow was birch, backed with pine which had been applied with fish glue.

One type of wooden bow has attained legendary status even though no artifacts survive: the Welsh bow. The legend stems mainly from an account written by Gerald de Barri, also known as Giraldus Cambrensis, or Gerald the Welshman. An Englishman, he journeyed through Wales in 1188, and described a siege at Abergavenny Castle in 1182. Pursued by Welsh archers, two soldiers ran into a castle tower and slammed the oak door behind them. The enraged Welsh let fly and sent their arrowheads completely through the door, which Gerald said was "a hand," or about four inches, thick. Such hostile encounters were common. The English and Welsh fought like cats and dogs for generations.

Gerald said the Welsh bows were made of elm "rough and lumpy, but stout and strong" and capable of inflicting severe wounds at close range. Hardy argues that Gerald's Latin, correctly translated, also says the bows could shoot a long distance.

If a real Welsh bow is ever discovered, it will be archery's biggest archaeological find since the Meare Heath. Some writers say the Welsh bow was short. This speculation is based on drawings. Hardy shows such an original drawing of a Welsh archer. The bow seems short, but the artwork is not to scale. The bow is as thick as the archer's wrist and the arrowhead is bigger than his fist. Elmer would agree such depictions are completely unreliable.

Rausing said Gerald wrote that the Welsh weapon was a flatbow. Hardy attacks Rausing's translation, and implies he thinks the English yew descended from the Welsh bow.

Leaving such squabbles aside, let this writer assure you of one thing: For a heavy, unbacked elm bow to shoot as hard as it possibly can, the bow must be wide-limbed and man-sized, in the tradition of the Holmegaard, Meare Heath, De Zilk, and Asby-Stigtoma. Such a bow can indeed be "rough and lumpy," as are many such elm bows I have made. If the Welsh elms were flat but narrow, or wide and short, efficiency would drop noticeably. If they were made like the English longbow, efficiency would fall even more, in direct proportion to increases in draw weight.

COMPOSITE BOWS

Composite bows were around in early Europe. They appear to have originated from troops fighting for the Romans, and from invading eastern tribes, such as the Huns.

We should leave Europe for a moment and travel to the Lena Valley in Siberia, between 3,000 and 2,000 B.C. Hunters were using short bows with bellies made of antler. The antler remnants of these bows were found in graves. Rausing said sixteen "bows" have been found. The antler is always smoothed on one side. The other side is always flattened and roughened, for gluing. Fifteen of the bows were made of two pieces of antler, and the remaining bow used three pieces. All evidence suggests the bows were straight-ended, without recurves or siyahs. On one bow, nocks are cut into the antler. In the others, presumably nocks were cut into the wood protruding from the ends. The length of these bows ranges from 40 to 59 inches. This, combined with the antler bellies, increases the suspicion the bows may have been backed with sinew. Conceivably, the bows could have used wood and antler only.

Either way, the composite bow concept is extremely old.

One of the earliest types in Europe was the Yrzi bow. It had a horn belly, wooden core, and sinew back. There were no recurves or siyahs, but the bow was shaped like a C bent toward the back when unstrung. The bow used laths of bone for the limb tips, and the nocks were cut into the bone.

These bone pieces have been found in ancient Roman camps. They have also appeared in Russia, China, and Hungary.

Rausing says Hun bows also used bone reinforcements at the handles. An eastern tribe called the Avars invaded Europe at the beginning of the Middle Ages, using composites with recurved ears. Rausing says the Hun bow was straighter at the ends, similar to the Yrzi bows.

Like the Welsh bow, the classical Grecian bow has become legendary although no artifacts survive. Homer described it as two ibex horns joined at the handle. Rausing said this cannot be done because of the shape of ibex horns. He apparently did not know that horn and baleen — like wood — can be steamed into a new shape. Tim Baker once sent me a small piece of baleen about a foot long that he had recurved. I cut nocks and strung it. It pulled about three pounds. It shot an arrow weighing about 50 grains with a force that surprised me. If the mechanical problems can be licked, I have no doubt a solid-horn bow could be extremely effective.

But Rausing may be right when he says the Grecian bow was a composite. To be sure, the scores of Renaissance artists who depicted the Grecian bow never saw one.

ARROWS

Perhaps the most surprising thing about ancient European arrows is that the bifaced stone arrowhead — so familiar in America because the Indians used them — was a late development.

The earliest European arrows used heads made of retouched stone flakes. The bifaced head usually has a lens-shaped cross section with scars on both sides.

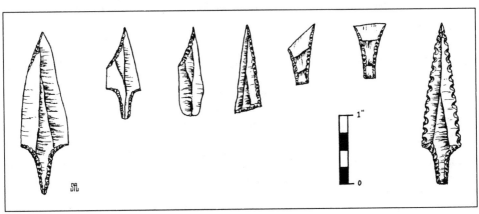

Neolithic arrowheads made from touched-up flakes.

The oldest European stone heads were made by taking a flake knocked from a core, and working the edges only. These heads typically had a smooth surface on one side and fluted scars on the other. By the Bronze Age, bifaced arrowheads were finally in widespread use.

Chisel-shaped stone arrowheads such as these were used extensively in Stone Age Europe. They are easily made from small flakes.

Perhaps we should say "proven bifaced arrowheads," because a collection of artifacts more than 15,000 years old tantalizes the imagination.

From a cave in Eastern Spain emerged a number of beautifully made bifaced points which were the right size for arrows. Clark shows several at actual size, with some 1.5 inches long and one only 15/16ths of an inch.

These points are from the Late Solutrean industry. Earlier and later industries (specifically, the Magdalenian) concentrated on blades knocked from cores. But the biface was in its glory in the Solutrean, with superb bifaces of all sizes produced.

Some publications say the Solutrean diet included deer and goats. Conceivably, the small Solutrean points could have been used with an atlatl on deer and goats. They cannot be accepted as arrowheads without more evidence, which does not exist.

The earliest definite European arrowheads are described in *"På jagt med stenalder-våben"* (*A Hunt with Stone Age weapons*), or *"Macro and Micro Wear Traces on Lithic Projectile Points,"* published in the Journal of Danish Archaeology Volume 3, 1984. The authors are Anders Fisher, Peter Vemming Hansen, and Peter Rausmussen.

This paper divides the flake arrowheads into two types. One is the Brommian point, made from a fluted flake. Sometimes, a tang is chipped into the base. Larger Brommian points were probably used on spears or darts, or as knives. The second is the transverse, or chisel point. The sharp edge faces the path of the arrow, like a chisel. (This type seemed most common among the Danish Holmegaard-era archers.)

The authors conducted a number of tests (including shooting replica points into recently killed animals) and concluded the wear traces shown by many transverse and Brommian artifacts are those that would have resulted from hunting. Four arrows have been found with chisel-shaped points still attached. The Danes also note bones have been found which were struck with chisel-shaped points.

The blade, burin, and microlith stone technologies predate archery. Apparently the earliest archers simply modified these flakes and microliths as arrowheads. I made and shot a few Brommian points into a dirt embankment, and they all broke quickly. By comparison, a good biface — even if made of glass or obsidian — proved more durable. This may be why the biface replaced the flake head.

Brommian style heads were found with the Stellmoor arrows. At the same excavation, splinters of stone were found in reindeer bones.

Microliths — flakes even smaller than Brommian heads — were found on an arrow from south Sweden, Clark says. A pointed piece was used as the tip with a longer flake positioned on the side of the shaft as a cutting blade. Both were set in the shaft with resin.

Clark says an arrow found at Zugerburg-Gasboden Switzerland had a bifaced head mounted to the shaft. The end of the shaft, the wrappings, and all but the edges of the biface were covered with resin. This may have been an attempt at improved penetration, by creating a smooth surface.

Split wood such as pine, ash, and yew were typical European arrow shafts. The Danes used guelder rose, which is a viburnum. Many of these arrows may have been worked from a shoot.

The Stellmoor arrows seem unique among ancient European arrows, because they were spliced. Both shaft and foreshaft were made of pine. Foreshafts seemed to range from 6 to 7.8 inches long. The longest surviving Stellmoor arrow, out of more than 100 found, is 29 inches long. Perhaps the Stellmoor archers carried spare foreshafts, in case a miss broke the foreshaft.

Ancient arrows tended to be on the long side. An incomplete Holmegaard arrow is 86 centimeters (33 inches). Another Danish arrow was 102 centimeters (39.7 inches).

This is consistent with primitive arrows used elsewhere. North American Indian arrows were frequently long for the draw. Arrows used in South America and New Guinea are often quite long.

My experiments with wooden bows and untipped arrows have convinced me that using extra-long arrows makes accuracy easier because the arrow's center of gravity is in a more favorable position (which is to say, closer to the bow than the string as the bow is drawn). This is supported by the accounts of Maurice Thompson, who said he and his brother Will used untipped reed arrows about a yard in length.

Ancient European arrows seem to have been fletched with split feathers. One Danish arrow shows fletching 16 centimeters (6 1/4 inches) long. Clark notes many white-tailed eagle bones have been found at Danish Stone Age sites, suggesting this bird provided a favorite fletching.

The authors of *"På jagt ..."* note one arrow was found at Vinkelmose in Denmark that had a barrelled shaft, tapered on both ends and thicker in the middle.

Socketed metal arrowheads were found with the Danish and German Iron Age bows. With the composite bow came the first use of socketed three-blade heads in a style that would be familiar to many bowhunters. The greater striking force of the composite bows made three-blade heads an effective option. Since a wooden bow hits with fewer foot-pounds of force, penetration would suffer with three-blade heads. Two-blade heads are far more effective with wooden bows, then and now.

USING THE DESIGNS TODAY

Even if you have no interest in "duplicating" ancient European bows, you can still make good use of ancient European designs and techniques.

American archery writers for many years scorned woods such as ash, hickory, elm, and oak for bows. There was logic to this criticism, because Osage orange and yew can stand higher levels of strain than these "white" or "second-string" woods. This means the white woods are not the best candidates for the narrow-limbed designs favored by the bowyers who used Osage and yew.

However, if we make a white-wood bow from healthy wood with a moisture content of about 9 percent, and we make the bow man-sized with limbs about two inches wide, things change. Now, the white wood can stand the strain of shooting. If the bow is well-made, there will be very little string follow. And the white wood bow will shoot just as fast as a narrow Osage or yew bow of similar weight. It will also be just as durable. (See Vol. 1 chapters on Design and Performance and Other Bow Woods.)

Whether you intend it or not, this design is the descendant of the ancient European bows. If the limb width is fairly constant along most of the limbs, you have a bow that mimics the Meare Heath or Asby-Stigtoma design. If limb width tapers more sharply from mid-limb to tip, you have a bow that mimics the Holmegaard design.

When available, board staves of woods such as oak and hickory can make fine bows. They can be unbacked and edge-ringed, when the cut-through rings appear as straight lines on the back, parallel with the limbs. This edge-ringed technique was used by the Stellmoor bowyers.

Tim Baker wrote in Volume 1 about the advantages of removing the high crown from the back of a bow made from a small log. Creating this flat back improves distribution of strain in the limbs, improving durability and makes it easier to minimize string follow. The trick is to make the cut-through rings appear as straight lines on the back. Baker says it is also quite important to make the back as parallel as possible with the fibers running end-to-end along the stave. Baker and others who use this technique are duplicating the double edge-ringed method used with the Neolithic yews.

It is a method with valuable potential. It allows the bowyer to make a flat-backed, wide-limb bow from a small-diameter tree.

RECONSTRUCTIONS

If you want, you can make bows exactly like the ancients.

A Holmegaard replica has a special requirement. The ancient Holmegaards did not have rings appearing 100 percent as perfectly straight lines on the back. Most of the rings did appear as straight lines, but the Holmegaards were often made with the center rings on the back disappearing into feathered points. Sometimes these points were aimed at the handle, sometimes the tips, sometimes both.

This is a close-up of the back of an elm Holmgaard replica. The rings of growth feathering off were also found on the back of some originals.

Here's the special requirement: If a Holmegaard is made this way, the limbs must be almost identical in length, and the limbs must bend evenly. If the bow is not made this way, the feathered points of grain on the back may tend to separate.

All drawings and photos of Holmegaards I have seen show limbs virtually the same length.

A backward bow will also have these feathered points of grain. The backward bow is also safer if the limbs are the same length.

If a Holmegaard is made so no feathered points appear on the back, odds of success will be better in case one limb is longer than the other. This requirement

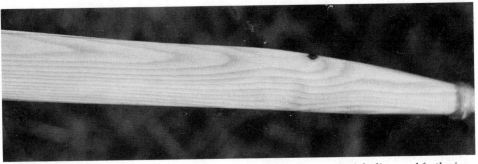

The growth rings on the back of this Neolithic yew replica appear as straight lines and feathering points near the limb tip.

was revealed to me when I made an elm Holmegaard replica with one limb about an inch longer than the other. A feathered point on the shorter limb began to lift up slightly. I was puzzled, since the original Holmegaards had backs made this way. I couldn't decide what to do until I remembered a couple of earlier bows given strong pulls when the limbs were unequal. One bow splintered on the back. On the other bow, a limb snapped in two. With each bow, the damage occurred on the stiffer limb. The limb causing the trouble on the Holmegaard was the stiffer limb.

I shortened the longer, more limber limb. I closed the damaged feather point with cyanoacrylate glue and sanded it smooth. It stayed closed. End of problem.

If a Holmegaard or backward bow is made correctly, it can yield other surprises.

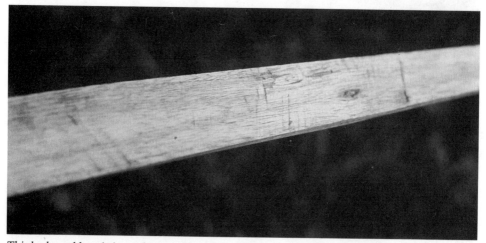

This backward bow is in no danger of breaking despite the tool marks on the back.

This ash Holmegaard replica cracked in the back above a knot entering from the limb's side. In retrospect, this spot should have been left raised.

Tim Baker sent me a backward bow made of walnut. The back is interesting. It has many tool marks that would break a bow following one ring on the back. But this bow is in no danger of breaking.

This example inspired me to completely flatten some small knots on the elm Holmegaard, to see if they would splinter or deteriorate. The bow is thoroughly broken in, and the knots show no sign of damage.

This was an interesting test, but another bow yielded different results. An ash Holmegaard split almost immediately on the back above a knot that came out of the side of the limb. Another knot on the ash — which looked almost exactly like a knot on the elm — also began to crack immediately.

Therefore, the safest practice with a Holmegaard has to be raising the knots on the back. This is done exactly like raising a knot on a normal bow. With one exception: You're not following one ring.

Baker suggests ash is a poor candidate for a Holmegaard bow. He suspects odds of success are improved by sticking to woods with a better tension-to-compression ratio, such as elm, hickory, yew, oak, or Osage.

Some writings note the original Holmegaards were made of elm grown in the shade, with fairly fine grain. However, thin rings are not a requirement for a Holmegaard or backward bow. They can also be made successfully with thicker-ringed wood. In terms of performance, adequate limb width is more important with an elm Holmegaard.

I attempted to glue a riser onto the back of a backward bow, to create the Holmegaard look. The wood cracked under the riser at the first small bend.

If cut-through rings feather off the back of a Neolithic yew replica, the safest plan has to be to make the limbs equal length.

There is also a benefit to making sure the bow is made so the arch of the rings are centered in the middle of the bow. If they are off center, I have found the bow may warp to one side. This is not a functional liability, but cosmetics are affected.

It is worth mentioning there are no "snake" bows or "character" bows among available depictions of ancient European bows. Some of these bows look pretty rough. But the bowyers tended to use very straight-grained material. It is easiest to imitate the ancients and use the straightest grain you can find.

However, character wood can be used if workmanship meets the challenge. Keep the bow limb parallel with the grain. If the rings show a bump in your Holmegaard stave, best to make sure the finished limb has the bump left in it. If you make an incorrect diagnosis of how the grain runs, the back of the bow may splinter.

You do not need yew for a double edge-ringed bow. You can use virtually any wood and get good results by following Baker's advice. If not using yew, you can expect best results from a flatbow design. If using a white wood, you can expect best results by making a long, two-inch wide flatbow.

The question can be asked if Neolithic yews could have been built in some style other than that depicted in the illustrations. The answer is yes.

Tim Baker's earliest readings on the subject simply said Neolithic yews were all heartwood. So he grabbed some yew and cut all the sapwood off. He was left with the outer heartwood rings forming the back. The back did not follow one ring perfectly, however. A few rings, perhaps three or four, had been cut across in a number of spots. But the back was nonetheless quite parallel with the rings.

The bow worked fine. Baker has concluded that unless badly tillered or grossly abused, such an all-heartwood yew bow will be durable and perform well. Most of Baker's bows made this way are fairly light, quite long, or both. I gave the theory a sterner test by making a 67-inch bow that pulled 60 pounds. There is no sapwood and several heartwood rings have been cut across on the back. Aside from that, it looks like an English longbow. It has been shot about 1,000 times and is in perfect condition.

A successful variation of the Neolithic yew technique is to remove the sapwood and allow the outer yew heartwood rings to form the back of the bow.

My bow had knots in the back. I raised them by leaving them surrounded by a mound of white sapwood that protrudes from the heartwood back. This proved a superb way to produce an unbacked yew bow when the original stave had knots in the back. Before learning this lesson, the only thing I could think of was to put rawhide on a yew bow with knots in the back.

If making a Holmegaard, backward bow, Neolithic yew, or all-heartwood yew, there is a step you can take that can help you a great deal. A very great deal. Like a 15 on a scale of 10.

I have gotten away with bloody murder on unbacked bows by giving them long stringing time before I give them long draws. These bows had less than ideal backs. The rings were particularly thin, or the spring growth was thick, or the rings had been cut through here and there.

Let's say we have a new, unbacked bow. The tiller looks great on the tillering board. We string the bow, and the tiller still looks good. It's not too heavy. We pull the bow to half-draw a few times, and everything looks rosy.

If all this is true, my next preferred step is to set the strung bow aside for at least six hours.

Keep in mind that when I'm hunting, my bow will be strung for six or eight hours at a stretch. It is my belief that if an unbacked wooden bow cannot stand long stringing time like this, it's hardly worth owning.

Also keep in mind that if an unbacked wooden bow is designed well and built well, long stringing time is not a problem. The bow will not take on excessive string follow, because a good bow is made to stand the strain. It is long enough for the draw length and wide enough for the draw weight. And when the bow is used for hunting, it will be thoroughly broken in. That new unbacked bow we just put aside is not thoroughly broken in. The wood under compression is providing more resistance now than it will when the bow is broken in. And because it provides more resistance, it will put more strain on the back now than it will later. The back will be able to take it later. It may not be able to take it now.

I once finished two unbacked bows simultaneously, made the exact same way. The wood was the same, and the condition of the backs was identical. One was given eight hours stringing time before I gave it a long draw. It held up fine and is still a fine shooter. The other bow I braced for the first time. All was OK. I pulled it to half-draw. All was OK. I pulled it to full draw. It exploded.

My all-heartwood yew bow mentioned above gave me the heeby-jeebies when I first finished it. "No way is this gonna work," I warned myself. At 5 p.m. on a Monday, I braced the bow for the first time. I sat down, trying to work up the nerve to draw the bow. I finally worked up the nerve at 5 p.m. Tuesday. The bow had sat braced all that time. This bow still follows the string 1 1/2 inches, and I sigh in ecstasy when I think about how fast it shoots. So 24 hours of stringing time was not too much. Another large part of this bow's success resulted from not bending it very far when it was still too heavy (before attempting one of these bows, it would be a good idea to read, then re-read, the chapter on Tillering in Vol. 1).

It is certainly true that pulling the new unbacked bow to half-draw 200 or 300 times, then increasing the draw with more pulls, probably works as well. OK, I'm lazy.

It is also true that a fellow could make 20 or 30 unbacked bows and pull the daylights out of them when first braced and experience no trouble. As for myself, better safe than sorry.

Those of us devoted to wooden bows often shake our heads when some compound or plastic-toting writer refers to bowhunting as "an ancient sport."

Hunting with a space bow is a sport only about 25 years old.

Hunting with a fiberglass bow is a sport only about 40 years old.

Hunting with a wooden bow is a sport thousands of years old.

If ancient or traditional is what you seek, what better bow to hunt with than one conceived in ancient Europe?

COMPOSITE BOWS

Charles Grayson, M.D.

Whether the idea of the composite bow, or one constructed of different materials, was of unicentric or multicentric origin is moot. It seems most likely that the original site of development was Central Asia and that it spread widely by incursions or migrations of nomadic peoples such as Persians into India, Assyrians into North Africa, Ghengis Khan and predecessors across the Steppes into China, Korea, and Malaysia, and by ancient migrations across the Bering Straight into North America.

TURKISH BOWS

Of all the different variations of the horn composites, the best known are the Turkish flight bows described in the writings of Klopsteg who, as an archer, mathematician, and engineer, reviewed the German translations of Hein of the original sixteenth century Arabic treatise of Kani.

The use of the bow for warfare in Asia waned about five hundred years ago, but the sport of archery was kept alive in Turkey by competitive shooting for distance. The old field of competition, the Ok Meidan, exists to this day in Istanbul. Thus the majority of composite horn bows still available for study and examination are the flight bows, about two hundred years old, rather than the war bows. Examples of the earlier heavy war bows such as the Crimean Tartar are occasionally seen. They are fifty to sixty inches long as compared to the forty-four or forty-five inch flight bow. The heavier bows also have a small added pad made of bone, ivory or wood at the angle of the recurve for the string to rest on when the bow is braced and during the early part of the draw.

The flight bows were designed to take advantage of the maximum tolerance of the horn, wood, sinew, and glue to the stresses applied during use. Some bows are still intact after two hundred years, speaking well of the meticulous construction which often required four years from start to finish.

Theoretically, the most efficient bow is one in which the string rests on the face of the bow at the braced position, gradually lifting off of the tip during the draw — the recurved bow. Since the force of the string has the least effect on the limb when parallel to it (in contact) and the most effect when at right angles to it, the configuration and flexing of the bow limb should be such that the string is at 90 degrees to the tip of the limb at full draw, and in contact with as much of the limb as possible at brace position. A further concern is that there should be

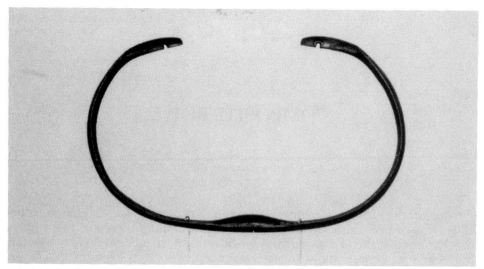

Old Turk flight bow, relaxed shape, 45" long. About 200 years old, varnish only over sinew back.

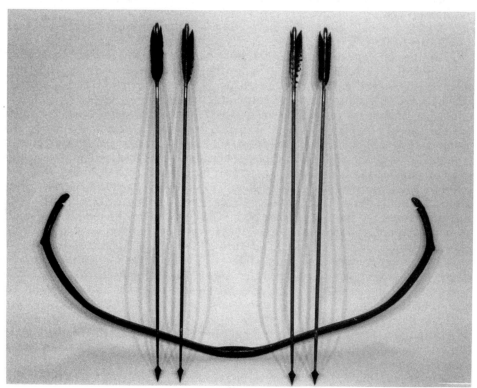

Crimean Tartar bow, signed and dated, about 200 years old. Red leather covering with gold floral design. Horn on face left uncovered. 62" long. Arrows 35" long.

uniform stress, compression, and tension throughout the limb at full draw. For this to apply, the thickness of the limb should be the same throughout, but the limb would diminish in width toward the tip. The ideal limb shape would be an arc of a circle at rest and a straight line at full draw, with the bow string at right angles to the bow tip. Such a bow would be deflexed at the center as an angular bow. The bow would be efficient but, in fact, unstable, tending to twist and "un-string" in the hand during draw or release.

The Turkish bows included some of these attributes but not enough to cause more than a minimal amount of instability. There existed almost no reflex at the center. The reflex curve was long and blended smoothly into the recurve. Though the string contacted the surface of the limb for only a short distance at brace height, it lay parallel to the limb enough to shorten the effective length during the first part of the draw. Also, the limb flexed almost entirely in the middle third, so the string was at right angles to the tip at full draw, a simple principle of leverage.

The Turkish bow was built on a wood core usually of five pieces joined together by dovetail or "V" joints. The center section, about eight inches long, an inch thick, and three-fourths inch wide, also served as a grip with a riser on

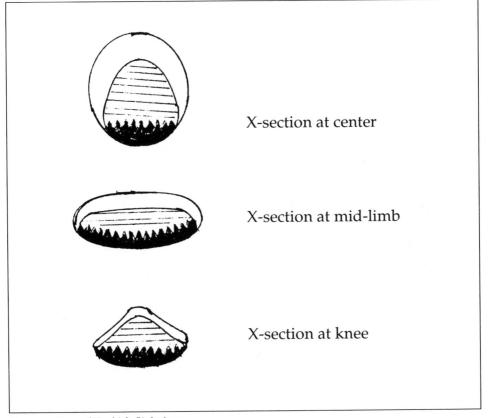

X-section at center

X-section at mid-limb

X-section at knee

Cross-sections of Turkish flight bow.

back. Limb sections were flat, about an inch wide and one-fourth inch thick and fifteen inches long. Notches cut on the outer end of each accepted the long tips, or siyahs, glued in at an angle to form the recurve. They were left thick to allow for subsequent carving of all ridges. All five pieces were carved to blend smoothly together.

Before any further tapering, the bowyer deeply grooved the front face with a tool like a coarse wood saw blade with teeth about twelve per inch. About one twelfth inch deep, the grooves formed a 60-degree angle. A strip of horn for the belly was identically grooved to fit the wood grooves. This grooving doubled the area of glued surface and altered the force of separation from a direct pull to a shearing force. Of all the old Turk bows I've examined, none showed any sign of separation of this glue joint.

The horn was glued to the wood and compressed by wrapping with a special cord into which a short tool was inserted and twisted, which acted as a lever. Wayne Alex, Alaska, says he can obtain enough pressure to deform the wood in the grooves with this method if there is not an exact fit. Even clamps will not exert this much pressure, nor will they provide such evenly distributed pressure.

Usually a gap of about a sixteenth of an inch existed between the ends of the horn strips at the center. Whether left purposely or the result of further reflexing of the bow, this gap is not explained. It was filled with a narrow piece of bone or ivory to help prevent splaying of the horn when the belly was subjected to tremendous compression during a shot. A fifty pound bow with two foot limbs and a one inch thick (front to back) grip will undergo about 2500 pounds of compression on the belly. The sinew back undergoes a similar degree of tension, if the neutral plane is halfway between the front an back of the bow (keep in mind that the sinew and horn nearest the surface perform most of the work). Horn tolerates about 4000 pounds of longitudinal compression before collapsing. Antler is less tolerant, depending upon its age and treatment during processing.

In preparation for the sinew backing, the bowyer reflexed the bow by tying a cord between the nocks. The sinew, extracted from the back legs of cattle, was dried, pounded, shredded and set aside in bundles. Scrap pieces of tendon, simmered for several days, yielded the glue. Fish glue and hide glue were sometimes added to the sinew glue.

Glue soaked bundles of sinew were applied to the back of the bow, beginning at the grip and extending outward to the siyah, each succeeding bundle overlapping the preceding one. The bowyer combed the sinew to make the fibers straight and parallel. The first layer of sinew was allowed to dry, the bow reflexed more and held in place by the cord while another layer was added. The bowyer increased the reflex with each added layer of sinew until the bow tips touched or crossed.

The Turks allowed the sinew to dry for six months or a year before tillering and finishing the bow. On some bows the horn was scraped down to the wood core near the tips during tillering, so that the grooving could be seen. A horn faced bow could also be balanced for even tiller by heating the horn on the belly. The bow tips were narrowed to about a half inch for a distance of three or four inches. The bow string had a long loop that lay on each side of this segment

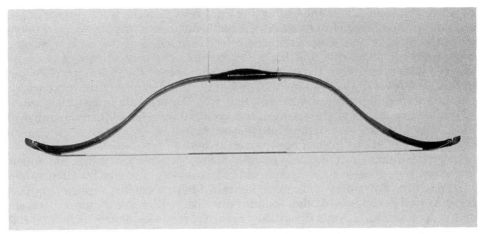

Turkish replica by Helmut Mebert, about 1940. Composite, thin rawhide covering, 47" long.

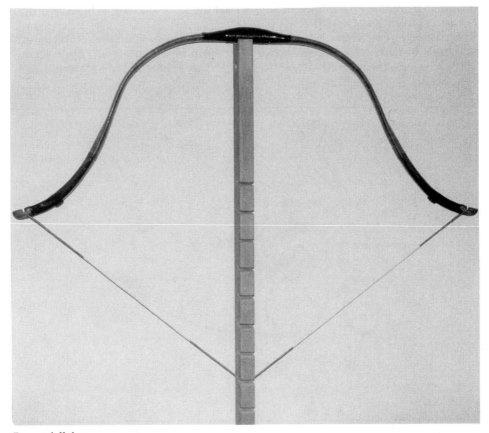

Bow at full draw.

down to the knee, where the connecting knot rested on the front surface of the limb or on the bridge, if present. As the bow was drawn, the string lifted away from the recurve and lengthened the effective portion of the limb while the angle between the string and the tip increased. The central part of the bow showed little reflex, since the distribution of sinew over the riser limited flexing in this area. Most of the bending occurred in the middle third of the limb, which resulted in a reflexed, recurved bow that was the ultimate in combination of efficiency and stability. The result of this configuration is best demonstrated in the energy storage graph of the Chinese bow, to follow.

How far would the finished bow cast an arrow?

Using the thumb draw, a special barreled arrow of twenty-five inches, and a four inch overdraw, ancient stone markers indicate distances over nine hundred yards!

About fifty years ago, a German, Helmut Mebert, created replicas of Turk bows as well as replicas of other Asiatic bows that, with some minor repairs, are still usable today. Today, Edward McEwen, Wayne Alex, Jeffrey Schmidt, and others are constructing composites following details of the old bowyers.

The best flight bows were "conditioned" by warming, presumably to dry out the sinew. It would be interesting to determine whether the warming and drying process really shortened the sinew backing or allowed the horn facing to expand to its original length.

The question of which is the best natural material or combination of natural materials in making composite bows is far from being answered. More testing and experimentation needs to be done, much as synthetic bow materials have been researched.

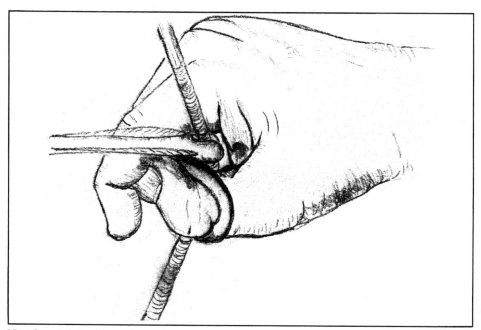

Use of an Asiatic thumb ring to draw and release an arrow.

PERSIA AND INDIA

Persians bows were similar to the Turkish flight bows, but with wider and longer limbs and longer ears or siyahs. The horn facing consisted of several thin strips rather than one solid strip, and the grooving of horn and core was less prominent, less geometric. Otherwise, not much descriptive difference could be noted between the two types. It has been said that the Persian bow was more efficient, but that seems doubtful and has not been substantiated by actual testing.

The bows of India were also closely related to the Turkish, but the general construction was even less precise. The most common type had an extreme

Fully armed mounted archer, Persian or Indo-Persian. Note shape of bow tip between quiver and horse's back. From lithograph by Carle Vernet (1758-1835).

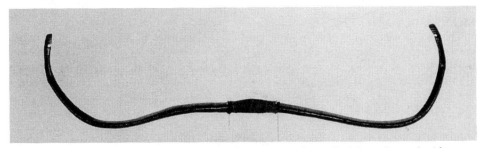

Old bow showing Persian-type "angle" rounded, not as angular as Crab bow. Covered with rawhide and decorated. Poems written on each limb.

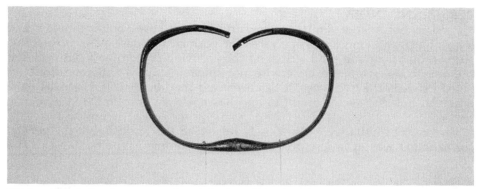

Old bow from India, shape at rest. One tip broken off. Such configuration gives the name "Crab" bow. 51" long, 1 3/4" wide limb.

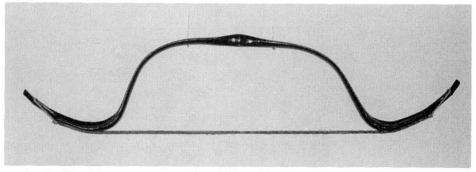

Similar intact bow braced.

angle at the knee or base of the siyah and was descriptively referred to as a "crab bow." One form of sinew-backed wood bow from Northern India had the general shape and cross-section of an English longbow only reversed, with the flat side of the "D" on the face or belly. A thin layer of sinew covered the back with the whole bow being beautifully and completely decorated. These bows may be from Kashmir where some of the most intricate and beautifully decorated arrows were made.

MONGOLIA AND CHINA

The composite bows of Mongolia and China, though basically of similar construction to the preceding types, were much longer, about five and a half feet, with heavy, cumbersome ten inch long siyahs. They were made to cast heavy arrows, not the light cane arrows of Asia or India. The horn or bamboo cores were not grooved, merely roughened. Most bows were backed with sinew, but one type was backed with hemp fibers, the backings usually finished with a covering of birch bark cut into oblique strips. The prominent ridges or shoulders measured about two inches wide and an inch high. Of note are the special warming cabinets the Chinese employed for allowing return of reflex and recurve lost during use.

Chinese archer "war lord." From painting on silk mat, 17th century (author's collection).

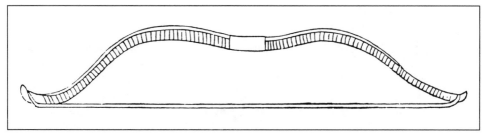

The "Yellow Birch" bow.

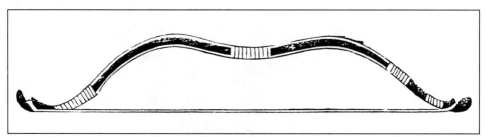

The "Black Lacquer" bow.

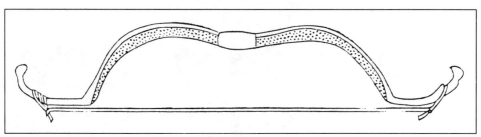

The "Kaigen" bow. Possibly the "Practice Bow."

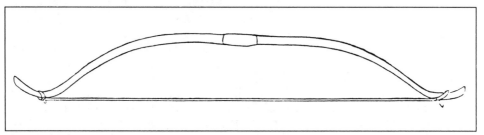

The "Big Nock" bow. (The Collection of Books of Archery, first published in Chinese in 1637, translated into Japanese in 1789 by Saria Ogyu).

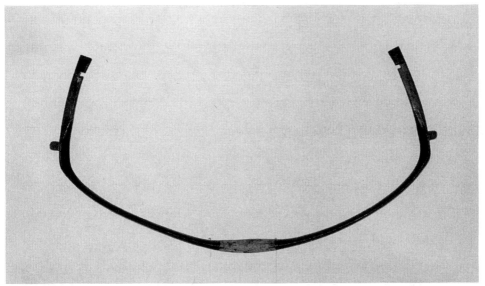

Tartar bow, Northern China. Very heavy bow, 4 1/2 pounds physical weight; 90 pounds at 20" draw. Full draw 34-36". Estimated full draw weight over 150 pounds.

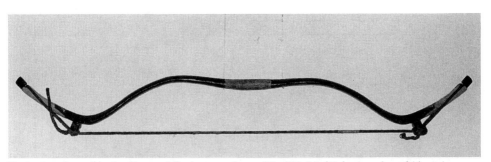

Tartar bow braced by heating and flexing over forms (Teplik). Multiple strand rawhide string 3/8" in diameter. Used only to build and demonstrate strength.

The older Chinese bows had shorter ears but retained the reflex and recurves of the Asiatic bows. Some idea of their construction and other details of archery techniques is gathered from old books such as the two volume work *The Collection of Books of Archery*, first printed in China in 1637, and later translated into Japanese and annotated in 1789 by Saria Ogyu. The Japanese version has recently been partially translated into English.

These two volumes indicate that several types of bows were made. Some were self wood, some were wood backed with birch as practiced by Siberian natives up until modern times. Some comments indicate that the horn facing was of two pieces meeting at the center of the bow. Backing was usually sinew although hemp fiber was also employed. The diagrams illustrate some of the different types.

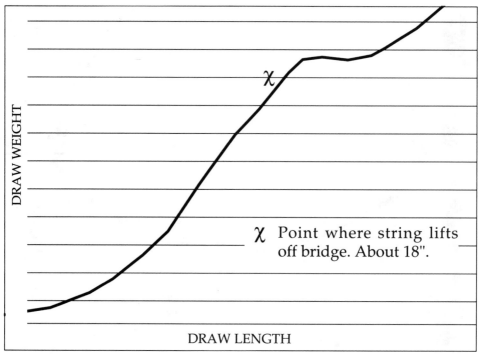

χ Point where string lifts off bridge. About 18".

Energy storage curve of Chinese bow, clearly showing point at 18" where string lifts from bridges.

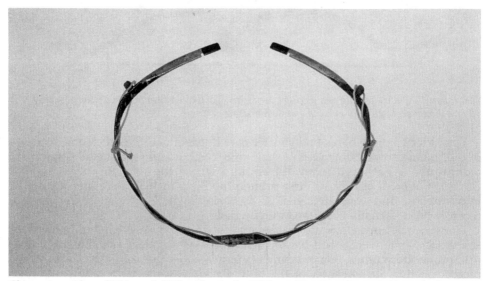

Chinese target bow, 70" long, 1 3/4" wide, siyahs 11" long. Note long loops tied into single cotton string. Beautiful decoration on birch bark over sinew-backing.

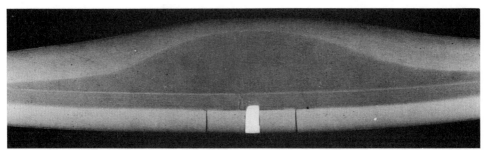

Chinese bow, X-ray at grip, side view showing sinew over riser (top). Glue line between riser and bamboo core is dense, indicating added metallic substance (lead?). Butt splice in bamboo core faintly visible.

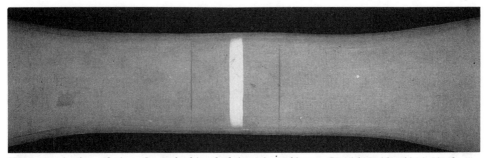

X-ray at grip, frontal view. Central white slash is a piece of ivory. On either side of ivory is short sections of horn, used to fill the gap when main belly strips of horn were too short. Dark lines are air gaps.

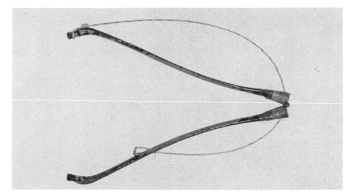

Chinese hinged bow with siyahs cut short, no bridges, rawhide string (see also Take-down Bows, Vol. 3).

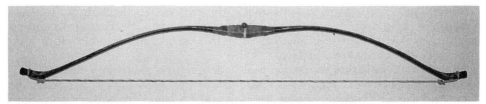

Same bow braced, 51" long.

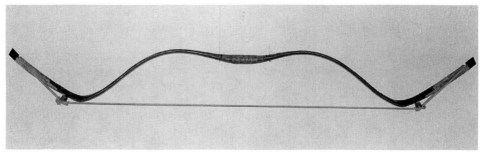

Chinese bow braced.

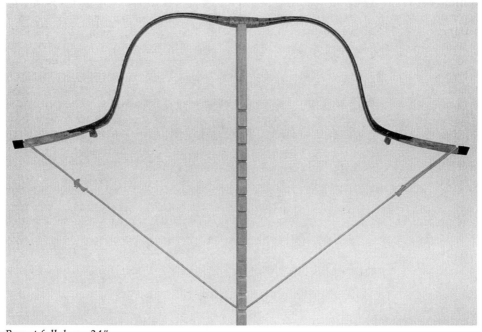

Bow at full draw, 34".

Heavy and cumbersome in appearance, the arrows had fletching up to fourteen inches long and an inch high. These contrasted to the Persian or Indian fletching, which measured as small as three inches long and an eighth inch high — or were even absent completely.

Mongolian bows were more commonly covered on the back by snake skin and had bridges up to four inches wide. The arrows were also about three feet long. And though this type of bow was fairly stable, the long bridges prevented the bow from unstringing in hand if a twist developed in the limb.

KOREA

The Korean bow was of unique and singular design which, today, seems geographically out of place, being situated between the long cumbersome Chinese composites and the long, seven and a half foot Japanese bow.

More so than the other composites, the Korean bow had the greatest reflex concentrated just above and below the grip. The central part of the limbs was almost straight, and the recurve was pronounced. The core and ears were mulberry. The bridges were of hard (chrometanned) leather covered with red cloth. The horn of buffalo, left uncovered, extended out to the ears, but the back was covered with birch bark or thin leather. One broken bow, the core exposed, showed the surface to be flat and smooth. These bows were very unstable and had to be perfectly balanced before use.

Though all the bows obtained for my collection were old and showed defects which made them unsatisfactory for use, one new bow was obtained about twenty years ago. This was warmed overnight in an electric blanket, aligned, balanced and shot a number of times. For this study, this bow was warmed over a heating element, balanced, and braced. However, when drawn, it reversed, and the horn broke near the grip. Three other bows were braced, but each one let down at the site of the reflex, the sinew lifting off the core or pulling the core apart. The damage was easily repaired by running in some thin synthetic glue, increasing the reflex and wrapping with a rubber band for a day. Then the area was wrapped with linen cord, gut, or sinew and the bows braced with no repeat of the separation. It was noted that some other Korean bows were similarly wrapped, showing that the original owners had much the same troubles. Being unable to obtain an energy storage curve, dependence on the word of others and photographs demonstrate what seems to be the superiority of the Korean bow.

In Korea, at archery meets, a man who wishes to brace a bow sits in a cross-legged position with the recurve over one thigh and the grip under the other. They grasp the ears with their hands and pull the bow to position for placing of the string. This bracing was similar to the step-through method of the Chinese, Scythians, and others, but in a sitting position. A charcoal brazier stands close

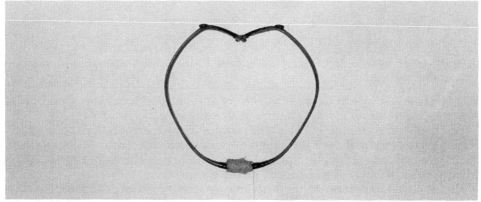

Korean bow relaxed. Profound reflex near center section, long recurve, short siyahs, bridges or shoulders at angles.

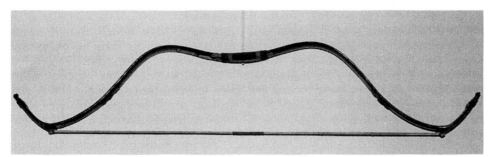

Korean bow braced.

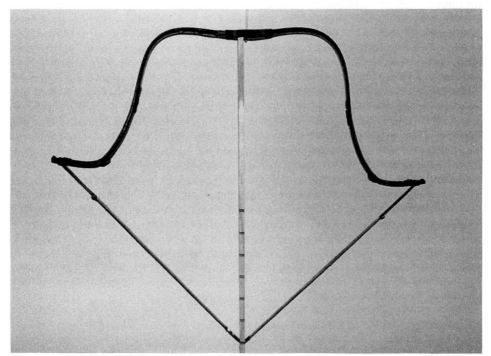

Same 50" bow at full draw, 32". This is the most flexible of the composite horn bows. Mongolian release with thumb ring.

by over which to warm the bow to correct any imbalance or twist. The bow is then handed to the archer who returns it after the shooting is over.

The usual target range is 161 yards, with a 33 inch arrow. One photograph shows an archer at full draw with the arrow elevated only about 20 degrees. The same bow will cast the 33 inch arrow over 600 yards, according to the late Col. Milan Elott. The bow seems to uncoil just like a spring.

Archery was important to the Koreans, as archery clubs persist to this day. Members of the Imperial Court wore a belt with a small ornate quiver of beautifully made arrows and a bow case containing a miniature bow of about half size.

JAPAN

Though the contemporary bows of Japan contain no sinew-backing or horn facing, they are truly composite bows with single strips of bamboo replacing both horn and sinew. The lamination between the two layers of bamboo consists of small sections of bamboo with strips of mulberry wood on the outside edges. About six inches at the ends of the bows are of solid mulberry. The mulberry used for bows is special, and is not the type cultivated commercially for silkworm food (mulberry is botanically related to Osage orange).

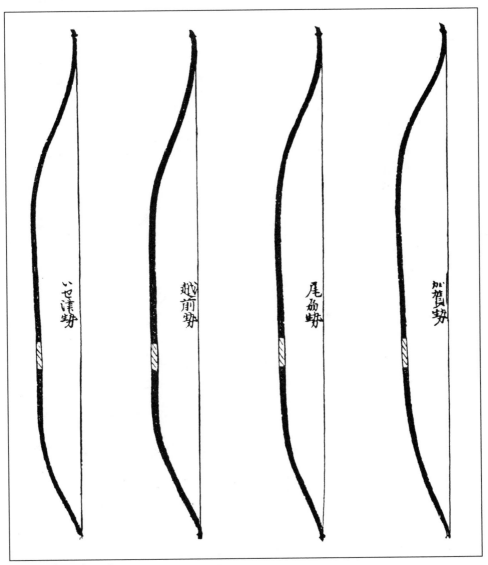

Japanese bows braced.

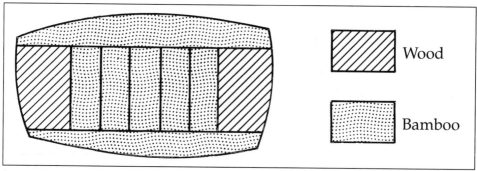

Japanese composite (see also Laminated All-wood Bows, Vol. 3).

In contrast to the short Korean bow, the Japanese bows are seven to seven and a half feet long. One old bow, dated 1839, was almost eight feet long. All were recurved and mildly reflexed when at rest. The grip is located about one-third the length of the bow, measuring from the lower tip. The reason for this is obvious, considering the length of the entire bow. It would appear that such asymmetry might make for poor delivery of the arrow. However, the draw is smooth with little stacking and the arrow flight is flawless.

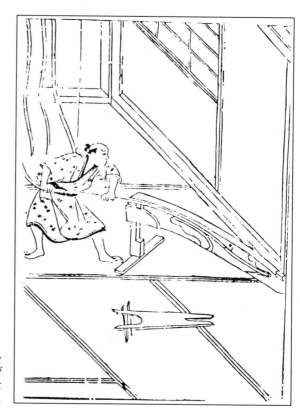

One step in shaping the bow during manufacturing process (Handbook of Japanese Archery and Horseback Riding, Edo, 1787).

Bracing bow, two-man method. One end of string is held in mouth, ready to slip over nock when bow is bent (All About Laws of Shooting, Masashika Asano, 1689).

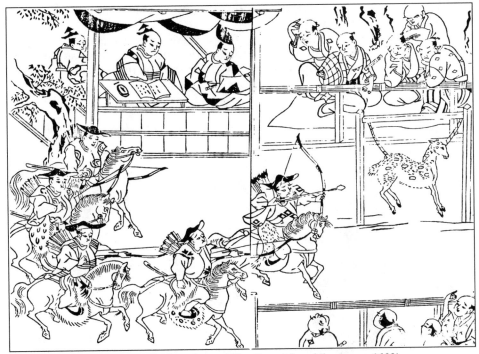

Mounted Japanese archers (All About Laws of Shooting, Masashika Asano, 1689).

Shooting stance. Note bare left arm and chest.

The laminated bows are thought to have been in use for 800 to 1000 years. The earliest bows, of which there are surviving examples, were fairly simple round staves of a variety of yew or syringa.

The draw is Asiatic, or a thumb draw. The release is unique in that the wrist of the hand holding the bow is slightly extended so that, upon release of an arrow, the entire bow rotates in the grip until the bowstring rests on the back of the forearm.

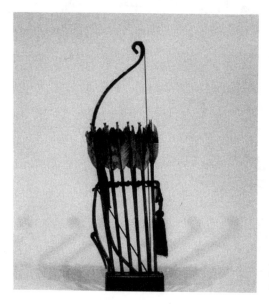

Japanese Rimankyu set, 20" long. Used as a sidearm in Sedan chair. Bow and rack all of baleen. Note belt hook on back of rack.

EGYPT

Wallace E. McLeod has examined and defined the structure of Egyptian composite bows from the ancient tombs, some dating from about 1500 B.C.

Most types showed horn facing and sinew-backing on a wood core. The wood was a single strip or as many as four strips glued together. Some bows had several horn strips incorporated into the belly. Birchbark covering over the entire circumference of the bows suggests that they were imported, possibly from Assyria, though McLeod concluded that the bows were later manufactured in Egypt. Most bows were angular in configuration, with a deflex at the grip and straight limbs.

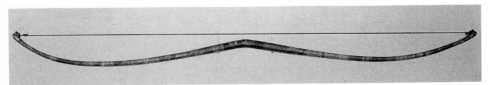

Replica of Egyptian horn composite angular bow by Edward McEwen. Deflexed, recurved, at rest, string on backwards.

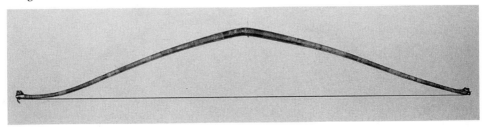

Bow braced.

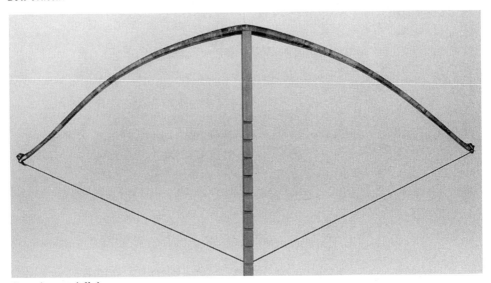

Same bow at full draw.

OTHERS

The bow of Hunza (Afghanistan) embodied the main characteristics of composites, but the horn facing consisted of several strips of ibex horn on a wood core. The sinew backing was coarse and rough with the entire bow wrapped with whole tendons. The ears show little backward angulation, and there was little or no recurve or reflex. However, such bows are still in use.

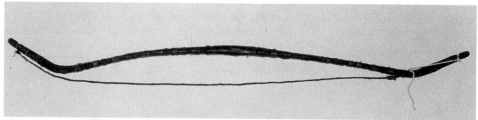

Rare old bow from Hunza (N. Afghanistan), rough sinew backing, thin strips of Ibex horn on belly, bound with whole tendons. Release method unknown. Arrows 30-31" long.

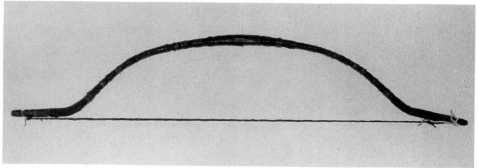

Same bow braced.

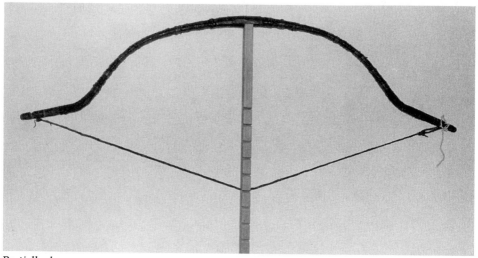

Partially drawn.

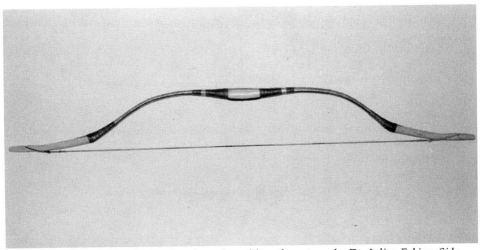

Replica of prehistoric Hungarian Avar horse bow, fifteenth century, by Dr. Julius Fabian. Side plates of siyahs of antler, blue ox horn facing.

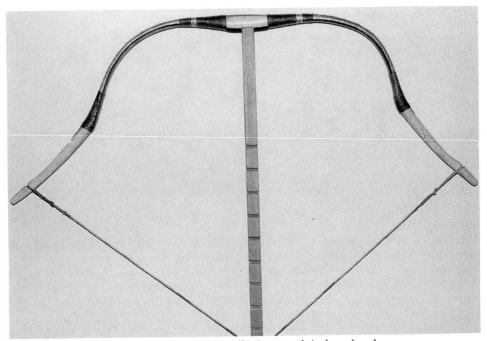

Bow at full draw. Loops on string too short so effectiveness of siyahs reduced.

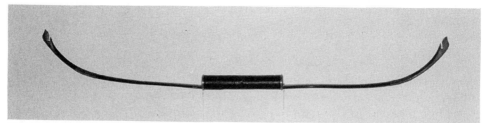

Horn bow, Java. Long center section of wood with brass rings to hold limbs together. Limbs spliced about center of recurve and wrapped with strong cord.

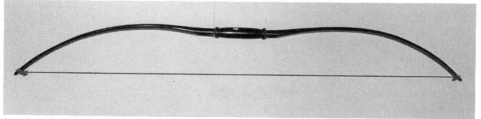

Java horn bow, take-down type with ferrule, braced.

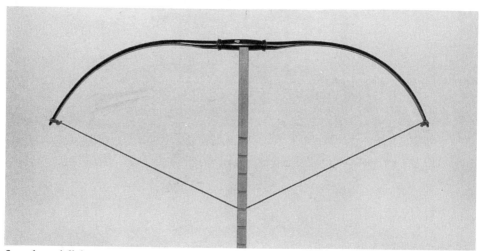

Same bow, full draw.

The copy of the prehistoric Hungarian Avar bow by Dr. Julius Fabian is incorrect. He did not know the proper angle for the ears, as he wrote in a personal letter, and wasn't sure how much reflex was present on the original bows found in burial sites. Not realizing that the string loops on the originals were long, perhaps eight or nine inches, the usefulness of the ears on his reproduction was never appreciated.

It should also be noted that self horn bows were made in the same areas as the composites, Arabia, Africa, India, Java, and Japan.

NORTH AMERICA

Had not Columbus, among others, led Europeans to the settlement of the Western Hemisphere instead of some explorer from Central Asia, the modern North American archer might well be using short, recurved, composite bows and a Mongolian release with a thumb ring or guard. However, until recent decades, the English type longbow was the most common bow form along with the Mediterranean or some variant of the three finger draw and release. The straight bow was here before the arrival of the Europeans, who only perpetuated the straight longbow form present on the Atlantic side of the continent south through Florida, Central America, and South America down to Tierra del Fuego.

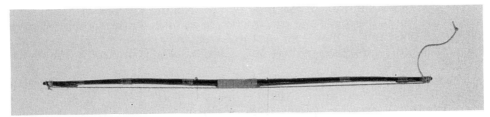

Century-old Apache bow, 38" by 1". Repaired and restored.

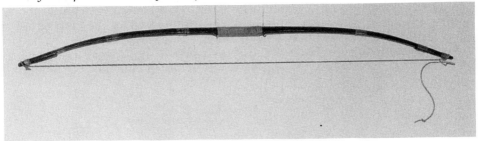

Same bow braced.

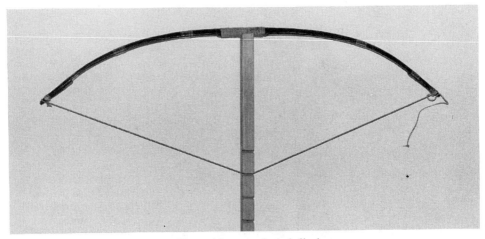

Bow at 16" draw, despite uneven tiller and long cracks in belly from age.

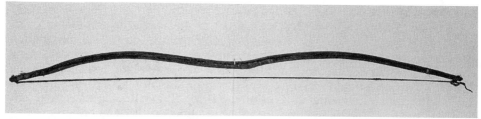

Southwest U.S. Apache bow of mesquite or ironwood, central reflex, string follow. Thin sinew backing and sparse sinew wrap, 44" long, 1 1/4" wide at center, 5/8" thick. Over 100 years old.

The idea of the short, recurved, reflexed bow coming to North America from Asia is evident in the shape and construction of many bows throughout Western North America and in the Arctic east to Greenland. The two types may have blended in the Central Plains where our present interest is directed to the sinew-backed horn bows.

The great majority of the old composite bows south of the Canadian border were wood backed with sinew. Many varieties of wood were used, but the best were from slow growing, bushy trees or shrubs, woods of fine, sometimes almost invisible grain, tough, resistant to splitting and permanent compression.

A small proportion of the composite bows were made of sheep (Bighorn) horn, or elk antler with sinew applied directly to the back of the horn or antler strip, a simplified form of the Asiatic or Oriental three layer construction having a wood or bamboo core. However, if short pieces of horn were used, such as buffalo horn, a wood core was still necessary to avoid cumbersome reinforced splices.

Buffalo horn bow at low brace height with old Cheyenne arrow. Horn sections laminated to wood core, then sinew-backed.

Buffalo horn bow at 23" draw. Full draw is 25-27". Bow is 44" long, 5/8" thick at center, 3/8" thick at mid-limb, 15/16" wide at center, and 5/8" wide at tips.

The composite horn or antler bow, though less common than the wood composite, was widely distributed throughout the Northern Plains and westward to Idaho and Oregon. One elk antler found in Oregon showed a long strip crudely cut out on the front side estimated to be at least twenty-four inches long. A second shorter strip was partially cut for removal on the back side of the same antler. It is important to note both strips appear straight as far as any lateral deviation is concerned.

Good strips of elk antler are not now easy to find because antlers are sold to Oriental markets for medicinal purposes, and hunters keep good sized antlers as wall trophies. Adequate strips can be cut from mediocre antlers beginning on the main beam and extending out onto a large tine. A flat bend in such a strip is not of much consequence. Two pieces of antler as short as seventeen or eighteen inches are enough for a sinew backed bow.

It would be interesting to reexamine the old elk horn bows to be sure they really were of elk rather than caribou. Caribou provides longer and straighter

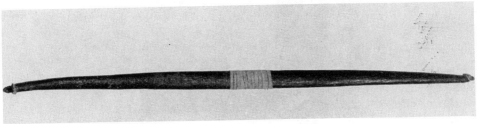

Old sheephorn bow of single piece, no reflex, slight recurve, 32" long.

139

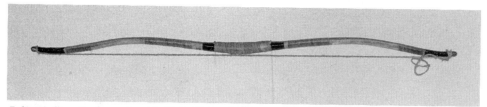

Relaxed elk antler bow, sinew backed, slight reflex and recurve. Made by author.

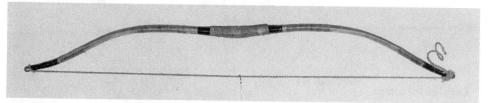

Elk antler bow braced, re-tillering needed after much use.

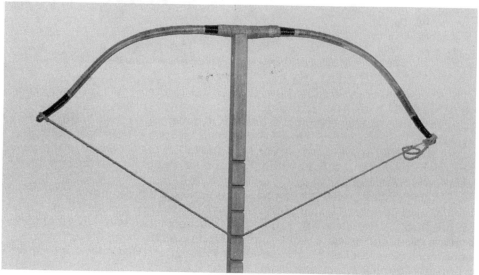

Same bow at full draw.

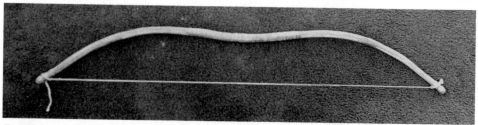

Recreation of rare type of composite found on the Northern Plains; buffalo ribs glued to wooden core, sinew backed, 36" long. Made by Jim Hamm.

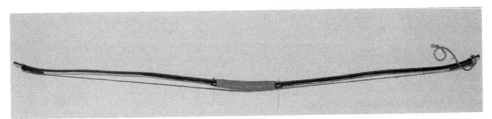

Caribou antler bow, reflexed, recurved, heavy sinew backing. Made by author.

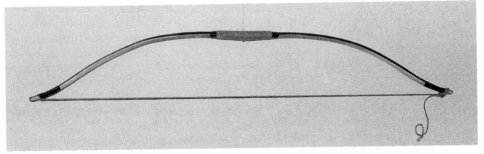

Bow braced. Right side is lower limb.

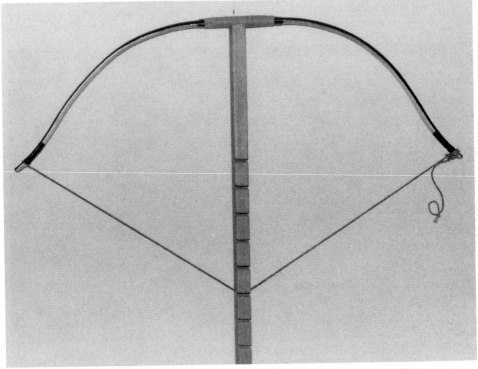

Bow at full draw. Needs thicker riser at center and retillering for more bend toward tips.

pieces of antler. Woodland caribou shared the same area with elk, and a remnant of one herd still persists and migrates across the Montana-Canada border.

Original sheep horn bows probably came from the Rocky Mountain sheep since the Stone or Dall sheep ranged much farther north. The Dall horns are less massive, less apt to be broomed, and generally provide a longer strip of good horn. Jack McKey, from Alaska, prefers making bows from Dall sheep horn despite the narrow tips.

The construction of a sheep horn bow is a long process requiring much care and understanding of the materials. If Dall sheep horn is selected, the narrow tips may be left stiff to act as ears as in the Asiatic composites. Whatever horn is used, the pair must be carefully examined for soundness and absence of damage from insects. The outside strips can be cut off with a band saw and trimmed to a degree where they can be heated by boiling and gradually uncurled. The band saw cut is not an easy process. The saw blade tends to run off to one side due to the spiral of the horn; thus, a pair of horns may be inadvertently ruined. A series of contiguous holes, about half an inch in diameter, drilled into each side of the horn along the intended cut will prevent the saw blade from binding. The horns can even be split along this line with a chisel.

Only a thin strip of horn is needed for the wider middle and central part of the bow limb. About one quarter inch is usually enough. If a stronger bow is eventually desired, more sinew may be added on the back. The addition merely moves the neutral plane more toward the back of the bow, and the sinew over which it is applied acts as a thicker spacer or core. There is little or no tension or

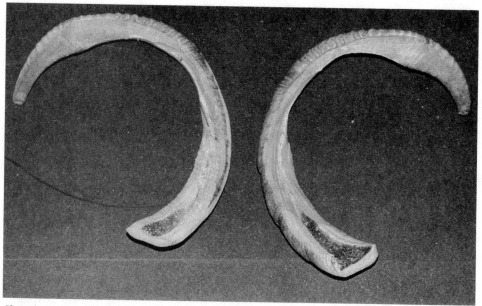

Sheep horn, rough cut, 24" outside. Note 90 degree twist from base to tip.

compression near the neutral plane. Most of the tension and compression are nearer the surface of the sinew and horn respectively. A good example of this principle can be seen in the early aluminum bows in which the cross section was the shape of a flattened "I" bar, the centerpart being a spacer instead of a wood core or, in this case, sinew or horn.

Two strips of horn about twenty inches long, spliced at the center, will yield a bow. Old spliced bows are about 38 to 40 inches long, though one in the author's collection was made of a single strip of sheep horn only 32 inches long backed with a thin layer of sinew, then covered with a waterproof layer of pitch.

The rough-cut horn strips are left as wide as possible so any lateral curvature can be corrected by trimming the sides rather than by heating.

When the two strips are shaped, they are spliced at the center or grip, usually by a simple lap splice which may be covered by a short piece of horn or antler as a riser. The splice is held by glue and/or pegs of horn, bone, metal or antler through all overlapping thicknesses. The riser stiffens the center of the bow and reduces the flexing in this area.

If the two horn strips are shorter than desired, a butt splice may be used, also covered by a riser. Even a short third section of horn may be interposed at the center and lap spliced to the two limbs. Now the horn base can be tillered slightly, but since it is unprotected by sinew, the horn will not tolerate much tension on the back. The neutral plane at this point is somewhere within the horn itself.

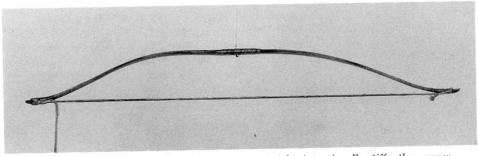

Bare horn base strip braced and tillered. Lower limb, at right, intentionally stiffer than upper.

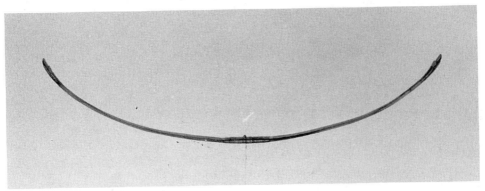

Finished strips reflexed, recurved, ready for sinew.

After gentle tillering, score the back surface with a sharp saw blade placed crosswise and dragged along the length of the horn.

Now the sinew may be applied, but some comments are in order for a better understanding of the use of sinew, glue, horn and antler.

Collagen is an extracellular, insoluble, fibrous protein found in bone, cartilage, teeth, tendon, skin and in most mammalian tissues or organs. It is also found in tissues of other vertebrate animals such as fish. When denatured by boiling, collagen becomes gelatin, a complex protein soluble in hot water and which also swells in cold water. It is a colloid made of a system of particles having linear dimensions of molecular or microscopic character. The particles may be large molecules such as proteins, or solids or liquids which remain dispersed indefinitely and take up water to form gelatin or gel. The structure is comparable to graphite which is one arrangement of carbon atoms held together by electro-magnetic bonds in a linear arrangement.

Antler is like bone in that it contains a considerable amount of collagen and, like bone, contains about 60% calcium phosphate. When antler is heated to alter its shape, it is possible to boil out the collagen and leave little but the brittle bone mineral salts. The result is partly the cause of breakage when stresses are applied to the finished bow in use.

Conversely, a bone soaked in vinegar or acetic acid dissolves the calcium phosphate and other mineral salts leaving only the supporting collagen structures. The remaining "bone" is flexible like a piece of rubber. So, antler strips should be heated in water but not boiled repeatedly or for long periods.

On the other hand, horn is keratin, a scleroprotein found in claws, nails, feathers, hoof, horn, and outer layers of skin. Horn will not make glue but can be heated and re-heated without appreciable structural damage.

Since animal glues and sinew are so closely related chemically and structurally, they bond well when placed together under proper conditions. Animals glues bond well to wood by allowing penetration of glue into the porous surface.

Horn does not have a porous surface which allows glue to penetrate, and the chemical dissimilarity does not allow bonding. The horn surface must be roughened or grooved as clearly shown in the Turkish bows where the grooving doubles the contact surfaces and changes the force of separation from a direct pull to a shearing force.

The best glues are made from hides, the poorest from bone. A mixture of animal and fish glue was preferred by most old time bowyers. The Chinese added lead powder, probably lead sulfate, to some of their glues for added strength.

The best sinew for bow backing comes from the back leg of elk, moose, or caribou. It should be removed before the legs are cut off preparatory to quartering or butchering. Make a cut through the hide on the back side of the leg from the dew claws up the hock to expose a large flat tendon about ten inches long. This tendon and the one under it are usually referred to as the Achilles Tendon. In comparing to the human anatomy, this is not the Achilles Tendon which extends from the hock up on to the ham muscles. Removal of this will not interfere with hanging the animal on a hook or gambrel. Under this tendon is another round tendon extending from the dew claws to the hock where it passes through a tunnel on the inside of the hock and fans out on and into the ham muscles. Cut this tendon off with some muscle fibers which can be scraped off later. The tendon can then be pulled back through the tunnel. The tunnel may be opened if necessary. Now the tendon can be cut off above the dew claws. There is another small tendon parallel to this which can also be used. Several very thin loose layers of tissue sheathe the tendons. Remove these as far as possible. Tendons up to 24 inches long can be removed in this manner.

Don't forget to wash the tendons in Clorox water or a similar antiseptic and wash the hands after handling tendons or legs. These animals can carry bacteria or disease very serious, or even fatal, to humans.

Tendons can be dried or frozen and kept almost indefinitely. The dried tendons can then be pounded with a light hammer or wood mallet and teased apart with hands or pliers. The shredded tendon can be degreased, though this is usually not necessary. The Turks used a weak lye solution (ashes) which saponifies the remaining oil. However, one product of saponification is glycerine which might be left behind, though glycerine is sometimes used in glues. Oil removal may be hurried by washing with acetone, but the washing must be repeated since just one rinse of acetone evaporates, leaving the oil behind.

Backs strap sinew can also be used for bow backing, but leg sinew has more frayed fibers that hold the entire backing together better. Unless a generous supply of sinew is available, that from the back is reserved for strings, wrapping feathers and points, and for sewing quivers or other leather objects.

Some bowyers like to use hot glue for sinew backing. This requires less time but doesn't leave time to express excess glue. Liquid hide glue seems preferable, provided allowance is made for slower drying process.

First, a thin, watery layer of glue is applied to the back of the horn. Thicker glue fills the scoring and partially obviates its usefulness. A bundle of the shorter fibers is then completely soaked in glue, placed on a flat surface, held with a finger near the center, and "combed out" flat toward both ends with fibers parallel. This flat bundle is then laid on the bow, and similar bundles are laid on, overlapping about one third to one half, like shingles. The first sinew is applied at the bow tips and successive sinew layers applied toward the center of the bow. The long sinew bundles are applied last. These will usually reach from the bow tips to the center and actually overlap at the grip. With liquid hide glue, there is no reason why the complete sinew job can't be done in one session. The cold liquid hide glue does no damage to sinew.

Now the entire bow must be wrapped to squeeze out excess glue. Indians of the West Coast employed strips of bark, and one old bow I've seen from Northern California still showed marks of cord wrapping in its sinew back. The Turk bowyers used strips of linen cloth about one inch wide. The excess glue oozed through the cloth. Wrapping with strips of rubber about an inch wide (cut from an old inner tube) does a better job since compression is preserved even as the excess glue is squeezed out, and the remaining glue dries and shrinks. It is best to begin the wrapping at the grip and wrap toward the tips making each wrap abut on the preceding one. Even a second layer of wrapping might be applied over this. The excess glue will ooze between the laps. By beginning at the center and wrapping toward the tips, the sinew is squeezed out lengthwise so no waves or squiggles are introduced.

Sinewed sheephorn bow after tillering.

Braced. Note lower limb slightly less flexed than upper.

Bow must be perfectly balanced, or it will flip-flop. This demonstrates the remarkable flexibility of this type bow.

Sheephorn bow at full draw of 20"+.

In twenty-four to forty-eight hours, carefully take off the wrapping and remove the ridges of excess glue. Reapply and remove the wrapping every day until the sinew backing is firm. The wrapping may be left off with sinew exposed for several hours each time between applications to permit faster drying. At this point, smooth out and further compact the backing by rolling with a small roller about two inches wide and an inch or so in diameter such as a paper hanger uses.

When the glue is dry enough so the bow can be handled, small strips of sinew from the back strap are removed, dampened, soaked in glue and flattened out to wrap the grip at its upper and lower ends and the tips for about two inches. Moving the ribbon of sinew from side to side while wrapping results in a flatter, smoother surface. The wrapping prevents the sinew-backing from lifting at the tips and at the recurve. Some California Indian bows and some Korean bows are completely wrapped with sinew.

The backing may extend over the sides of the horn to help prevent lifting along the edges as drying occurs. It does not help much in preventing recurrence of any lateral curve taken out in the process of shaping horn or antler. The belly has a "memory" of its original shape and will sometimes revert to it after a bow is finished and has been used for awhile.

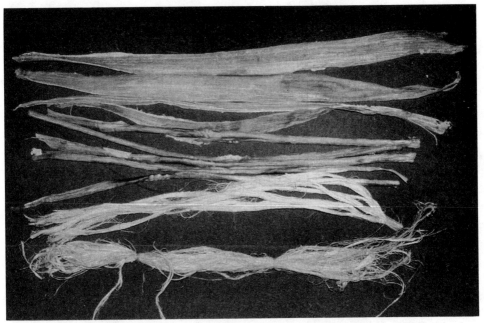

Elk sinew (top to bottom), back strips 22" to 24" long, leg tendons, leg tendon pounded and partially shredded, bundle of shredded leg sinew.

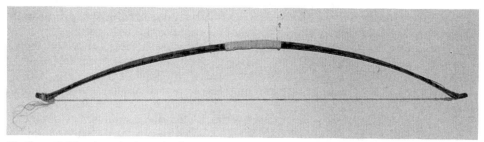

Northern California style sinew-backed bow braced, 40" long, 3" maximum width. By author.

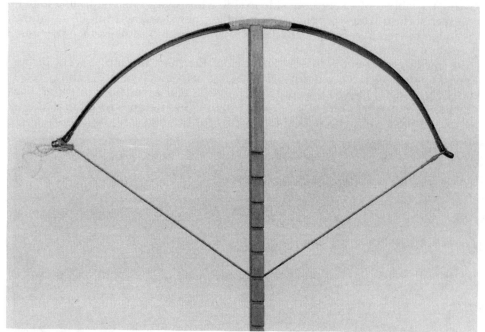

Same bow at full draw showing typical arc.

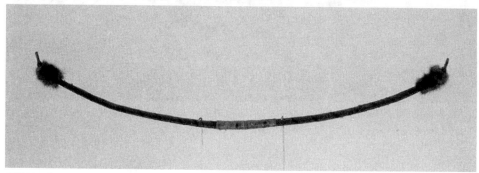

Old Northern California sinew-backed yew bow completely wrapped with sinew. Strips of mink skin used as string silencers.

Once the sinew is in place, the bow can be put away to dry for two or three months, held in reflex shape with a temporary cord on the reverse side.

When ready to brace, final tillering can be done by scraping the horn or by warming while braced. If the bow is too light, more sinew may be applied, using long fibers as before.

After the sinew dries, fine, longitudinal fissures may appear in the backing. These are of no concern but may indicate that all the excess glue wasn't removed. The California Indians used a mixture of powdered clay or chalky soil (diatomaceous earth?) mixed with glue to fill in and smooth out the roughness of the backing. A mixture of inorganic (mineral) pigment and pitch was used to draw designs on the bow and at the same time served as a waterproof covering.

Incidentally, the California Indians also used a glue made of the air bladder of sturgeon dried, cut in pieces, and boiled to the consistency of cream. This dries slowly but is a good glue.

Elk antler is also an excellent base for a sinew backed bow and may have been used almost as frequently as sheep horn. The bend in the strip can be changed by heating in hot, not boiling, water.

Once the antler strips are obtained, they are treated almost like the sheep horn. Unlike the sheep horn, the central part of the antler is porous or honeycombed. This is of minor concern as long as the dense cortex or outer layer is on the front surface of the strip. This is the part that takes the brunt of compression. The spongy core acts merely as a spacer since it is in or near the neutral zone.

Caribou antler provides strips superior to elk. The cortex is thicker, more dense, and has few grooves or channels on the surface from blood vessels present under the velvet. Very long strips can be obtained with only a single arc and no secondary side curve. These come from large bulls, especially those that do not have the usual small tine on the back side of the main beam. I am convinced that some of the so-called elk horn bows might have been of caribou antler which was commonly used farther north in Arctic regions.

Other materials of short lengths can and have been used for bow facing. But these require a supporting wood core to which the short segments such as buffalo horn or rib bone are glued. The ends are butt joined and sinew applied to the back of the wood core.

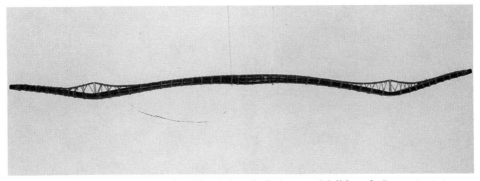

Eskimo bow, 58" long, wood, single cable of sinew lashed to wood full length. Ivory struts to support cable at angles.

After a year or so of use, most horn or antler bows require adjustments or realignment due to a tendency to return to the original shape of the horn. This may require at most the complete dismantling of the bow, rejoining the limbs and replacing the sinew. Sometimes, only heating and bending the tips slightly may suffice.

In the author's experience of making horn and antler bows and restoring or repairing old ones, the sheep horn bow seems far better than antler bows. Antler bows seem to stack at full draw, but horn bows do not have such an abrupt limit. Perhaps the horn has better or greater compressibility before rupturing or crushing. Measurements on the caribou antler bow show the sinew stretches 1.8%, and the antler compresses or shortens only 1% at which point the antler at

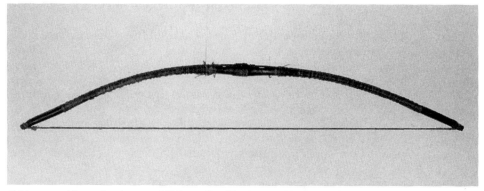

Eskimo wood bow, Arctic type, 45" long. Double sinew cables twisted opposite directions and fixed permanently.

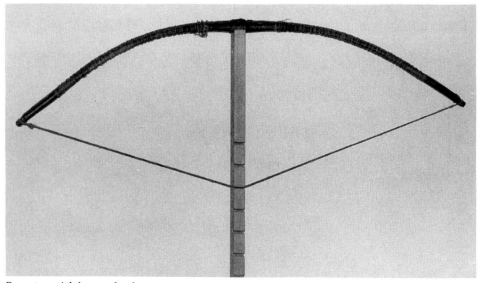

Bow at partial draw only, due to age.

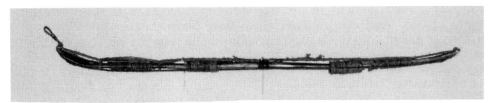

Eskimo bow, Arctic type, 29" long. Made of five pieces of musk ox horn and one tip of caribou antler. Sections are butt spliced with antler pieces overlaid and pegged on, then wrapped with sinew. Loose backing and string of braided sinew.

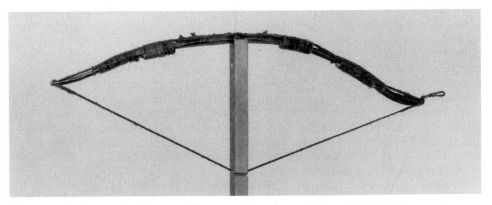

Bow at partial draw only. This type of bow usually used as a set bow, held at full draw and released when an animal tripped a trigger.

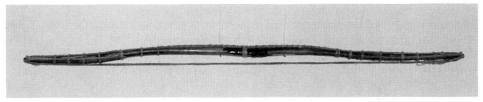

Eskimo bow, 40" long. Musk ox horn, "V" splice at center, caribou antler tips, lap spliced. Loose braided sinew cordage bundled on back.

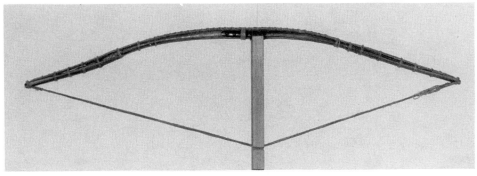

Partial draw only, as 100 year old bow is fragile.

the bow center begins to disrupt. These figures also point out that the neutral plane lies only about one third of the way from the front of the bow. Not enough antler for the amount of sinew! Correction can be made by allowing the tips to bend more or stiffening the center section by adding antler as a riser.

Composite bows of horn or wood and sinew north of the Canadian border and on into Arctic usually had loose sinew backing of braided cordage. The base may have been of combined sheep horn plus caribou antler, musk ox horn plus caribou antlers, caribou antler alone joined together, or even baleen. Most of these bows showed traits of the eared or angled recurve bows of the Chinese or Asiatic design. The tips did not bend or work, instead, all of the bending was done in the central part of the limb. Some bows were simply straight, with no reflex or recurve. Sinew was usually from caribou, with back sinew braided rather than twisted into cords. The cordage was applied from end to end as tightly as possible, sometimes with the bow slightly reflexed. The cords were pulled against the bow, and held by sinew wrappings. Often there were two ropes of cordage twisted in opposite directions by inserting "sinew twisters." If the cordage were twisted rather than braided, one would become looser while the other became tighter or shorter. These sinew twisters were left in place while the bow was used and removed later to allow the cords to relax. Single cables on the back may have been twisted tight and held permanently in place by a strip of rawhide inserted through the center of the cable at the grip and wrapped around the bow several times.

Some of the bows with back angled tips had struts under the cable. When the bow was braced and drawn this mechanism further tightened the cable with much the same effect as a rigid "ear" of the Chinese bow.

The baleen bows of Greenland consisted of two strips of baleen about an inch or more wide, which overlapped through most the length of the bow to the backward angle of the tips; the tips were of one thickness only. Each strip was about a quarter inch thick. Loose sinew backing was applied on the baleen base the same as on wood or horn bows and bound to the baleen with transverse wrappings. Fine strips of rawhide "babiche" from ribbon seal were sometimes used instead of sinew cord. Remnants of these baleen bows found in Greenland

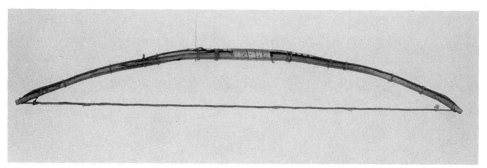

Eskimo bow, Arctic type, musk ox horn, the pieces spliced by overlapping 5" splice which is riveted. In order to obtain each limb of 24" by 1 1/2", a very long pair of horns must have been used. Cordage applied on back and tied on flat.

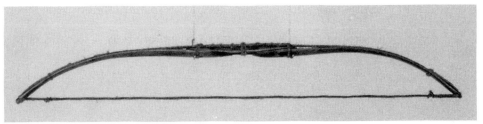

Eskimo bow, 33" long, three pieces of caribou antler, lap spliced, copper riveted, then wrapped. Braided cord backing and string.

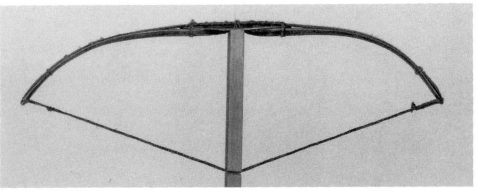

Partial draw only.

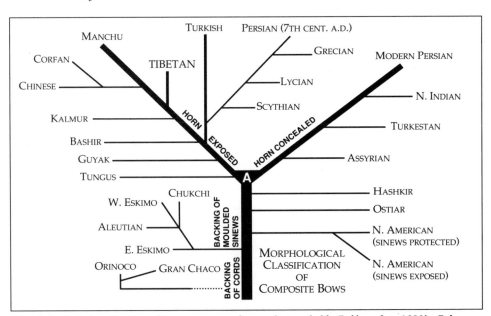

Morphological classification of bows, source unknown but probably Balfour, late 1800's. Below "A" the bows are of wood or horn, above "A" the bows are of wood and horn.

are sufficient to show the construction, though no complete bow has been reported.

The composite horn bows of North America constitute only a fraction of the many more sophisticated composites of Europe, Asia, China, Russia, Korea, and Japan.

To understand the underlying reasons for details of construction of a composite bow, one must be an archer, know some engineering principles, and know a bit of chemistry. But, above all, one must replicate one or more of the old bows to really appreciate the old bowyer's ingenuity.

BENDING WOOD

Paul Comstock

It is true that a perfectly pipe-shaped log is generally capable of producing the straightest, most symmetrical wooden bow possible. It is also generally true that such a piece of wood can be made into a good, reliable bow with the least amount of effort.

Other pieces of wood can be more "difficult." They can require a higher level of skill and bowmaking smarts to produce a reliable weapon. And such wood often produces a bow that is not perfectly smooth and straight, but is lumpy, twisted, gnarled, and crooked. To a veteran bowmaker, these bows are also interesting and unique. It is no accident that as bowyers become more proficient and experienced, they also grow less fussy about the symmetry and appearance of a stave.

My own bowmaking experiences have led me to the strong conclusion that a bow's appearance does not have any influence whatsoever on how the bow functions as a weapon.

In terms of function, what is really important? That the bow is long enough and wide enough to stand the strain of bending and that it be constructed well. Such a bow will have a minimum of string follow, or set, after being strung for long periods of time. It will have good tension early in the draw and pull smoothly at the end of the draw. Its cast per pound will be above average. Its stability will make accuracy easier for the archer. It will be extremely durable.

And perfect cosmetics are not needed to achieve any of these things.

I submit that demanding a perfectly smooth and symmetrical bow is a symptom of fiberglass mentality. This is what fiberglass-laminated bows look like. Someone who can't shift out of the fiberglass gear may think wooden bows have to look the same. They *can* look like fiberglass. But they do not *have* to look like fiberglass. The bowyer who is prepared to deal with more challenging pieces of wood is going to make more bows than the fellow who demands "perfect" wood. Because "perfect" wood is rare.

There are a number of techniques that can turn less-than-perfect pieces of wood into perfect wooden bows. Among these techniques are heating and bending, and steaming and bending.

By using these bending methods, a crooked piece of wood can be turned into a straight piece of wood. A deflexed piece of wood can be turned into a reflexed piece of wood. A straight-end piece of wood can be turned into a recurved piece of wood.

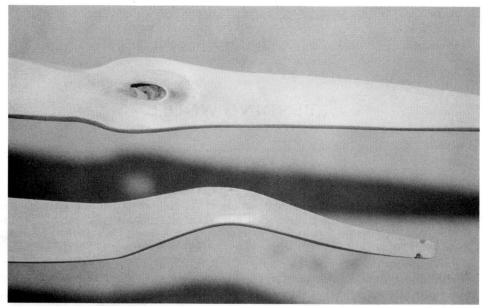

Marvelous character bows which would never have been attempted by anyone afflicted with "fiberglass mentality." These weapons, by the way, were both made by beginners.

If wood becomes hot enough, it becomes pliable and can be bent into a new shape without breaking. And when the wood cools, it can keep the new shape.

This method has a considerable number of possibilities for wooden bows. But heating and bending has the highest odds of success when limited to these applications:

• Putting a reflex into the handle of the bow.

• Recurving the ends of the bow.

• Removing large or long deflexed sections of a limb.

• Straightening crooked sections of the bow. The main requirement is that when the bow is strung and viewed from the belly, the string bisects the handle. This prevents the bow from turning in the hand. In this regard, it makes no difference what a limb does between the center and the tips, as long as the string lies across the handle (refer also to Tillering chapter in Vol. 1).

There is a catch to heating and bending. It weakens the wood because heating and bending deforms the wood cells.

If the wood is only bent a few degrees, the wood is weakened by a very small amount. And often there are no ill effects. For example, I have repeatedly used steam and bending to straighten deflexed sections of bow limbs. When the bow is finished, the repaired limb acts as if it had always been straight.

But this sort of approach may only work well under certain conditions. For example, my success with removing deflex may depend on the fact I always straighten the wood before I begin tillering the bow. If one waits until the bow has been tillered and bent — and then tries to straighten a deflexed spot — odds are high the deflex will eventually return.

In the same fashion, others have tried to steam and bend reflexed curves into small sections of the working limb. In most cases, the normal compaction of the wood, which makes the bow follow the string, will pull out this artificial reflex. Odds of success are higher when the entire limb is bent into a reflex.

Bending the bow from one side to the other—to straighten a crooked spot— also has good odds of success in most instances if the limb is not too wide.

It should be mentioned that most tropical woods are notoriously contrary about bending with heat, in particular lemonwood and goncalo alves. Lemonwood was bent in the old days not by heat but by a chemical treatment. These problems virtually never occur with North American wood.

Generally speaking, the most successful heating and bending is done in a spot where the limb is working very little or none at all. In other words, at the handle and limb tips.

THE HANDLE

Building a bow with some set-back in the handle is an effective way to keep string follow at a minimum. It is a rule of thumb that when comparing two identical staves — one with set-back in the handle and the other perfectly straight — the bow made from the stave with the set-back in the handle is always going to have less string follow.

In Volume I, Tim Baker explained that the level of string follow shown by a bow is — on average — the greatest single indicator of how efficient the wooden bow will be. My own performance tests — described in *The Bent Stick* — support this premise 100 percent. If you want good cast per pound, keep string follow to a minimum.

When a new bow has some set-back in the handle, the limb tips are farther forward than a perfectly straight new bow. And this makes it easier to keep string follow low.

There are other factors in keeping string follow to a minimum. They include: good bow design (such as making the limbs wide enough, and keeping the belly as flat as possible), good tillering and workmanship, and not subjecting the bow to excessive strain during the construction process.

How much set-back is enough? Lay the bow stave on the floor, belly up. Measure the distance from the back of handle to the floor. In theory, the set-back can measure anywhere from 1/4 of an inch to about six inches or so. But six inches is more dangerous than three inches. And three inches is more dangerous than 1 1/2 inches. Severe set-back places more strain on the back of the bow. A stave with six inches of setback can make a bow, but the tillering must be absolutely flawless. If one section of the limb is overstrained a tiny bit, that section of limb can easily break.

It is much safer to keep set-back at reasonable levels. I think 1 1/2 inches is a good rule of thumb that will produce the desired results under a broad range of circumstances.

One of the best methods ever described for steaming set-back is also one of the oldest. It is described in the 1936 book *The Flat Bow*, written by W. Ben Hunt and John Metz. Hunt and Metz describe steaming six-foot staves that were about 2 or 2 1/2 inches square. The stave was steamed for at least an hour, then quickly put into a press and tightened with either a vise or two nine-inch clamps. The wood was bent so each limb tip moved three inches from a straight line. The wood was left in this position until it cooled.

Even though the limb tips were moved three inches, they would tend to move toward their original position when removed from the press. So the final set-back would be about 2 or 2 1/2 inches. These distances are well within reason for a six-foot bow.

Remember what you just read: A piece of wood can move back toward its original position after it is heated or steamed and bent. When steaming a crooked piece sideways, it is a good plan to bend it slightly past the straight position. Then the piece will be straight when cool.

It should be mentioned that a finished bow can sometimes be improved by steaming set-back into the handle. This can increase draw weight, decrease string follow, and improve arrow speed.

I once had a yew stave that had a natural deflex of about two inches. Since any yew is valuable in my area, I made a bow from the wood. This was an English style bow that worked slightly in the handle. It followed the string about three inches. I was frustrated because the bow was a mediocre performer, and so decided to steam a reflex into the handle and see what happened. I steamed the bow and clamped it into a press so the limb tips were in a straight line with the handle. Ultimately, the string follow fell to about two inches. The bow gained about three pounds in draw weight. Performance improved significantly. I was a happy camper.

THE LIMB TIPS

There are two kinds of recurves which can be put into the ends of a wooden bow.

The first type is the static recurve. The bow limb itself bends, but the static recurve does not. It keeps its basic shape throughout the draw. The second type is the working recurve. The working recurve does bend as the bow is drawn.

There are two ways to make a working recurve. One way is to steam a slight reflexed "kink" about three to six inches from the limb tip. The bow is tillered so this kinked spot flattens slightly as the bow is drawn. This method is not too difficult to accomplish.

The second way is to make the recurve rounded, similar to a glass-laminated recurve. This must be done carefully for best results. If the wood of the recurve is too thin, the recurve can be pulled out by bending the bow. Perhaps worse, the recurve can warp sideways. This is caused by the weakening of the wood cells described earlier. If the recurve warps sideways, it can be impossible to keep the bow strung. It is just plain difficult to make such a working recurve wooden bow. Static recurves can also have an angular or curved appearance. But with a static recurve, the wood is thick enough not to bend.

In the 1930s and 1940s, it was not uncommon for even static recurves to be pulled straight by the strain of shooting. For this reason, bowyers often laminated extra wood on the belly side, to keep the recurves from losing their shape.

If a recurve is bent only slightly, it can be done handily with dry heat. If any recurve is to be bent severely, steaming and boiling are usually safer methods.

It is possible to repair a bow's tiller by recurving only one limb tip. Let's say we have a good flatbow, but the lower limb bends too much. Using dry heat or steam, you can warm up the lower limb tip and bend a slight kink into it about two inches or so from the tip. Let the wood cool thoroughly and string the bow. Draw it a few times. You can expect the lower limb to bend less and the upper limb to bend more.

PRESSES, FORMS, ETC.

While not 100 percent necessary, it is often helpful to use presses and forms when heating or steaming and bending wood.

It is possible to bend wood by hand and hold it in position until cool. In his book *Bows and Arrows of the Native Americans*, Jim Hamm is shown holding a hot piece of wood (with potholders) and bending it over his knee until cool. In *Cherokee Bows and Arrows*, Al Herrin shows how to straighten wood by bending it in the fork of a tree.

Jim Hamm demonstrates his "Jim Dandy" bow straightener to Ron Hardcastle (photo by Paul Brunner).

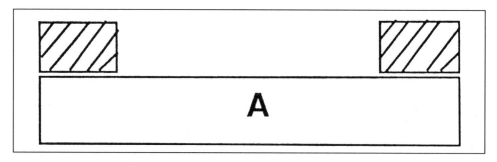

The Flat Bow depicts husky presses capable of bending wood over 2 inches square. Note the illustration. "A" is a bar 14 to 16 inches long. It is made of either iron or 4-by-4 oak. The blocks on each end of the bar are oak. The stave is bent toward the bar by either a vise or a pair of 9-inch clamps.

If bending wood no thicker than an inch, the press can be more modest. I made a press patterned after *The Flat Bow* presses. But the bar is only a piece of oak plank. I can successfully steam and bend wood up to an inch thick with this press. I use 4-inch clamps and one clamp is usually enough. Sometimes the bar of the press bends slightly during the process. But it poses no problem.

This is the press I use to remove deflex from sections of the stave's limbs. This is done after the bow is roughed out, but before tillering starts.

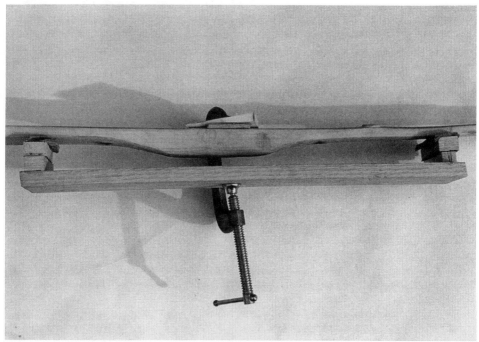

This press is handy for reflexing bows and removing deflex from limbs. For reflexing thicker pieces of wood, a huskier press is needed.

This bow was simultaneously reflexed and straightened at the handle by using a two-way press.

Sometimes it is necessary to bend a piece of wood in two directions. For example, when a stave is deflexed in the handle, and also crooked in the handle.

The bowyer will typically be frustrated by such wood. He will steam the deflex out. Then he will steam the wood sideways to straighten it, only to find the deflex has returned.

I licked this problem by building a two-way press. This press is a two-sided trough. Short oak planks were epoxied together. Small blocks of wood are taped into place before the press is used. In this manner, the blocks can be moved later to accommodate different bending needs. The wood is steamed, put into the press, clamped one direction, then clamped the second direction.

I was pleasantly surprised to find that 95 percent of the time the first clamp stays in the correct position when the second clamp is tightened.

Recurve-bending is also easier with a form, and is discussed fully in the next chapter.

In *The Book of Primitive Archery,* Jay Massey shows a form that can be used to steam a reflex into an entire limb.

It is important to remember that steaming makes wood soft. If you are going to secure the wood with a clamp, the clamp will put a dent in the wood. This is not a problem if the clamp rests on the belly or side of a roughed out bow. Later woodworking will remove dents left by the clamp.

If the clamp must be put on the bow's back, you can protect the back with shims. Cut some oak or other tough wood into pieces about 1 1/2 inches square and about 1/4-inch thick. Put thick leather between the bow and the wooden shim, and secure the clamp onto the shim. In this way, the surface of the bow will not be damaged.

Also remember when you remove wood from steam or boiling water, you have to act fast. If you are going to bend a limb tip into a sharp recurve, you must do it in about 30 seconds or the wood will cool enough to crack as you bend it.

Make preparations to avoid delays. Have your clamps opened to the correct distance, and have any needed shims and leather close at hand.

If steaming a set-back into a handle—or straightening a section of limb slightly—you won't be as rushed. You can take up to 90 seconds or so to finish these tasks.

Straightening a limb from side to side is more easily accomplished with fairly narrow limbs. And steaming a propeller twist straight is probably easier to accomplish with a wider, flatter limb.

Many bowmakers are extremely fastidious about steaming out all propeller twists and sideways curves in the limbs. I would submit that this is simply the fiberglass mentality mentioned earlier.

If we make up a list of the things that will break a wooden bow, being slightly crooked or propellered are about the last on the list. There is a benefit to having the string bisect the middle of the handle when the bow is strung. This is possible even if the bow is somewhat crooked or propellered.

If your main concern is a functional, durable bow, cosmetics in the form of laser-straight lines and micrometered limbs have little value.

STEAMING AND BOILING

If a stave is about two inches thick, it should be steamed or boiled at least an hour before bending. If bending a limb tip into a sharp recurve, it is also safest to boil or steam the wood for at least an hour, to prevent fractures. If the wood is an inch thick or less and is to be bent only slightly, it can be steamed or boiled for 30 minutes.

The most simple set-up for steaming is to place a pan or pot on a stove or burner. Put water in the pan or pot. Position the wood over the pan or pot. Cover the top of the pan or pot with aluminum foil, keeping the wood under the foil.

The aluminum foil does not have to be air-tight. A certain amount of steam can leak out with no problem.

Keep an eye on the water level. A lot of water can steam away in an hour. If you have to add water to the pot, heat it first in a separate pot. This will keep your steaming set-up from cooling off. Use the same trick when boiling the wood.

If you let all the water boil out of your pot, you may wind up with charcoal instead of a bow.

When steaming wood, the water in the pot does not have to boil hard. It only has to be hot enough to steam. This is usually going to require that the water be boiling only slightly.

Steaming on a stove by covering the bow with foil.

Tim Baker's method of using stovepipe fixtures to steam an entire bow.

I use a pan about 12 inches long, six inches wide, and two inches deep. This is big enough to let me do any type of steaming I please. It may be the position of your stove in the kitchen prevents you from steaming wood. If so, spend a few dollars on a single-burner hot plate. It will make water hot enough to steam copiously.

Tim Baker sometimes likes to steam an entire limb. To do this, he constructed a steaming rig out of stove pipe. The stove pipe goes into a pipe wall fitting, the same sort of fixture builders use where a stove pipe enters a wall. The wide

Two methods of boiling wood outdoors over a fire; a large pot suspended by a tripod for recurving tips, and a long, open trough to boil a limb or even an entire bow.

fitting covers the steaming pot. The stove pipe sticks into the room, resting on the back of a chair. A towel closes off the open end of the pipe, from which the bow protrudes.

Al Herrin describes capping a long piece of pipe, filling the pipe with water, putting the capped end of the pipe in a fire, and boiling an entire bow or limb. Jim Hamm says it is safer to place the wood in cold water and bring them to boiling temperature together. Cold wood may crack if plunged into already boiling water, he says.

If your steaming pot or pan is shallow, take care that flame from a fire or gas range does not lick up the sides and scorch the wood.

Boiling also can be used when splicing billets. If the handle splices to not fit together well, boil them for 30 minutes. Pull them out of the water and clamp them together. The softened wood will mash together for a much tighter fit. After the wood dries thoroughly, disassemble the billets, then use the normal gluing and clamping procedure.

When bending yew or Osage, the wet wood can usually be removed from the press as soon as the wood cools with good results.

With other woods — including the white woods such as elm, hickory, ash and birch — it is safer to leave the wood on the press until it is completely dry. Removing these woods from the press when wet may allow the wood to resume its original shape.

DRY HEAT

In addition to boiling and steaming, bending can be done with dry heat. Bending wood with dry heat requires precautions. If the wood gets too hot, it will scorch or ignite. Dry heat can also remove considerable moisture from the wood. Which could make the bow break. This danger does not exist with steaming and boiling.

Bending wood significant amounts with dry heat takes a careful approach, like that described by Hamm in *Bows and Arrows of the Native Americans*. Hamm uses an outdoor propane grill whose temperature can be carefully monitored, and sets the grill on low or medium heat. He suggests this procedure be used only with bows that will be backed, because of the danger of the wood losing moisture. Hamm says green or half-green wood bends more easily and with less cracking than drier wood — regardless if steam or dry heat is used.

Bending small distances with dry heat can be accomplished if the heat source is right. I once had a 1,500-watt space heater that would make wood almost too hot to handle. Wood at this temperature could be bent about as much as 15 degrees off a straight line. Eventually, this heater broke. And I have not yet been able to find another like it that would get wood as hot.

For the first-timer best results can be expected by boiling or steaming the wood.

For the primitive technician interested in aboriginal methods, there is the hot rock method. A large rock can be heated (though not red-hot) in a fire, then removed from the blaze. Hold the limb against the rock and apply pressure. The warmer the wood gets, the easier it will bend. The wood is then held in place until the rock begins to cool.

Another method was described by Steve Allely in his chapter on Western Indian Bows in Volume I. Wet moss is placed on the section of the bow to be bent. A red-hot rock is placed on the moss, creating steam. After a few minutes of steaming, the limb can be bent by hand or tied to a form.

Even if a bowyer's career begins with perfect staves or lumber for bows, eventually he'll grow adventurous and attempt "character" bows, or recurves, or set-back bows. This is when wood-bending techniques show their value.

RECURVES

Jim Hamm

Many people are surprised to learn that a recurved bow can be made from anything other than fiberglass laminations — the way all modern recurves are fashioned. But this style of bow is an integral piece of archery history, from the four thousand year old wooden bow found in the mud at the bottom of a lake in Italy, to the Turkish composite bows, to the sinew-backed bows made by the West Coast Indians. The beautiful recurves from the 1930's and 40's were the highwater mark of wooden bows, and today there is a resurgence of interest in these lovely weapons with the ancient lineage. An all natural-material recurve can rival the performance of the most up to date fiberglass bow on the market; good news for those who insist on true "traditional" in their tackle.

A recurved design holds some very important advantages, which helps explain why it has survived for so long.

Depending upon the degree of recurve, this type of bow shoots considerably faster than a straight bow of the same weight, the equivalent to shooting a bow 10% — 40% heavier. In fact, adding recurves to a design stands as the single most effective way to increase the cast per pound of draw weight. Because the string is under greater tension from the beginning of the draw, such a bow stores more energy early on, resulting in more total energy stored and faster arrow flight (see Bow Design and Performance in Vol. 1, for a complete discussion of the factors which contribute to an arrow's velocity).

The effect a recurved design has on arrow speed depends upon several factors. The more severe the angle of the recurve, and the higher the percentage of the limb which is devoted to the recurve, the more energy it stores. In general, the more the string contacts the tips of the bow the faster it will shoot an arrow.

Aside from the advantage of increased speed, recurved bows are usually shorter than straight-limbed bows, which makes them easier to transport and use in the field. Their maneuverability in a tree-stand or in thick brush improves considerably over a straight longbow's. The shorter design calls for shorter pieces of wood, which are naturally less difficult to find.

Recurves alleviate the stacking effect as the string angle at the tips increases during the draw. Though a recurve can add considerably to arrow speed, perhaps an equally important attribute may be in allowing a shorter bow to function without the normal stacking. These bows are very "smooth" to shoot, meaning that poundage increase per inch does not rise dramatically at the end of the draw.

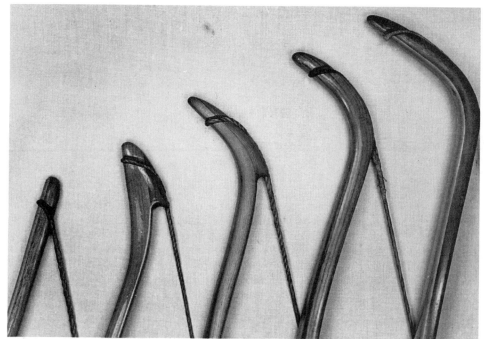

From left to right the bows will shoot progressively faster, all else being equal, as the length and angle of recurve increases (courtesy Bear Archery and the Fred Bear Museum).

A recurve will have very little hand shock due to its shorter length. One reason for this is that the shorter limbs have less mass or physical weight; the less mass in a bow's limb, the less hand shock. And, as described in the Design and Performance chapter in Vol. 1, a recurve's limbs have vertical movement, in addition to the forward movement, as the tips coil up just as an arrow is released. Both of these factors contribute to a recurve's reduced jar or vibration.

Adding recurves is also an excellent way to increase the poundage of a bow which has been tillered to a lighter than desired draw weight. How much the weight rises depends upon the angle and length of the recurves, but it can often be increased by ten or fifteen pounds.

Though recurving a bow's tips is perhaps the single most effective way to improve efficiency and speed, as with almost every aspect of archery design something gained in one area means something lost in another. The increases in speed from a recurve are accompanied by decreases in stability and accuracy. This is due, in part, to the shorter limbs. Longer limbs tend to act as stabilizers, which hold the bow steady during and after the shot, while shorter limbs amplify any small errors of grip or arrow release. Another potential problem is that the higher string tension makes correct arrow spine more critical as the shaft must flex to a greater degree due to the harsh shove on the nock at the last moment of string contact, unlike the soft send-off of a longbow with a bit of string follow.

Though recurving a bow's tips will usually add speed, it is not a cure-all. In fact, in some cases, there is little or no benefit to recurves. For instance, the speed of a full-length bow of 67" drawing 50 pounds, outfitted with short, low-angle recurves, might well remain the same due to greater string follow resulting from increased strain on the limbs and thicker, more massive tips. At best, the speed would only rise by a couple of feet per second. However, if shortened to 60" in addition to the recurves, and re-tillered to the same weight, then such a bow will gain a bit of speed, about 5 fps. It will also show considerably more string follow, if it doesn't break outright from the additional strain on the working section of the limbs. Resolve this problem of durability and string follow by substituting wider limbs or using more elastic material. To reduce or eliminate string follow entirely, sinew-back the bow or make the working section of the limbs even wider and increase the total speed gains to around 10 fps. Or the handle can be set-back, in addition to all of the above, and the speed gain will be about 15 fps. As you can see, recurves alone are only modestly effective but become increasingly useful when added to shorter bows with wider or more elastic limbs, sinew-backing, and set-back limbs. The point is that each of these refinements add to the string tension early in the draw and improve the speed, but each also contributes to decreased stability and accuracy. There is no such thing as a free lunch, and nowhere is this more true than in archery designs.

For purposes of illustration, imagine a a 68" straight-limbed flatbow, with 1 1/2" of string follow, at one end of the spectrum, and a 44" highly-reflexed and recurved Turkish bow at the other. Everything else being equal, the short bow will be much faster and the long bow much more accurate. As examples, short, highly-reflexed Turkish bows are on record as having shot arrows almost a thousand yards, while in the 1930's, Gilman Keasey used a longbow to place six out of six arrows into a nine inch circle at eighty yards. As we move from the longbow toward the shorter bow, the instability gradually rises and the angle and percentage of the recurve must gradually increase to reduce stacking. Still moving along the spectrum from the longbow toward the Turkish bow, the limbs must become wider, or be made from more elastic materials (such as horn/sinew), to withstand the increasing forces. As bow weight rises, limbs should also become wider or be of more elastic materials. There are no hard and fast formulas for constructing a recurve. An individual design depends upon bow weight, material, length of recurve, angle of recurve, percentage of the limb devoted to the recurve, speed requirements, and accuracy requirements, just to name some of the more important variables.

What, then, is the best design for a recurve? There have been many hours of long distance phone conversations between the authors of the *Bowyer's Bible* series, agonizing over this very point. The merits of longbow vs. recurve, accuracy vs. stability, stacking vs. smooth-drawing have all been considered at great length. Though there is some divergence of opinion on this issue, based largely upon personal tastes, I'm prepared to go out on a limb here. Perhaps the best trade-off between speed and accuracy is a recurve of 60" to 64", measured before the tips are bent (this is for a 28" draw length). The smooth draw provided by the recurved tips gives the feel of a longer bow in terms of accuracy and stability. The speed gains will depend upon the configuration of the recurves, but the

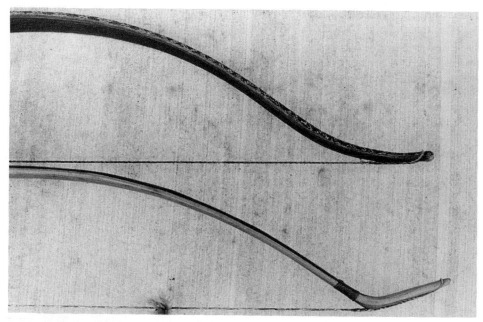

A working recurve (top) and a static recurve.

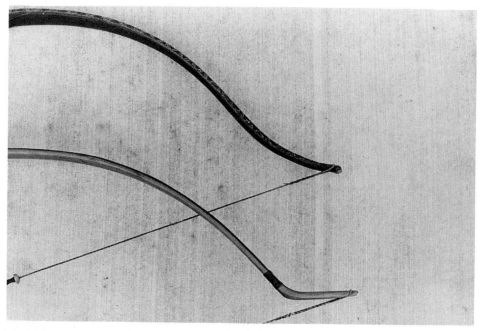

The working recurve's tip uncoils during the draw while the static tip remains stiff. Note how the string angle in relation to the tip is lower for the static recurve, thus giving a smoother draw with less stack.

arrow will fly noticeably faster. Naturally, the resulting flatter trajectory makes aiming at different distances easier, and thus eliminates much of the factor most responsible for missed shots. This, combined with the smooth draw, allows a recurve of this length to be as accurate as a longbow, while giving greater penetration per pound of draw weight due to increased energy storage and speed. A recurve of this length may be best of both worlds.

Beyond the shooting factors, recurves are generally more trouble to construct. The manufacturing time of a bow can increase anywhere from a couple of hours to a couple of weeks, if the bow is also to be sinew-backed. A recurve places greater strain on the working section of a limb, making it more prone to breakage. Sinew-backing solves this problem, but raises some others, such as difficulty of construction and the effects of moisture upon the sinew and water-soluble hide glue which holds it in place. An all-wood recurve with no sinew backing is possible, though the working section of the limb must be appropriately wider to withstand the increased tension and compression. This adds to stave preparation time. Lining up the tips so the string tracks properly around the curves may present another difficulty and add to manufacturing time. And, since the working section of a recurved bow bends farther, the belly comes under more compression than a straight-limbed design, making it much more likely to chrysal, or exhibit compression fractures. This is especially true with any of the weaker woods such as ash or elm.

Recurves, in general, generate more noise when an arrow is released than straight-limbed bows, which can be a consideration for a hunter trying to place a tag on a wary game animal. The recurve's speed compensates for this somewhat, since a faster arrow gives an animal less reaction time, but it may be more difficult to dampen the sound of a recurve than a longbow.

Despite a few drawbacks, the first time you feel the smoothness of a recurve, and, most of all, see the arrow screaming toward the target, you'll instantly know what your next bow project will be.

So, let's roll up our sleeves and press forward into the actual construction.

There are two basic types of recurves; one which uncoils as the bow is drawn, or a **working recurve,** and one which remains stiff throughout the draw, or a **static recurve.**

WORKING RECURVE

A working recurve is easier to construct and more suitable for a bowyer's first efforts.

A working recurve's tips bend, or uncoil, so they can be about the same thickness as a longbow's. I normally floor-tiller a bow to be recurved in this way, or even string it and roughly tiller it at half draw. This allow the tips to be as thin as possible before they are heated and bent, an important point to be remembered during all phases of wood bending. The thinner a piece of wood, the less heating time required to bend it, and the less the wood will be disrupted and weakened.

It is a smart idea to leave the tips wide during the bending process. This helps them bend only in one plane, at right angles to the limb, instead of twisting to one side. After they are shaped they are narrowed to the final desired width.

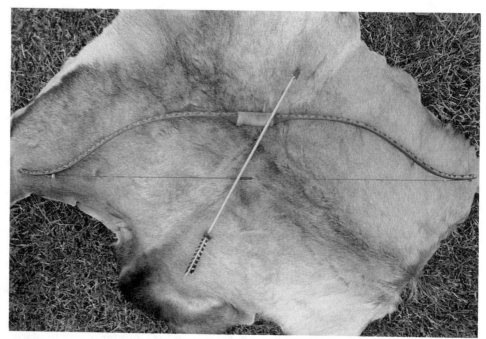

A working recurve bent by hand using direct heat.

The simplest way to construct working recurves is with direct heat. Though an open flame can be used, I prefer a propane grill since it traps the heat and allows it to soak into the wood more slowly. Remove the metal grillwork from the propane grill, as it can scorch lines across the bow's tip, creating a hamburger patty appearance. Set the temperature on low. Keep in mind that when wood is heated slowly, so that it is the same temperature throughout instead of hot on the outside and cool on the inside, the bend is more stable and enduring. I coat the section of the bow to be bent with grease of some sort; bacon grease or any type of fat will work, but canned shortening is the easiest. This helps keep the wood from scorching while aiding in the penetration of heat, and also traps inherent moisture in the wood rather than allowing it to be forced out, rendering the wood dry and brittle.

Heat only the section of the limb to be bent, in this case the tips. There is no need to heat-stress wood which will not be bent. After placing the tip of the bow in the grill, turn it occasionally, every minute or so, then check it after a couple of minutes to see if it is hot enough to bend. If it isn't hot enough, and it probably won't be, return it to the grill for additional heat. Continue regularly checking the flexibility of the wood; you want it just hot enough to bend and no more. Remember, the less heat used, the better. Also, watch closely for any scorching or darkening of the tip. If this occurs, and the wood still won't bend, either the heat is set too high or the wood is too thick.

When the wood is pliable, bend it with potholders or towels to avoid burning the hands. Hold the tip in the bent position for a minute or two, after that it will usually hold its shape until completely cool. At least this is true for Osage orange. It seems a bit of a paradox that the woods normally the most contrary to work, such as Osage and yew, are among the easiest to bend. Hickory, though it grows straight and fairly knot-free, is more difficult to bend with direct heat than Osage. A wood which proves obstinate can be boiled or steamed, which will be discussed under static recurves.

There is no reason a form cannot be used to clamp the bow tip once it is heated and pliable. But I have found it easier to make the mild bends by hand. Once one tip is bent satisfactorily, the other should be heated and shaped to match. After both are turned, one end can be re-heated, if necessary, so that the tips will be identical. If steam or boiling is used, then the bow must be clamped to a form to hold its shape until dry and cool. Or the bend can be held under cold water for several minutes.

Be aware that with a self bow unbacked with sinew, some of the recurve may pull out after a number of shots. The only way to insure that the bend remains entirely intact in a working recurve is to sinew-back the bow.

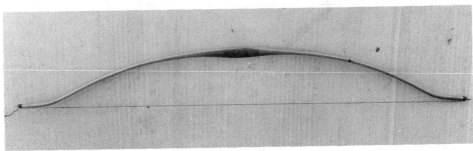

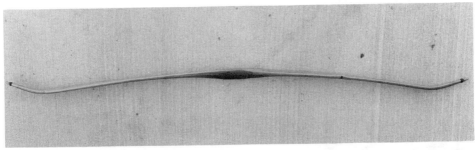

A fine example of a reflex-deflex design, a yew self bow made by Tim Baker. This bow is a dead ringer for a four thousand year old bow found in Italy.

Perhaps the most efficient, and accurate, working recurve design is the reflex-deflex, similar to one of the Bear Kodiak™ fiberglass laminates. The recurves add speed while the deflex maintains high stability and accuracy. One way to attain this shape is to boil a length of wood, without a thickened handle section, then clamp it to an appropriate form. In fact, a stave could no doubt be heated and placed in a fiberglass bow press. When cool, glue a handle section to the stave and, if desired, add a layer of sinew to the back of the bow. An alternative is to splice together two billets with a bit of deflex built in, then recurve the tips. Fred Bear spent a lifetime developing and perfecting this design in a fiberglass bow, and it is an excellent model for all-wood or wood and sinew working recurves.

STATIC RECURVE

The tips of this design are thick enough so they do not bend when the bow is drawn. These static ends keep the angle of the string in relation to the tips low at full draw and provide a smooth draw, but place more strain upon the shorter working section of the limb. Though very efficient, it is difficult and time consuming to make.

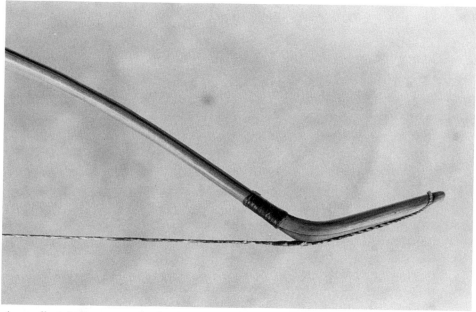

An excellent design; an angular bend of about 60 degrees at the tip.

My favorite design for this type of bow, for a 28" draw length, is made from Osage, 63" long, about 1 3/4" - 2" wide at the widest section of the limb, and sinew-backed. The "ears," or stiff tips of the bow, are 4" long and bend fairly sharply at about a 60 degree angle. These tips are made narrow and just thick enough not to bend, which helps save mass and add speed. My personal preference is a weight of about 55 pounds, which shoots a hunting weight arrow at around 170 fps.

Since the tips of this bow design are thicker than a working recurve's, so they won't bend, they must be heated with steam or boiling water. Thirty minutes of heating for each half inch of wood thickness is a useful rule of thumb. Some type of support for the belly of the bow is a necessity, as bending the limb

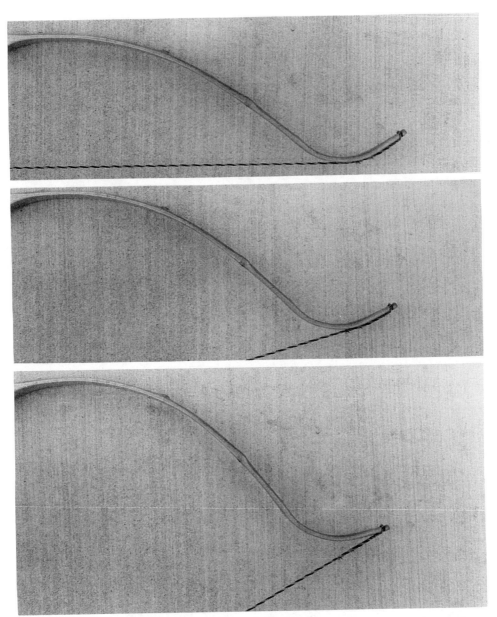

The static tip remains stiff throughout the draw. Note the design; tip was formed around a smooth arc.

backward into a recurve will pull up splinters on the belly without it. This is equivalent to drawing a bow which has the growth rings on the back badly violated. A strap of band metal, such as a used bandsaw blade as wide as the end of the bow, will hold down splinters and handle the problem. Clamp one

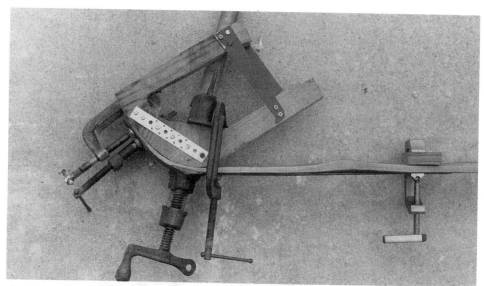

Apparatus for recurving tips. The very end of the bow is secured to the form with two "C" clamps. After boiling in a large kettle for twenty minutes the pipe clamp is added and tightened to the degree shown, then the entire device returned to the kettle for more boiling. Note strap of metal around outside of bend, held at the tip by the first clamps holding the end of the bow. The other end of the strap is held by a single clamp along with a block of wood to protect the back of the bow, both placed far enough up the limb to clear the form as the bend progresses.

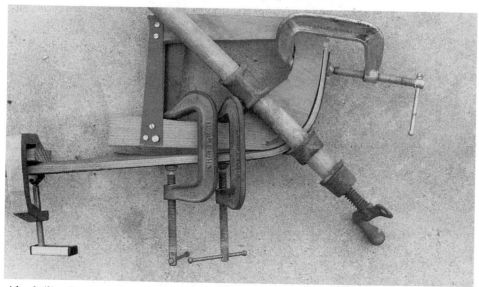

After boiling for about fifty minutes, the bend is nearly complete. Each time the bow is removed from the kettle the clamps are only tightened until snug, then the tip returned for ten minutes more boiling. When the bend is complete, the bow is left clamped to the form for twenty-four hours. The finished bow is pictured on the front cover.

end of the metal to the form along with the tip, then clamp it further up the limb with shims to protect the wood. As the wood is heated, the strap automatically pulls tighter and tighter as the wood is bent farther. It acts much like the backing of a bow, exerting tension to hold down splinters. Keep in mind that tips which are of uniform thickness are less likely to crack and will bend more evenly.

Ron Hardcastle's method for securing tip of bow and metal strap to the form.

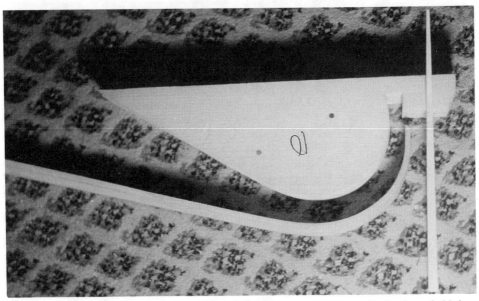

Recurving jig devised by Tim Baker. The long wedge is jammed crossways in the slot to hold the bow's tip. As explained in the text, Baker rarely uses a metal strap to support the belly of the bow, but, if desired, one could no doubt be secured by the wedge at the same time as the tip.

A bending method which has worked well for me is to clamp the bow tip and metal strap to the form, place them in a pot of cool water, then apply heat until the water boils. Raising the temperature of the wood along with the water, rather than plunging cold wood into boiling water, decreases the chances of cracks along the radial grain. Once the water begins boiling, occasionally raise the contraption from the container, tighten the clamps until they are snug, then immediately return it to the water for more boiling. Every ten minutes or so tighten the clamps further, using potholders to protect the hands from the hot metal, until the tip is shaped around the form. Pipe clamps work very well for this if you have a pot large enough to submerge the entire device. I use an old cast-iron pot, which holds about fifteen gallons of water, suspended by a tripod over a firepit, but a large pot on a stovetop works as well.

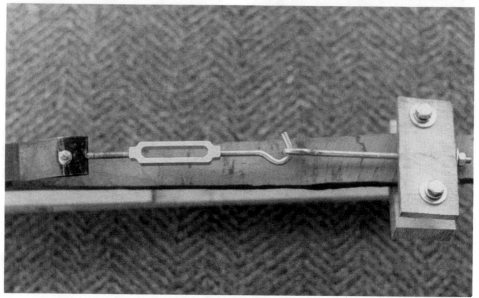

Malcolm Smith's ingenious metal strap attachment. The bolts are tightened to secure the clamp to a billet near the handle, then the hook of the turnbuckle (whose opposite end is attached to the end of the strap) goes through the eye-bolt.

Malcolm Smith has a slightly different technique. He boils the bow tip, with supporting metal strap in place but without the form, for about two hours. This long heated period is necessary because Malcolm bends a relatively thick piece of wood for the tips of his bows. When ready, he removes the wood from the water and immediately clamps the tip, along with the supporting metal strap, to the form. Working quickly so the wood will not have time to cool, he tightens a turnbuckle to snug the strap (a notable refinement to his system), then pushes the limb down to the form, achieving all of the bend at once. He leaves the wood clamped to the form until cool. (The old-time method also involved constantly pouring boiling water over the wood as it was placed in the form and bent. This prevented the outside of the wood, which must do the most bending, from cooling off until the bend was made).

Smith's bending jig with clamps in place.

After extensive boiling, the tip of the bow, along with the strap, is clamped to the form, the turnbuckle on the metal strap quickly tightened, then ...

... all of the bend is achieved at once.

The bow is clamped to the form and the billets (in this case) are set aside until cool and dry.

With seasoned and dry wood, Malcolm soaks the portion to be bent for several days prior to boiling to saturate the outside pores with water, which is an excellent strategy. He feels this eases the bending process with less danger of cracking. On a related subject, it is much easier to bend relatively green wood (12 to 20 percent moisture content) than completely dry wood (seven to ten percent moisture content). A good approach might be to bend wood into recurves when it is still between 12% and 20% moisture content, then air dry it as you normally would before finishing the bow.

Chuck Boelter, a dentist by profession (though he should have been a brain surgeon judging by his static recurves), has yet another method. He prefers to steam the wood, rather than boil it, believing this to be a faster, easier method. He steams the tip at least thirty minutes, or more for drier wood. Chuck, too, uses a metal strap around the belly side to prevent splinters from lifting up, then

Chuck Boelter shooting one of his static recurves.

places the tip in a form and achieves all of the bend at once. When the bend is achieved, he places the tip, along with the form and clamps, in cold water for 15 minutes, then removes and allows it to dry for 24 hours.

It is possible to produce a static recurve without a form — and even without the supporting metal strap around the belly — with a method Tim Baker has devised. He works the belly of the bow to one growth ring, as well as the back, boils the tip until pliable, then, using potholders to protect the hands, he bends the tip over a knee, then plunges the recurve under cold tap water until it cools. By working the belly to one growth ring, the yearly layers of wood do not try to pull apart when bent and a severe recurve can be introduced. This technique of working the belly prior to bending can also be employed with a form.

No matter which method is used, once both tips are bent it is a good idea to let the wood dry for several days, depending on local conditions, before attempting to bend or string the bow.

A word about bracing a recurve. If you normally place the lower tip against the instep of the left foot, then pull on the handle with the left hand while pushing down on the upper tip with the right and slipping the string into place in the nocks, then two grievous events can take place if a recurve slips in the grip. First, a loss of control during stringing can cause one or both tips to twist, which can result in a dead bow when a tip breaks off. I once shattered all existing records for sustained cursing, freestyle division, when during bracing my hand slipped and I broke the upper tip from a new bow I had been working on for three weeks. It was not a sight for women and children. But an even worse calamity can strike if a recurved bow slips using normal stringing methods. If the bow slips from your grip, the highly-stressed upper limb will fly forward, and the tip is aligned precisely to strike the end of your nose at Mach 2. This is no small matter, as the tip can permanently remove teeth and/or eyeballs in an instant. With a recurve, a much safer stringing method is to "step-through" the bow, which allows more control and less chance of injury to bow and bowyer. A commercial bow-stringer, which fits over the bow tips, also works well.

Normally, if a bow is to be sinew-backed, I never pull it until the sinew is in place. But this is not the case with a sinew-backed static recurve. A bow of this design must be tillered so that it can be strung to judge the alignment of the tips. Fashion string grooves on the belly side of the recurves with a chainsaw file before the first stringing, as this helps the string "track" properly. But quite often (read usually), when first strung, the bow will still twist slightly and the tips will not track as they should. The cure for this is to mark the tip which seems to be out of alignment with the direction it needs to be bent to correct the twist. Sometimes both tips require adjustment. Then unstring the bow, coat the tip with grease, and heat with direct heat to bend it. When it has cooled completely, restring the bow and check the alignment again. It may well still be incorrect. Sometimes the tips must be heated and bent four or five times before the string alignment around the recurves is satisfactory.

I have always performed this heating and adjusting of the tips before the sinew was applied, feeling the heat might damage or destroy the backing. This is one situation where a sinew-backed bow is tillered, at least enough to allow it to be strung, before the backing is in place, though even a static recurve should not be drawn until backed. Chuck Boelter, however, backs his bows before lining up the ears. After the sinew cures, he strings the bow to determine which direction to bend the ears, then unstrings it and gently heats the belly side only over an electric burner. He recommends rounding off the wood's edges on the belly side, as sharp corners are more likely to scorch. When the wood is hot enough to bend, the sinew will just be warm and unaffected. He clamps the tip until cool, then restrings the bow. The tips will often have to be reheated several times before alignment is perfect, and the adjustments during heating are quite subtle. He notes that shorter bows seem easier to straighten and that leaving the tips a bit wide at this stage is also a good idea.

Whether sinew-backed or not, be aware that wood with twists or other abnormalities will sometimes look fine when unstrung, but when strung the tips will be twisted. By the time they are finally bent properly, the tips may look badly out of kilter when the bow is unstrung. This is unimportant. All that matters is how the string tracks around the recurves when the bow is braced.

There is a useful refinement to the sinew-backing of a static recurve. Since the tips are thick enough not to bend, and are in no danger of breaking, the sinew need only go to the base of the recurves if you wish. This saves on weight at the tips, since sinew and glue weigh about twice as much as wood. The area where the sinew feathers out at the base of the recurves should be wrapped with sinew for security, to prevent it from pulling loose and possibly causing the bow to break.

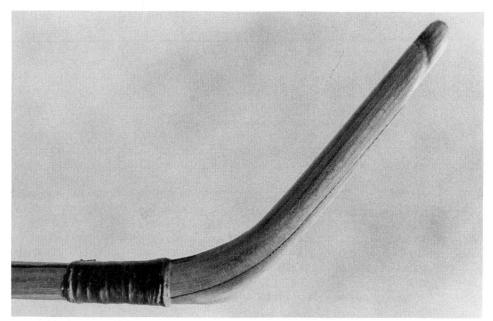

One of Boelter's recurves, showing thin glue line where extra piece of wood was added to stiffen the tip. Two things are noteworthy. First, the tip is thickest, and strongest, right at the bend where the greatest leverage is exerted, then becomes thinner toward the tip to reduce weight. Second, the dark wrapping secures the end of the sinew-back, as the backing only reaches the base of the recurve and does not go over the tip.

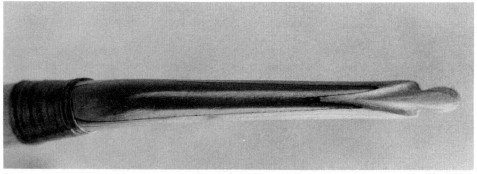

Belly view of same bow, showing nock and string groove around recurve.

Back view.

View of very tip of bow, showing shape and depth of the string groove at the top.

Another option exists for constructing a static recurve. Work the tips down to the thickness for a normal bow, then boil or steam them and bend them on a form. These thinner tips are easier to bend, with less danger of splitting. Shorter pieces of wood are bent on the same form, then glued to the belly side of the tips to stiffen them. Chuck Boelter bends both pieces at the same time, with the standard metal strap around the outer piece, so the fit will be exact. Epoxy or Resorcinol glue can be used to attach the short section to the tip once the wood is dry.

Rather than bending them to the desired shape, the short section can be cut out on a saw to the precise shape of the tips. The same type of wood as the bow can be used for these tip stiffeners, though a different species can be visually appealing. Mesquite or walnut stiffeners on an Osage bow make one attractive combination. There can also be some small performance advantage to different woods. For example, spruce stiffeners can be used because they are both strong and light in weight, which slightly improves performance.

Graceful design devised by Nels Grumley in the late 1930's to stiffen recurve and prevent brush from snagging at the tip. Known as a Brush Bow, Bear Archery sold this model for $50 in Osage orange or yew (courtesy Tom Baldwin).

A variation of this "glued-on" static design became popular in the 1930's and 40's. Known as the Grumley tip, after its inventor Nels Grumley, who was Fred Bear's chief bowyer during this time, the tip had a concave configuration at the base of the recurve to guard against snagging brush between the string and the bow (modern add-on brush buttons perform the same function). This alleviated a very real problem with carrying a recurve in the field. Others bowyers of the era copied the design and it became known as a brush nock. These tips are quite graceful and serve a useful purpose, even though a fraction larger and heavier than a standard static recurve. But, since the built up "bridges" at the tip cause the bow to shorten sooner during the shot, the speed may be about the same as a bow with standard recurves.

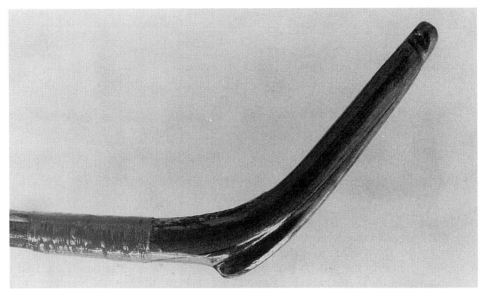

A Grumley-style bow made by Chuck Boelter.

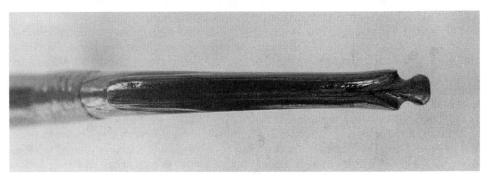

Belly view.

View of base of recurve, looking toward tip. Note how wood was removed from sides to reduce weight.

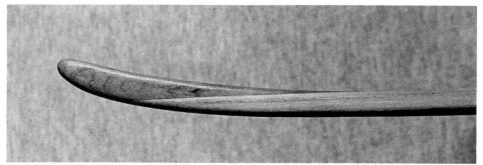

A Tim Baker recurve made by gluing a flat piece of wood to the back of a lumber stave, then cutting to shape with a bandsaw.

Tim Baker glues flat sections of edge-ringed wood on the back of lumber stave tips, then cuts out the recurved shape with a bandsaw. At first glance, it seems as though the tip would fly apart when a glue joint failed, but Tim advises that if applied properly the glue is stronger than the wood, and he has never had a problem with a bow of this type. Speed and ease are the main advantages to a bow made in this way; Tim says he can construct one in a day. This method yields the advantages of a slight recurve as well as extending stave length by up to 4" — quite a valuable trick in itself.

The tips of a static recurve of any design should be narrowed and thinned as much as possible as long as they are still strong enough not to bend. Notice in the photos that the thickest section of the tip lies right at the bend, where the greatest leverage is exerted. Recurves are often left too thick, which greatly increases hand shock and reduces speed. In one really severe case of which I am aware, a bow's massive recurves lowered its speed 8 fps below that of a straight-limbed bow of the same weight.

No matter which style of tip is used on a recurve, it is very important to make the belly of the bow perfectly flat during final tillering, with no crown whatsoever. This allows more wood to resist compression, which reduces string follow and guards against potentially fatal chrysals on the belly. This flat belly design is an aid to any type of bow, but none more so than the recurves, whose limbs undergo significantly greater stresses. Chuck Boelter also cautions, and justifiably so, not to overly weaken the outer one-third of the working section of the limb when tillering, as beginners are especially prone to do.

If you plan on making many bows, no doubt a recurve is on the list. And well it should be. Their speed is legendary, and their beauty hard to resist. You'll never regret falling in love with the ancient recurved design.

STRINGS

Tim Baker

Although we struggle with words to express it, each of us senses the magic in a wooden bow. And we all share the ever-fresh thrill of the flight of an arrow. But archery has a third area of wonder, the effect of which is not often felt in modern times, originating as it generally does far out of sight in distant areas of manufacture. This third wonder is the simple string.

This may be difficult to accept until you see a string suddenly alchemized into existence, appearing from the magician's gesticulating fingers, rising up from the seemingly useless linear dust of animal or vegetable fibers.

During any bowmaking class there are moments when eyes suddenly brighten with insight, but never as brightly as when grasping the concept of string.

"Useless" fibers are taken in hand. The students are told a bow string is being made, but they don't quite see how this can happen. Not a real string. Not from such refuse!

The twist-and-reverse action is visible, but the results are concealed for a time by the hands, then suddenly revealed to the skeptics. They are startled by abrupt comprehension; by such perfection of form rising from such rude makings; by the elemental mechanics of the process, yet the far-reaching implications of the results.

There are exclamations of surprise, sublime smiles, and suddenly-eager fingers. There is magic in the air.

THE PRINCIPLES OF STRING

If loose, parallel fibers are twisted together into a single-ply cylinder or cord, the resulting internal friction prevents the fibers from slipping past each other when strained. In addition, the cord tends to elongate when pulled, causing its diameter to contract. This applies even more friction against internal fibers, somewhat like a Chinese finger tube toy. As a result, the breaking strength of the twisted cord can approach the combined breaking strengths of its constituent fibers.

A crude bowstring can be made from such a simple, single-ply cord. Its main body will hold together surprisingly well, but at the nocks it quickly frays and weakens. If single-ply cordage is not kept actively and permanently twisted, it tends to untwist into its original useless disconnected fibers.

To make durable, practical cordage early man had to invent a way to prevent

The miracle of reverse twisting transforms apparently useless chaff into a cord having both strength and beauty.

such untwisting. And to our good fortune this very important development would have occurred not just accidently, but inevitably.

Twist up a cylinder of fibers. Continue twisting the cord until it begins to kink. Then simply let go of both ends.

The cord will instantly wrap around itself, creating a two-ply cord now having neutral twist. Some of the original twist will be used up in the process but enough will remain to supply necessary friction within each ply. A stable, durable, practical cord results.

Once this inevitably occurring principle of reverse-twist cordage revealed itself little refinement would have been needed to produce uniform, durable cordage of any length.

Useable cordage can be made simply by twisting loose fibers into a single-ply cylinder.

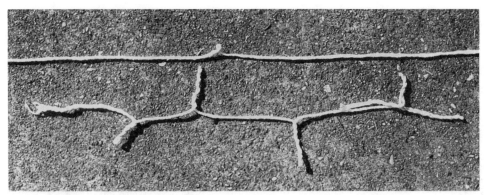

Stable, durable, reverse-twist cordage in the act of inventing itself.

To understand how cordage is made in practice it will be helpful to look closely at what happened when the primitive single-ply cord untwisted spontaneously around itself.

Each ply is twisted tightly clockwise, then allowed to untwist. If both plies are held side-by-side while untwisting they spiral uniformly around each other. If each separate ply was to continue unwinding, its constituent fibers would soon feel no friction, and there would soon be no cordage. The single plies do not continue unwinding, however, because the double-thick cord they are creating resists being twisted, and having greater diameter, it has greater leverage with which to resist. By the time a stable balancing of leverage is reached, the primary plies have used up only about 25% of their original twist. Sufficient friction remains in each ply to yield full-strength cordage.

Without this fortunate balancing of twists, practical rope, string, and thread would not have been available for early mans' clothing, shelters, containers, weapons, snares and nets.

It is unlikely that we have benefited more from, or taken anything more for granted, than this ancient, vital invention. Cordage is so useful that, if invented early enough, it no doubt was interactive in the selective processes that produced our very natures. It is possible that we are what we are partly as a result of cordage.

Perhaps the earliest evidence of cordage is seen on "The Venus of Lespugue," a 27,000 year-old small ivory statue of a European woman. She is wearing a loin cloth, its surface bearing the characteristic pattern used today to depict reverse-twist cordage. Perforated beads have been found in 35,000 year-old Cro-Magnon sites; their extremely small hole diameters suggests the possible use of cordage.

But there is reason to believe cordage is possibly far older: Prehistorian Dr. Errett Callahan was recently asked to examine a collection of 300,000 year-old stone artifacts from Africa: Acheulean hand axes housed at the Lowie Museum here in Berkeley. These are hand-sized, multi-purpose, bifaced stone implements made by Archaic Homo-Sapiens. Errett examined several axes, turning them at different angles to the light, running a thumb along first this flake scar then that. He was obviously in deep thought. Even an observer with

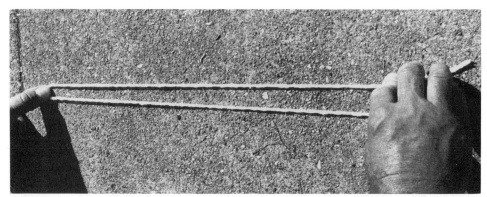

Twist up a length of single-ply cord from loose fibers. Twist until the cord attempts to kink. Fold the twisted cord into side-by-side plies. Note both plies are twisted in the same direction but both are struggling to untwist around each other in the opposite direction.

Slowly, as one, let the two plies begin to untwist together in your hand. At this point they are absolutely hungry to become string, wrapping around each other with certainty and eagerness.

only apprentice-level knapping skills could see that much forethought and preparation went into the knapping of these tools. Later, I asked him what he had been thinking. And he said he had been looking at the work of a brother knapper.

Making an Acheulean hand axe requires more knowledge, planning and effort than making cordage. Cordage would have been as inevitable. And cordage would have been as useful. Maybe some day we will find reverse-twist impressions in pre Homo Sapien-era clay.

There are many techniques for making cordage. Most are difficult to master through text and photos alone. But they are all based on the twisted-fibers-will-make-themselves-into-cordage principle. Once you twist fibers tightly all you have to do is get out of the way and string happens. Remember the common-sense of this when having difficulty grasping some particular cordage-making technique.

MAKING FUNCTIONAL CORDAGE

> SINGLE PLY CORD — a cylinder of parallel fibers twisted tightly enough to function as cordage.
>
> SIMPLE PLY — a single ply cord used as the primary building block of reverse-twist cordage. It can be thin or thick, an entire ply, or one of many in a simple parallel ply.
>
> SIMPLE PARALLEL PLY — many small, simple plies, the sole purpose being to give uniformity; they are used in parallel lines as if a simple ply.
>
> SIMPLE CORD — a cord made by reverse-twisting two or more simple plies.
>
> PRIMARY PLY — one ply in a simple cord, when this simple cord is one ply in a complex cord.
>
> COMPLEX CORD — where each ply is itself a finished simple cord.

Crafting a superior bowstring requires more than simply selecting the strongest fibers. It matters very much how the fibers are assembled.

Here are the variables commonly understood to affect cordage strength:

Finer fibers have more surface area, therefore more points of contact, therefore greater internal friction. When given the choice, select or shred fiber as thinly as possible without damaging the fiber. This is more important for vegetable fibers because cellulose is far less elastic than the keratin and collagen of animal fibers.

Smooth-surfaced fibers slip past each other more easily, and therefore must be twisted tighter. This weakens the finished cord.

Short fibers must be twisted tighter than longer fibers, also weakening the finished cord. Apart from weakening the string, excess twisting also shortens the string. This means a longer string is needed to begin with, which increases mass somewhat.

Excess twisting also makes a string more coilspring-like, causing a bowstring to stretch and absorb energy as it slams home after release. Energy absorbed by an elastic string is unavailable to the arrow, thereby reducing cast.

Beginning on page 203 in *Archery-The Technical Side,* Nagler, and other contributors, are puzzled when stronger threads sometimes make weaker strings, and vice-versa. I believe the theories and tests reported below explain this phenomena.

On the face of, it one could hardly imagine a more straightforward act than a string breaking. But when viewed in mental slow motion, a breaking string is a complex series of events involving many interacting forces and processes. But even a cursory understanding of the events in a breaking string will lead to better bowstrings.

Strings made up of many small-diameter plies, properly twisted together, are stronger than those made from fewer larger plies. But why?

The outer layers of a thicker cord have a larger diameter than inner layers. Therefore, when twisted, its outer fibers are asked to stretch and travel a longer, more spiraled path than inner fibers — the stripes on a barber pole, for example, are longer than the pole itself.

These outer fibers try to relieve strain by shortening their path. They accomplish this by: one, squeezing and contracting the cord's diameter, and two, by shortening the cord — central fibers are actually telescoped into negative tension.

When such a cord is strained in tension, its pre-strained outer fibers must necessarily break first, leaving fewer and fewer near-surface fibers to resist the load. A case of divide and conquer.

Inner fibers of thicker cords have not been twisted as severely as outer fibers, relying on compression from the more-strained outer fibers to create their cordage-making friction. Once these outer fibers break, inner fibers are able to pull apart more freely.

Since these inner fibers are, in effect, dead weight, such a string has less strength per mass.

Thread-thin cords, on the other hand, have smaller inner cores for outer fiber to wrap around. When twisted, outer and inner fibers therefore feel nearly equal strain, and nearly equal cordage-making friction. As a result, outer fibers do not break much more quickly than inner fibers. Thinner cords therefore have a lower percentage of central dead weight. They are stronger per mass.

As a visual clue to the more-equal behavior of inner and outer fibers in a thread-thin cord, notice that when spun very tightly, such threads do not become much shorter. A thick cord, on the other hand, shortens quickly when only lightly twisted.

Here is evidence of the greater strain placed on a thicker cord's outer fibers: The fibers in such a cord are smooth and parallel before being twisted. Once twisted, then untwisted, these outer fibers become slack because inner fibers now carry the load.

Outer fibers of thicker cords are more strained than inner fibers. This is easily demonstrated by twisting a thick cord of parallel blades of grass. You will see its diameter constrict, its length shorten, and its outer layers begin to break in tension. Notice that surface fibers are oriented at a strong angle to the cord, inner fibers progressively less so. Central fibers are almost parallel, and feel less friction once outer fibers fail. Meanwhile, a very thin cord of the same grass will accept considerable twisting without shortening or breaking.

Since a small-diameter cord can be twisted more revolutions per inch, fibers wrap around themselves more frequently. More points of fiber contact equals more fraction. More friction equals less slippage. Less slippage equals greater strength.

For graphic proof of this, cut unspun flax fibers to one-inch lengths. Twist up a thread-thin strand from these short fibers. This thread will be frizzy, but if tightly twisted will make useable cordage. Then try to twist up a half-inch thick cord. A cord this thick can not twist sufficiently for fibers to grip each other. No points of contact, no gripping can take place. No cordage can be made.

This extreme example illustrates the friction/strength advantages of smaller diameter cordage. If fine enough, and if twisted enough, thread strength will approach the combined strength of its constituent fibers. This thread will have a very high strength-to-mass ratio, precisely the requirement of an efficient bowstring.

Because outer fiber are more strained, primary plies should be twisted no more than necessary to prevent inner fibers from slipping. But they must be twisted up tighter than initially needed, because they will unwind somewhat when untwisting into a finished cord. And when making complex cordage, twist the simple plies slightly tighter still, because plies in the primary cordage will receive a slight net un-twisting in the process.

A cord's strength is due primarily to the twisting within its smallest component plies. Subsequent reverse-twisting adds less strength. Even the largest ropes could be made up of countless small, parallel, reverse-twisted plies. But such ropes would be ungainly, disorganized, and fray easily. Second and third level reverse-twisted plies in complex cordage and rope are there largely for convenience and durability, not inherent strength.

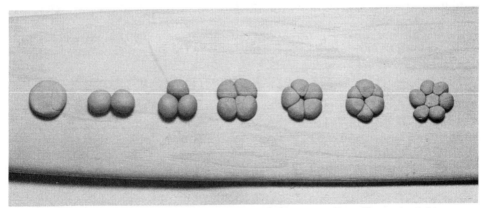

Ply diameter decreases as ply numbers increase. Smaller diameter plies will permits tighter twisting with less strain on surface fibers, but from four plies on, plies must be progressively more distorted as they attempt to fill an ever-larger hollow core. It seems likely that ply strength would be compromised by such distortion. With seven plies the problem solves itself: a single ply fills the void. This central ply becomes largely dead weight, but by equalizing stresses in the six outer plies, higher net cord strength results. With eight or more plies the cord's hollow core is filled with ever more dead-weight central plies.

But why doesn't larger-diameter reverse-twisted, simple and complex cordage suffer from the thicker-is-weaker problem?

For two reasons: One, the reverse-twist is not as severe as the initial simple-ply twist. Two, each ply is much smaller in diameter than the entire cord; this is especially true with cords having three, four, and more plies.

It seems reasonable that there should be no more than seven simple parallel plies in a ply, no more than seven plies in a simple cord, and no more than seven cords in a complex cord. If more than seven the cylinder becomes too thick, causing some plies to remain internal. When twisted, internal plies will not be strained in unison with external plies. They become merely dead weight. The thicker-is-weaker problem again.

Equally important to mass/strength is the uniformity of the simple plies. The following multi-strength property of string has been overlooked in the past. But an understanding of it is necessary for efficient bowstring design:

A spool of high quality, wet-spun, single-ply line linen had an "average breaking strength" of 5 lb.

But when a 50-inch long strand was tested, breaking strength dropped to 3 lb.

And when a series of 5-inch long sections of a long thread were tested, breaking strength varied from 3 to 7 lbs.

Even in this evenly-spun thread, strength varied by at least 3 to 7 lbs along its length.

If seven such plies are kept separate and parallel, as with an endless string, they will each break at their weakest point of 3 lb. Their collective breaking strength being 21 lb. But this 21 lb. string has the mass of a 35 lb. seven-ply twisted string.

If these seven plies are twisted tightly into cordage, with weakest-points placed next to strongest points, weak and strong will average out, and combined strength will be 35 lb. But the law of averages will not arrange things so perfectly.

The likelihood, however, of having advantageously distributed weak points increases with the number of plies. This is likely the reason the strongest-tested shoemakers' cord has 7 simple plies.

Here is a simple experiment to demonstrate the thicker-is-weaker/no-more-than-seven-plies theory:

Using single-ply natural fiber thread of 5 lb test, twist up simple cords containing 40, 20, 10, 7, and 5 threads. Twist each tightly enough to create cordage-making friction. Test each cord for breaking strength.

Results will be approximately as follows:

Thread count	Breaking strength	Breaking strength per thread
40	150 lb.	3.75 lb.
20	75 lb.	3.75 lb.
10	40 lb.	4 lb.
7	35 lb.	5 lb.
5	23 lb.	4.6 lb.

What we conclude from all this is that cordage made up of several, very small diameter simple plies will be considerably stronger per mass.

When commercial cordage is examined, stronger-per-mass samples prove to be made up of many small primary plies. For example, shoemakers' lock-stitch cord, the strongest-per-mass string yet tested here, has seven sewing-thread-sized simple plies, even though total diameter is little larger than kite string. And the same holds true for complex cordage. Final plies should be smaller in diameter, and greater in number, but not exceeding six or seven.

Testing Cord Strength, Stretch, and Set

When breaking a string to measure its strength, it's important not to disrupt internal strains when gripping or securing the string. The weakened string may not break where gripped, but as with a knot, it may break nearby, and at lower strength than it would otherwise.

Secure a thread or string to be tested around a smooth, round surface. Take a couple of turns before tying off. If secured properly breaks will occur *randomly* along the string's length. If secured improperly, breaks will occur near the fastened ends. Do not begin measuring until confident your method of securing the string is not contributing to its failure.

If a string is to be used by itself, or in parallel with others — as in an endless string — test section *several feet long*. This will reveal the strength of its *weakest point.*

If a string is to be twisted together with others in a cord, determine its **average breaking strength:** first break long sections to find its weak-link strength, as above. Then break several three to five-inch section to find its strongest-link strength. Take several readings, then average them.

When testing animal fiber, higher, truer readings will be obtained if the load is applied and released a few times, gradually building to the breaking point. This is true of vegetable fibers too, but less so.

To measure stretch and set — the amount a string will remain stretched when tension is released — lay out fifty inches of thread or cord. Fifty inches is long enough for accurate readings, and short enough for convenient handling. And each half inch of movement equals an even 1%.

Wrap one end of the cord twice around a smooth, round dowel before tying off at a nail or such. Attach the other end similarly to a scale. Place a ruler beside the scale. Pull the scale, applying tension slowly and repeatedly, building up to point of failure. Note the amount of stretch, and the amount of set as you proceed, as well as the point of failure.

Being more elastic, animal fibers such as sinew, gut, rawhide and silk can tolerate somewhat larger diameter primary plies. American Indian bowstrings were often a single-ply cord when made of sinew, but more often three-ply when of plant origin. This is true of weaker fibers, such as palm strings of Brazil. And it is true of the strong dogbane strings of the north.

To restate, a bowstring made of large, simple plies cannot be as strong as one whose plies are themselves made up of smaller simple plies. This is true for two reasons: 1, small diameter plies are inherently stronger, and 2, many small plies will average out weak areas inherent in simple plies.

Obviously there is a practical limit to the number and fineness of simple plies.

Shoemakers' linen was made of 5 lb. plies. But plies of up to 10 lb. are not seriously weaker. Above that weight the thicker-is-weaker problems becomes more serious. And above 10 lb. it's more difficult to arrange plies to add up to a designated bowstring weight — exact change is more easily made with nickels than quarters.

You may decide its too much trouble spinning the 100 or so yards of primary ply needed for a superior multi-ply string. If so you can buy pre-spun thread instead. But try spinning up your own at least once. Spinning is easy, fast, and enjoyable.

ROLLING YOUR OWN

With a little practice using a drop spindle you can spin a bowstring's worth of thread in about one and one-half hours. Or about 20 minutes using a spinning wheel, or the drill-wheel, to follow.

Any of the finer fibers lend themselves to spinning: flax, silk, ramie, hemp, milkweed, nettle, dogbain, iris, and many others.

Pull a fiber-bearing plant from the ground, pull a twig from a tree — for use as a spindle — and with this cave-man gear, thread can be spun finer and stronger than the finest machine-spun equivalent. Tell this to ten people and you'll get ten arguments, some suspiciously caustic and heated — modernism is a religion of the first order. Modern spinning methods are faster and cheaper but cannot equal the spinners of India, for example, whose Dacca muslins were woven of spindle-spun cotton so fine it measures 250 miles to a pound. Four-thousand five-hundred years ago Egyptian mummies were wrapped in cloth woven 540 threads per inch. Silk cloth from the Han Dynasty in China has been found woven 508 threads per inch. The best modern mechanical spinners and weavers can manage is 350 threads per inch.

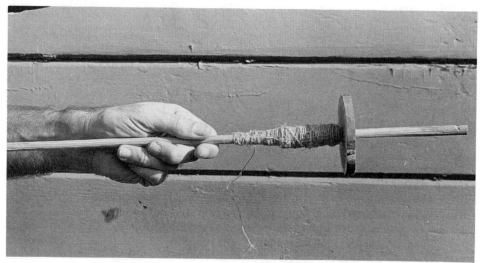

The drop spindle. Used in various forms for the last 9,500 years by almost every culture. Here, a section of small log is pierced by a straight twig. A drop spindle can be as simple as a rock or bone dangling from a string.

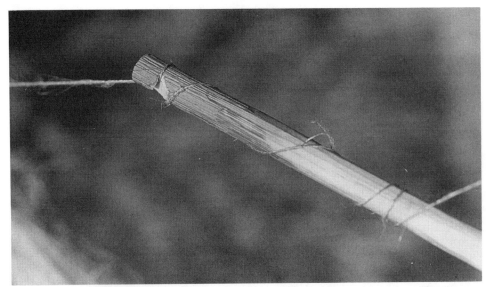

The notch prevents spun thread from slipping off the spindle. Carved as shown, it centers the thread for smooth, uneccentric spinning. Tie a starter thread just below the weight. Twist the thread around the spindle a few turns, then run it through the notch, leaving about eight inches free.

From a bundle of combed fibers, draw out sufficient fibers to lay over the starter thread. Twist both together lightly. Pinch and hold the end of the starter thread.

197

Let the spindle hang free. Twirl the spindle until the starter thread and fiber are twisted so tightly they try to kink. Do not let any of the twist escape up into the unspun fiber.

Quickly, before the spindle can untwist, switch pinching hands, and draw more fibers from the bundle. Pull to desired thread diameter, then pinch the stream of fibers just before they widen near the bundle.

Release the lower pinch, and let the pent-up twist run up into the newly-drawn fibers. Do not release the upper pinch or twist will run up into the fiber bundle, preventing the drawing out of new fibers.

Now you can switch into high gear. Using the flat of your palm roll the spindle forward along your hip, letting it fly free into the air when you run out of runway. With practice you will be able to impart terrific spin, which can be nursed through several drawing-out and re-pinching cycles.

When three feet or so has been spun, wind the newly spun thread onto the spindle shaft. Leave eight or ten inches free to store up twist for the next cycle.

Pulling threads from the bundle before you need to is the secret to fast, uniform spinning. Allowing pent-up twist to run up into un-pinched fiber is the secret to agonizing spinning.

A true spinning wheel is easier and faster to operate than a drop spindle. Wheels cost between two and four hundred dollars. But with the tools and skill

Operate this "spinning lathe" the same as a drop spindle. A slot lets the spun thread get past the front bearing. Hardwood shafts work best, acting as self-bearings. Shallow "U" grooves suffice as female bearing surfaces. The male bearings in this case are horn, but could be bone, antler, or hardwood. Or metal or plastic. Note most of the spindle weight is away from the axle, giving far greater flywheel effect. Roll the palm of you hand quickly over the shaft, as when hip-spinning the drop spindle. Make two or three passes and build up high speed.

Without the drop spindle constantly threatening to slow down and reverse, you can now take your worry-free time, concentrating on quality. Once you get the hang of spinning and can more easily operate a drop spindle, you will abandon this device. It is only faster and easier for beginners.

of a bowmaker you can certainly make your own spinning wheel, and in short order. Materials cost between five and twenty-five dollars. Look at one up close — it's self explanatory. Or weaving supply shops will steer you to a set of plans. While there you might also pick up a pamphlet on spindle and wheel spinning.

The main reason a spinning wheel is faster than a drop spindle is that thread can be fed directly to a take-up spool, with no need to stop and start the spindle.

A small pulley wheel is added to the ancient drop spindle. A big wheel, with a string for a belt drive, causes the small wheel and spindle to spin fast. A take-up spool rides free on the spindle shaft. Spun thread enters thru a hole in the tip of the spindle, as a way of getting past the spindle's bearing; once past, it exits through a side hole in the spindle.

The U-shaped flier arms are connected to the spindle. Spun thread is wound onto the spool by the flier arms. The spool rides free on the spindle shaft. In order to take up thread, the spool obviously must be made to spin somewhat slower than the flier. This is done by applying string friction against its grooved hub. By adjusting string friction take-up speed is controlled. When adjusted just so, the spinner, by resisting or giving in to the slightest tug, can cause spun thread to feed onto the spool at any chosen rate.

A simple foot treadle keeps both hands continually free, further speeding the process.

But maybe you don't have the patience for spindle spinning. Perhaps you don't want to go to the trouble of making a wheel. Possibly you're afraid your testosterone level might plummet. Or you dread the funny stories the guys might tell about you.

No problem!

The spinning wheel in these photos says Black and Decker on it!:

Here is a "drill wheel." It is a full-fledged, very efficient, no-apologies spinning wheel. It takes ten minutes to make. And is easier to use. The spool is harder to make than the spinning wheel itself. Weaving shops sell them for about $5.

The hollow spindle entrance, and the flier, are replaced by twisted coathanger wire. Quarter-inch metal shaft material serves as a spindle. Hammer the front inch of the shaft slightly flat, then the coiled wire to match. The spool spins freely on the shaft gripped in the drill chuck, its rate of spin, and thread take-up, is adjusted by the amount of string friction on the pulley.

The variable speed control. Don't laugh. It works great! Just slide it back and forth over the trigger. Fine-tune speed with a slight squeeze.

The secret to fast, uniform spinning is a smooth, even supply of fiber.

Arrange the mass of fiber to be spun in such a way that long, even columns of fiber can be pulled freely from it. To a large degree, internal fiber friction will pull fresh fiber from the bundle, or distaff, in a long parallel, uniform draw. Aid this process by selective hand feeding. This long lead-in of fiber should be kept from feeling any effect of the spindle's twist. Given a smooth supply line, spinning can proceed at about twenty feet per minute with linen, slower with shorter fibers.

Another secret to spinning with flax is to have a container of hot water near your left hand. Wetting the fiber with dampened fingers just before twisting activates the glue-like pectin surface of flax, leading to smoother, stronger thread.

When spinning, once a threshold tightness has been reached, small-diameter threads don't gain or lose much strength until twisted much tighter. A long plateau exists, but this becomes less true as thread diameter rises.

A more uniform thread will likely result if an example of a section of drawn-out, about-to-be-twisted fiber is taped in front of you while you spin.

When beginning a spinning session do a quick strength test of your work: Break short lengths which have been spun lightly, moderately, and tightly. See which is strongest, then spin the whole batch with equal twist.

In the same vein, some commercial strings benefit from tighter spinning. If a batch of string looks loosely spun it's wise to test it at different degrees of twist. One batch of 5-ply cotton, for example, rose from 12 lb. to 26 lb. test, only gaining about 15% mass per length — string shortens when twisted. Some commercial linen thread has also gained a similar percentage, but usually gains are much smaller. An entire spool of commercial string or thread can be quickly twisted tighter: run it through the spinning wheel, as if spinning loose fiber into thread. About fifty feet can be tightened per minute.

A spinning wheel will also speed up the making of the fifty feet or so of multiply string needed for an endless string. Imagine the agony of reverse-twisting this volume of 6-ply cord by hand. Instead, spin each ply, one at time, onto separate spools. Spin the plies tighter than normal. Set the six spools on six wire axles, or such. Feed the six plies as one through the wheel, now spinning in the opposite direction. At about twenty feet a minute the spool will take up perfectly formed 6-ply cord. This is about the only way the string for an efficient, completely home-made endless string can be made.

The top thread is highest-quality wet-spun commercial line linen. The smoother, more uniform bottom thread is hand-spun. Fully hand-made bowstrings can be superior to those made of machine spun thread. But, facing facts, a beginner's first efforts will not equal those of a machine.

When spinning is complete you are about fifteen minutes away from a flawless, first-class bowstring. See "Making Bowstring," farther on.

Following is the primitive method of making cordage. It yields a strong and tightly twisted cord. Due to its thicker and irregular plies such cordage is not the most efficient for bowstrings. Depending on the fiber, and skill of the string maker, cast will be lowered by an equivalent four to eight pounds of bow weight. Animal fibers do not suffer as much loss.

Using this ancient technique, completely serviceable strings can be made in the field under the most primitive conditions.

Yes, when you first try reverse-twisting cordage you will feel like a four-year old tying shoestrings. And you will feel worse after seeing "savages" spewing the stuff out by the yard on National Geographic Specials. But persevere. This is the real thing.

Tightly twist up a quantity of fibers, which when doubled will equal the thickness and strength of cordage wanted. Twist until the cord begins to kink.

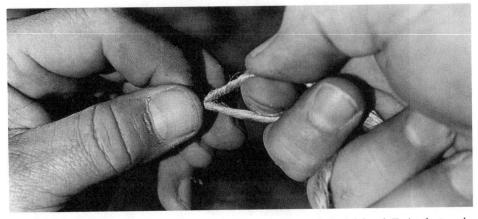

Fold the twisted ply in half at the kink. Pinch the kink tightly with the left hand. Twist the top ply clockwise, tightly.

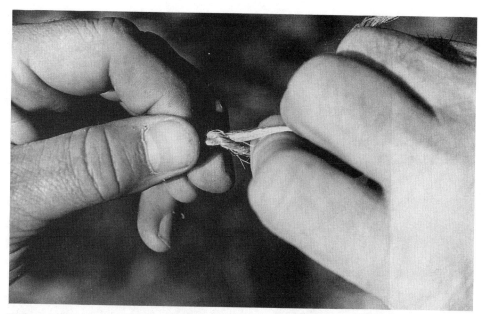

Without letting the top ply untwist, twist both plies counter-clockwise. Advance your pinch to prevent any untwisting.

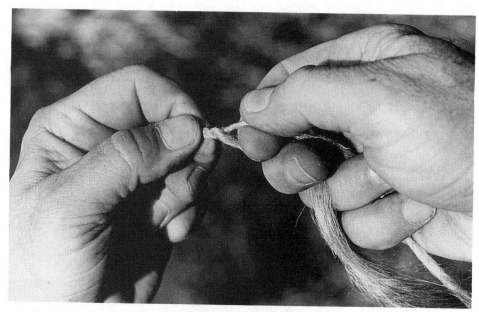

The "bottom" ply is now on top. Twist it clockwise tightly. Then again twist both plies counter-clockwise, and advance your pinch. Continue this process. Before twisting counter-clockwise get a grip on both plies and pull with mild pressure. This puts equal strain on both plies, insuring strongest-possible cordage.

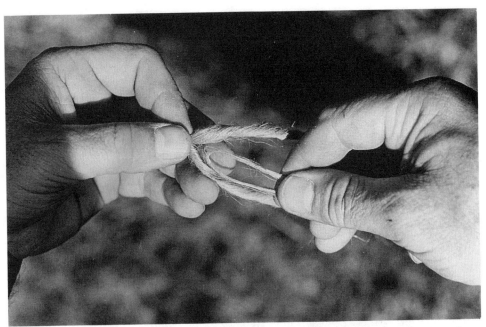

Proceed until cord diameter would otherwise begin to narrow, then splice in about ten percent new fiber. Bend the new fiber at the center of its length, creating a "V." Insert snugly into the cord's "Y." Take any twist out of the cord's unspun plies before adding the "V." This will permit full twisting of new and old fiber.

Continue reverse-twisting and adding new fiber when needed, until desired cord length is reached.

Take care to maintain equal diameter in both plies, otherwise they will not wind symmetrically around themselves. This places more strain on the straighter ply, weakening the cord.

The illustrated finger-twisting method gives a tighter net twist than the following method because each new twist of a ply re-tightens the slight unwinding from the last reverse twist. You can feel the ply twisting under the grip of your thumb, running back up into the last link of finished cord.

Longer fibers can be reverse-twisted into cordage much more quickly using another primitive method: rolling on the thigh, as shown in the photos.

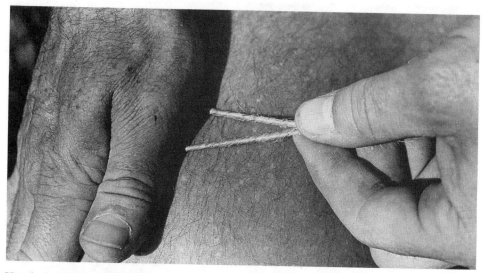

Here both plies are twisted at once. Pinch the "Y" tightly, then roll both plies forward on the thigh with the flat of your palm until they are twisted tight enough to kink. In order to get such a tight twist you might have to pre-roll each ply separately.

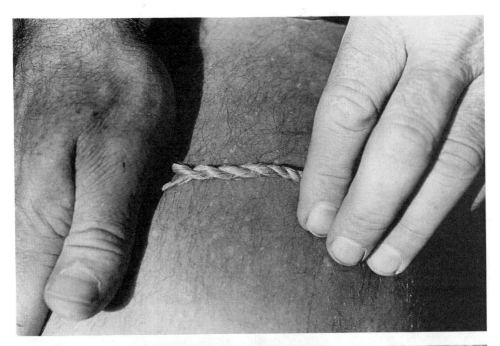

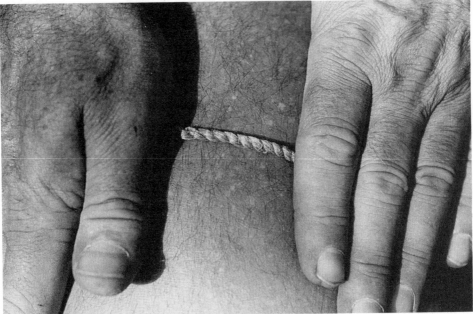

Release the pinch and the two plies will twist around themselves, forming new cordage. Re-pinch at the new "Y." Tighten this newly-formed cord by rolling it forward. Splicing proceeds as with the finger-twist method.

Primitive strings made of coarse fibers are usually covered with stubble. Moving the string slowly over a flame removes these fiber ends but does not damage the string body.

Strongest-per-mass strings are made of small simple plies of about 5 to 10 lb. test. There can be much variability in the size and number of simple plies, the number of primary plies, and in the complexity of the cord. In fact you will usually need to juggle these numbers to achieve correct string strength (see examples below). Feel free to juggle away — as long as simple plies are no more than 10 lb, and as long as primary plies contain no more than 7 simple-plies. Here are some sample configurations.

Designed with a reasonable margin of safety, straight-stave bows of normal length require strings with breaking strengths equaling four times draw weight.

A 35 lb. bow's 140 lb. string might be made as follows. Two 70 lb. plies, each containing seven 10 lb. simple plies. Which can be expressed as:

140 lb. = 2-70 lb. = 7-10 lb. = 140 lb.

A 3-ply cord would come out slightly over weight, but would still be satisfactory:

140 lb. = 3-47 lb. = 5-10 lb. = 150 lb.

A 50 lb. bow's 200 lb. string might be:

200 lb. = 3-66 lb. = 7-10 lb. = 210 lb.

If made of 5 lb. simple plies each primary ply would contain 14 simple plies.

Too many. The "7" limit is exceeded. Outer fibers would be over-strained and weakened; inner plies would be dead weight. Instead let each main ply be made of two sub-plies. In other words, each main ply would itself be a finished 2-ply cord:

> 200 lb. = 3-66 lb. = 2-33 lb. = 7-5 lb. = 210 lb.
> Or:
> 200 lb. = 3-66 lb. = 3-22 lb. = 5-5 lb. = 225 lb.

A 70 lb. bow's 280 lb. string might be:

> 280 lb. = 3-93 lb. = 3-31 lb. = 6-5 lb. = 270 lb.

If only 10 lb. simple plies were available then a four-ply string would be appropriate:

> 280 lb. = 4-70 lb. = 7-10 lb. = 280 lb.

A 100 lb. bow's 400 lb. string might be:

> 400 lb. = 4-100 lb. = 3-33 lb. = 7-5 lb. = 420 lb.

Or if using 10 lb. simple-plies it might be:

> 400 lb. = 4-100 lb. = 2-50 lb. = 5-10 lb. = 400 lb.

A 200 lb. test, primitive linen string (two simple, hand-twisted plies), made by a relative novice, will weight up to 300-grains. A 200 lb. = 3-66 lb. = 3-22 lb. = 5-5 lb. = 225 lb. string, made by an experienced spinner/stringmaker, will weight about 100-grains.

The difference in cast between these two strings will be unnervingly large.

In practice, primitive strings often do not shoot terribly much slower than prime strings. But for a very bad reason. They don't posses the same margin of safety, often having only half the breaking strength of prime strings. When primitive strings are made to high margins of safety they are very thick and heavy.

An anthropologist friend recently returned from the rain forests of South America. He had with him several Indian bowstrings. Typical of the design, they were longer than double length, half intended for bracing the bow, half for wrapping around the limbs as a spare. This anthropologist's Indian friends routinely harvest their meals from 20 yards and higher in the forest, shooting monkeys which do not especially want to be shot. The Indian strings were flaw-lessly made, but were almost one-quarter inch thick. They were designed not to break.

BOWSTRING DESIGN

Reading through scores of old and new archery texts reveals the desolation of precise bowstring information. Elmer, in *Target Archery*, gives the most comprehensive report. Gordon, in *The New Archery*, is a distant second. But with both sources, as with most writers on most aspects of archery, there is much opinion, much quoting, and little or no analysis, investigation, or testing.

A beginning bowmaker, unhappy with the cast of his new 49 lb. bow, stopped in to have it diagnosed. The bow was wide-ringed ash, 20 percent early growth, flat bellied, fairly flat crowned, 65" long, had a slightly working grip, was 1 3/4" wide above the handle, weighted 23 oz, was well tillered and had 1 5/8" set immediately after unstringing. At 27" of draw such a bow, based on the past performance of scores of same-design, same-set bows, must shoot a 500-grain arrow about 147 fps, give or take a couple of fps. Yet this bow managed only 135 fps. Its cast equaled that of a 39 lb. bow, give or take.

This bow was a dud by any standard. And a real dilemma, because on the one hand it *had* to shoot about 147 fps, yet was shooting only 135 fps. Only one possible explanation existed: the string.

As it turned out the string was made of artificial sinew, and weighed 320 grains. The bow might as well have been strung with a dead snake. Artificial sinew is made of nylon, and nylon s-t-r-e-t-c-h-e-s! And it is heavy. And if thickened enough to overcome much of its stretch it becomes very heavy.

A 170-grain linen replacement yielded a satisfying 148 fps, a 12 fps increase in cast. An astounding 10 pounds of equivalent draw weight.

Apart from durability, the above example illuminates the principle properties required of a good bow string:

A good bowstring must have high strength for its mass, and it must have little stretch during the shot.

A bowstring is more than simple cordage. It has special requirements. Making a superior bowstring taxes the limits of material, and the skill of the stringmaker, just as with wood and the bowmaker. But a bowmaker has control over many areas of design, each able to affect arrow speed by several fps. Only two such areas exist for the stringmaker: mass and stretch. This is where attention must focus.

In practice, stretch is not a large problem. Excepting nylon, straining fibers to near breaking will induce large, permanent sets. In this way, most of the stretch can be taken from even the most elastic string materials.

String Mass

For a 66", 50 lb. bow, strung with a 125-grain string, shooting a 28", 500-grain arrow,

A 20-grain rise or fall in string mass will affect arrow speed by about 1 fps.

Coincidentally, a one pound difference in draw weight affects arrow speed by about 1 fps.

Which means each 20-grain difference in string mass affects cast by about an equivalent one pound of draw weight.

Twenty-grain differences in string mass has less effect on heavier bows and heavier arrows, more effect on lighter bows and lighter arrows. And the cast-slowing effect of each additional 20-grains is slightly diminished as string mass rises. But "20 grains equals one pound" is a good rule of thumb.

The effect of string mass on arrow speed is about one-third that of arrow mass. Why just one-third? String at the arrow nock accelerates at arrow speed. If the string's entire mass was centered at this point, then string mass would affect cast the same as arrow mass. String near the bow's tips accelerates at tip speed, and has little effect on cast. Sixty five-grains added to each limb tip slows cast by only about l fps.

This is useful information. String loops reinforced to ultra-safety will not raise loop mass enough to measurably effect cast.

But why bother with all this? Why care if a string conforms to someone else's idea of perfection? After all, a too-heavy string will do the job. So what if a bow's cast is a few pounds short? Why make a simple thing complicated?

These are wholesome and proper questions. One answer is that once the principles are known, and with a little practice under the belt, it's about as fast and easy to make a good string as a poor one.

Another answer is that a well-planned, well-made string is a small reward, part of the larger reward of a well-planned, well-made bow. Asking, "Why bother making an efficient string," is just another part of the question, "Why bother making an efficient bow.

Yet another reason for making a quality string is that the difference in cast between a well made string and a poorly made string can easily exceed the difference in cast between a $100 stave and a $3 piece of pine shelving; or the most perfectly tillered bow and a wretchedly tillered bow, and so on.

Another answer has to do with the impulse for art and pride. The fibers in a growing stalk of flax, for example, express exquisite natural engineering and architecture. Somehow it seem inappropriate that they should end up as a lumpy, inelegant, slip-shod string.

String Stretch

Word has it that FastFlight™ is faster because it stretches less. After settling in, after taking all the set it is going to take, FastFlight™ stretches about 1.5% to Dacron's 4%, linen's 2%. and silk's 4%. FastFlight™ is faster, but the small difference in stretch between these fibers is not the reason. The reason is its low mass.

A 64" 40 lb. straight bow drawing 27" was strung with a 150 grain silk string. The string was made of twenty strands of 10 lb-test silk, in two moderately twisted plies. It cast a 500-grain arrow 134 fps. The string was removed and repeatedly strained to about 170 lb. pull, effectively removing any residual stretch from the string. When restrung cast remained at 134 lb. The string was removed and detwisted, letting all twenty strands run straight. Cast rose to 135 fps.

The bow was now braced with a 150-grain string, made of wet-spun line linen. Coincidentally, breaking strength was identical to that of the silk string, an estimated 200 lb. Also two plies twisted moderately. Cast was 135 fps. When strained to near breaking as with the silk string, cast remained unchanged. When the string was detwisted, letting strands run straight, cast rose to 136 fps.

The bow was braced with a *same-mass* FastFlight™ string, which also cast 135 fps.

Once broken in, the difference in stretch between silk, linen, and FastFlight™ strings had virtually no effect on cast.

But! At 150-grains the FastFlight's™ breaking strength equaled about 1,000 lb. A 75-grain, 500 lb-test version cast 139 fps. At 30 grains and 200 lb. it would have cast about 141 fps.

FastFlight™ is much lighter per strength than Dacron. It is also more resistant to cuts and abrasions. If you're going to use artificial string, FastFlight™ seems the best choice. If made into 300 or 400 lb-test strings, cost will be under $1 per string.

Lower-stretch strings would benefit recurves more than straight bows: both bows strain the string equally at full draw, but high early draw-weight bows slam home harder, stretching the string more, surrendering energy to the string instead of the arrow.

Word also has it that FastFlight™ is dangerous, that it has so little stretch it will break a bow. It's not quite that simple: FastFlight™, Dacron, and linen strings, each at 200 lb-test, will stretch enough to cushion a bow. Each strand of Fast-Flight™ breaks at about 55 lb. (about 35 lb. for B-50 Dacron). That's only 4 strands. But most stringmakers use 12 or 16 strands, bringing the bowstring to 600 lb-800 lb-test. Such a string is so overly strong, its already low stretch is reduced to virtually nil. As a result, bow limbs do feel more shock. One solution is to use only 6 or 8 strands, straining the string enough to make it give a little, with a side benefit of higher arrow speed due to lower string mass. To prevent its biting into the bow, and the fingers, loops and nocking point would have to be thickened considerably.

The above bow was braced with a string made of highest quality shoemaker's linen. At 200 lb. test this string weighed only 75 grains and cast 139 fps, identical to the same-mass FastFlight. A 200 lb-test Dacron string weighs 80-grains, waxed.

In other words, *highest-quality linen string virtually equals Dacron's performance.*

The strength per mass of this shoemaker's linen was surprisingly high. Quality linen thread is a rare commodity these days. All the linen previously tested here produced strings with a prewaxed weight of about 150 grains (for an average-length string, with 200 lb. breaking strength).

The first temptation was to suspect this new linen was Dacron or a Dacron-linen mix. Microscopic examination, however, showed both fibers visually identical in structure. The sure-fire test for synthetic materials was then applied: When burned the smoke of both fibers smelled pleasantly organic, not pungently plastic. Elmer talked of 70-grain bow strings, but I had assumed he meant very light, dangerously strained flight shooting strings.

This best-shoemaker's string was made of Irish linen, from Ireland. Despite its strength it is soft, supple and cushiony. Some brands of shoemakers' linen are hard and saw-like, and best kept parallel, as in an endless string, not reverse twisted.

This is a satisfying continuity: on the other side of the dark fiberglass void, writers earlier in the century reported Irish linen as being superior. Current books on the subject report France, Belgium and Holland still growing substantial flax crops, and that the finest quality is sent to Ireland for spinning.

Non-Irish shoemakers' lockstitch brands are hard, and weaker to varying degrees than the Irish.

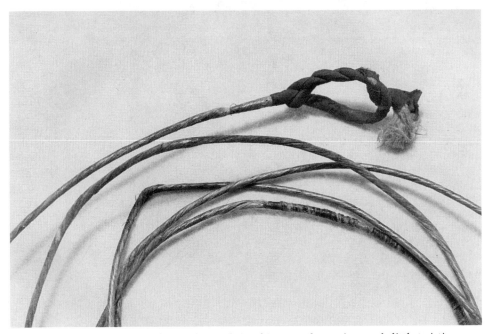

*Made of full-length strands of hemp, this traditional Japanese bowstring needs little twisting
(courtesy Grayson Collection)*

Traditional Japanese bowstrings are made of full-length hemp. They look to be a single, large simple-ply. However the string's central core is twisted in the opposite direction from that of its surface. This string will not change length when twisted, and should not twist in the fingers when drawn. These may be the reasons for this unusual design. Or this design may have been a clever means of curing the thicker-is-weaker problem:

The single-ply inner core is spun up first, and tighter than needed. The outer layer is added, then spun in the opposite direction. As with standard two-ply cordage, it will not twist far before its now larger diameter resists being twisted, soon yielding neutral twist. The final result being that both inner and outer fibers are more evenly strained, yielding less dead weight.

This design could possibly be idealized by progressively adding surface fibers to each ply as twisting proceeds. If done correctly each fiber layer would end up strained with equal tension.

This principle, if not this exact design, needs exploring.

"Reel" and rosin box for Japanese string (courtesy Grayson Collection).

MARGIN OF SAFETY

The old rule is that string strength should be four times draw weight. A 50 lb. bow, for example, needing a 200 lb. string. This allows for a comfortable safety margin on a straight-stave longbow. Slimmer margins were accepted for flight shooting. Sometimes very slim. When going for a new record string weight was reduced dangerously low. So low that strings often broke during the first, or subsequent shots, endangering the bow.

A bowstring is under greatest strain after release, as bow limbs slam home, jerking the string taut. But the force on a bowstring at that moment of "string impact" is determined primarily by the bow's early draw weight. If a bow is harder to pull early in the draw, it will impact with more force, and vice-versa. For this reason a lower-weight recurve, for example, can require a stronger string than a heavier straight-stave bow which follows the string.

String angle also affects needed string strength. Low-strung bows and long bows bring more leverage to bear against the string, causing higher string strain both when braced and early in the draw.

Different bow designs do need different strength strings per pound of draw weight. But until the time consuming tests needed to determine exact figures are done the following rule of thumb is likely adequate. Based on a draw length of 28", and computed for a reasonable margin of safety, string strength should equal:

Draw weight at 15", times ten.

Using this formula, a 50 lb. straight-stave bow with negligible string follow will weigh about 20 lb. at 15", times ten, equals 200 lb. Perfect!

A same design and weight bow having four inches of follow will weigh about 15 lb. at 15". A 150 lb. test string would do for this bow.

A reflexed and recurved 50 lb. bow might weigh 35 lb. at 15", times ten, equals 350 lb. A comfortably safe string for such a hard hitter.

These figures are for safe, durable, long-life strings. For flight shooting, string mass can be reduced by as much as one-half. Such a light string is far more likely to break, and will likely take the bow along with it.

A stronger string is needed when shooting a lighter arrow, because the bow slams home faster and harder. Weaker strings will suffice for heavier arrows.

Very thin strings sing like guitar strings on release. Very thick strings are dull and quiet.

Low braced strings are quieter, and cast faster arrows.

BOWSTRING DESIGN AT A GLANCE

- Breaking strength to equal weight at 15", times ten.
- Individual threads of about 5 lb. test.
- No more than seven sub-plies, or seven main plies
- Reinforce loop by 25 to 100%, timberhitch by 50 to 100%
- Serve arrow nocking point.
- Wax plies lightly before twisting, rub till wax soaks in.

MAKING BOWSTRINGS

Single-ply Cordage

Single-ply cordage is simply a cylinder of twisted fibers. It is quick to make, fairly durable in its body, but even when held together by knots this string tends to unravel at the nocks.

There are several near-solutions to this problem: Make several turns around the nock before tying off. Thicken these areas with extra fiber. Serve these areas. Reverse twist only these areas. Or add wax or glue.

Hemp fibers are often six, eight, even ten feet long. A single-ply cord of such full-length fibers is in no danger of losing strength by unraveling, but even here special attention is needed at the nocks.

With any of the strings mentioned here, a good finishing touch is to pull the finished string to about 4/5 of its estimated breaking strength. For two reasons:

One, if the string is going to break find out now, before putting a good bow at risk. Two, such pre-stressing strains the string far more than when in service. As a result the string takes a set; a lot or a little, depending on the type fiber used. This permanently removes most of the elasticity from a string, resulting in less stretch when fired. With experience, this amount of stretch can be planned for when determining initial ply length. It's important the string be pre-stressed AFTER it is made. This lets small disparities in fit and tension resolve themselves. Such near-breaking does not make the string more likely to break later when in use.

Straight Cordage

Standard cordage of two, three, or more plies. Simple or complex. Loops or knots are added when ready to brace the bow.

The Endless String

All strands in an endless string are parallel, each pulling independently. As a result, each is free to break at its weakest point. For this reason strands should be multi-ply cords, preferably of five to seven plies so that weak points in each ply are reinforced.

Fully home-made, efficient endless strings cannot be practically fashioned without first using a spinning wheel, or such, to create the needed 50-plus yards of multi-ply string. If unable to create such multi-ply string it would be best to use commercial Dacron, or multi-ply linen string, especially shoemakers' lock-stitch cord.

Many archers and writers of the past and present have assumed the loop of an endless string is weaker than the string itself. The following argument is presented:

The loop is only half as thick as the main string, therefore only half as strong. For the loop to have sufficient strength, string thickness has to be doubled, doubling the entire string's mass in the process.

This seems to make perfect sense, and if my engineer friend, Dick Baugh, hadn't set me straight on the matter the above argument might have stood. Many a fight, by the way, has been started down at The Bowmaker's Bar over just this subject.

It's easy to prove that an endless string's half-thickness loop is a strong as its full-thickness body: Determine the strength of a strand of string. Loop it over a smooth hook of a pull-scale, two strands handing down. Pull on both strands, noting scale weight at the breaking point.

This seems unfair, two strands against the loop's single strand, but the single strand will hold its own. Breaking strength will be double that of a single strand broken in a straight pull. Almost! Minor abrasion takes place where loop meets nock, and bunching, crushing pressures lower loop strength just slightly. This require loops to be slightly thickened, by thickening the whole string. A soft serving should be used to cushion the loop.

The Turks, and other composite bowmakers, used endless strings, usually of silk. These strings were made short, then attached to the bow with an auxiliary "Oriental knot." (see "Knots", to follow) An endless string has several valuable features:

1) A bowstring can be made to exact length.

2) If laid out carefully, tension is distributed evenly at all point on all strands, theoretically resulting in slightly less string mass.

3) By definition an endless string is not twisted. Each strand is therefore more like a bar than a coil. An endless string will therefore have slightly less stretch when shot.

4) An endless string requires less skill to make than a Flemish string.

Is the endless string better than the Flemish string? In other words, is it stronger per mass, is it more durable, is it easier, faster, and cheaper to make?

There are trade-offs with each design. Performance differences depend more on the experience of the maker than inherent benefits of the design.

Making the Endless String

The photos show how to make this string:

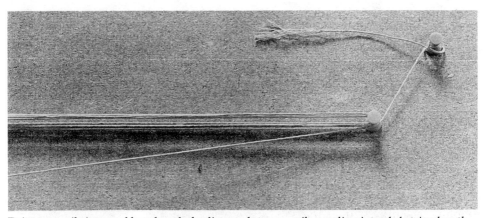

Drive two nails into a table or board, the distance between nails equaling intended string length. A special adjustable jig can be made for this, but unless you're going into the string making business there is little point. Determine the number of strands needed: breaking strength of one strand, divided into four times the bow's draw weight. Wind the string back and forth around the nails until desired strand number is reached. Be careful to apply equal tension on each strand.

Tie the two loose ends together.

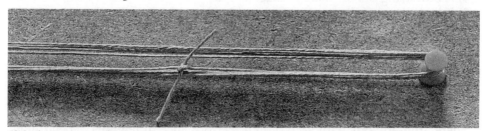

Slide the string around the nails a few inches so the knot can be covered by serving.

Serve for about three inches. Use medium-fine soft cotton, silk, or linen. Serve similarly at the other end.

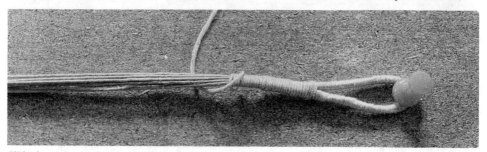

Slide the string back to its original position. Form loops by pulling the strings together and serving.

When loops have been formed at both ends of the string brace the bow and serve a few inches at its nocking point. Serve lightly. Any mass added here slows cast as if added to the arrow itself.

It is better to avoid twisting the string. But if too long it can be twisted to shorten. With practise exact lengths can be dependably made.

Roberts, in *The English Bowman* of 1801, makes this recommendation: "Fine glove-leather or any kind of tape or binding, wrapped round the eye of the string, will preserve it from being cut by the nock of the horn." Roberts had Flemish strings in mind, but his advice is also sound for endless strings.

The Flemish String

The design of the English warbow string is lost to us. Was it of old Flemish design? Quoting from Gordon, "Unfortunately, no bowstrings survive to us from the heyday of English military archery ..."

We know, however, that these strings must have been of very high quality. For safety under military conditions a 120-plus lb. bow would need at least a 400 lb. string. The remains of English military arrows are about 3/8" wide at the nock. Judging from photos of these nocks, strings were not over 1/8" in diameter. For a 1/8" string to safely draw a 120-plus lb. bow it must be made to the very highest standards. It would be nice to read a twist-by-twist accounting of the making of these strings.

The Flemish string is not mentioned in the 1833 *Archer's Guide*, London, But in 1845 *The Book of Archery* reports: "I believe few bowstrings are now made in England, the great mart being Flanders, where both materials and workmanship are excellent."

Duff, writing in 1930, claims that, "... for over five hundred years the Belgian bowstring makers have had an almost complete monopoly of the bowstring business."

Gordon believed that the "Flemish secret" rested, "... in the use of the long native-flax fibers worked and built into string directly from the distaff without the intermediate step of conversion into thread. It is this trick that gives the Flemish string its smooth 'whole' appearance and defied its analysis for a long time."

From what we now know of the need for uniformity, and of the thicker-is-weaker problem, we can be fairly certain that Gordon's interpretation of the "Flemish secret" was in error. Unless the flax was glued it had to be twisted, and if twisted it had to be spun into small diameter fibers to have decent strength. The flax spinners of Belgium were too expert not to know this. By the later 1,300's their product was so refined the king of France sent fine linen cloth to the Saracens as ransom for captured crusaders.

Many "Flemish" designs have replaced the original. The common denominator of these designs is, 1), A built-in plaited loop, 2), Some or all of its length is reverse-twisted.

The "Primitive" Flemish String

This string is made of two or three plies of unspun fibers, using the finger-twisting or thigh-twisting method, reverse-twisting its full length.

Since the primary plies in such a string are relatively thick, all fibers will not be strained uniformly. Because of this, and because of inevitable thinner/weaker spots in each ply, such a string can not be as strong as one carefully made from a larger number of smaller primary plies. To the archer this means a thicker, therefore more massive, therefore slower-shooting string. In the range of two or three times more massive, depending on the level of skill involved. Given an average weight bow and arrow, and assuming a proper margin of strength safety, this translates to five to ten fps reduction in cast. Cast reduces to as much as an 8 lb. lighter bow.

A High Quality Flemish String

Arrange two nails about one and one-third bow length apart.

To know how many threads will be needed per ply, perform a breaking strength test. Break several short lengths of thread to determine average strength. Determine the number of threads needed per ply or sub-ply.

Unwind self-spun or commercial thread around the nails, endless-string fashion, using no more than seven threads per ply or sub-ply. If using commercial thread, single-ply is preferred. When finished, pinch one end and snip or lift it free from its nail. Keeping the ply slightly taut, let it unwrap naturally around itself. Set this ply aside and repeat as needed.

There is no need to actively reverse twist each of the threads. Each ply in the 7-ply shoemakers' cord was actively reverse twisted, but need not have been if the seven plies were to be used as a primary ply, as here.

If making a simple string you will probably wind out three plies. If making a complex string you will probably wind out nine plies.

If complex, reverse twist the nine plies into three finished three-ply cords, then reverse twist these three cords into into a three-ply complex cord. For more uniform strain, and to save time, use the drill method.

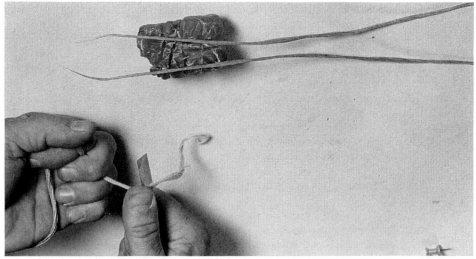

The plaited loop. Taper the last four inches of each ply. Wax the last twelve inches fairly heavily.

The plaited loop: Starting about nine inches from the tapered ends, make about three inches of reverse-twist cordage.

Bend these few inches of cordage into a loop, resting one "W" directly atop the other.

Continue reverse-twisting each double-thick ply as if they were one. The tapered ends will blend smoothly into the main string body. Stop just as the taper ends.

Secure the loop at the end of its taper, where reverse-twisting was halted. Tie a knot at each of the other ends. These knots should be at precisely the same place in each ply: plies shorten when twisted; you will know each ply has been twisted equally when all three knots are even. Each ply can be spun by twisting with fingers, on the thigh, by hand drill, or electric drill. Spin each ply separately. Spin until the ply is almost inclined to kink. Set the twisted ply aside, secured by a nail or weight. Once all three plies are spun individually in one direction, place all three together and spin backward until cordage is complete. Keep mild tension in the string. Again, use fingers, thigh, or drill.

The string can be finished by finger twisting, but the final product would not be as uniform, and would take twenty-minutes or longer to complete. The drill method is faster, and produces more evenly strained results. Secure the finished loop in a vise or such so that strain can be put on the untwisted plies without unwinding the loop. Reverse-twist the full string using the drill method, described earlier.

Plaited loops are somewhat sloppy and unevenly strained on four-ply and higher strings. When plaiting four or more even-numbered plies plait the loop as if making a two-ply string, separating the plies just before the splice tapers end. For odd-numbered plies, divide the odd ply temporarily among the other plies while forming the loop.

Tie a timberhitch in the string, about four inches short of bow length (see Knots, farther on). Brace the bow, low at first. The string will stretch. Adjust the hitch and rebrace. A low brace height puts greater strain on the string, removing stretch more completely. If you trust yourself, use this Jim Hamm trick: Hold the bow as if reverse-floor tillering, then press forward on the back of the grip. This puts tremendous strain on the string. If strung low enough, the bow can be made to strain the string to its breaking point. Once you know the limits this is a quick and simple way to remove all feasible stretch from a string. As you flatten the bow its new string will stretch, slowly lowering brace height. The lower the string moves, the greater the leverage brought to bear. Despite this, the string will become progressively harder to stretch, soon becoming rigid. You may have to break one string to learn the limits here. Keep you eye on both limbs and be certain that each is bending equally. If the string does break there is a good chance the bow will follow. Should this occur, note that Jim's address is listed at the front of this book.

Superior rope of any length or diameter can be made using bowstring-making techniques. Ropes need not be so mass-efficient, so each of the three main plys may be formed of many more than seven sub-plies. Self-made ropes of flax or hemp will be far stronger than those of the best commercial Manilla hemp.

A Utility Flemish String

The previous is a high-quality Flemish string. A slightly less efficient, but more quickly assembled version can be made with just two plies, of ten, fifteen or more strands per ply. Add 50% or more strands than normal, for insurance. This string will shoot slower, but it is easy and fast to make, and sometimes that's just what you want.

A Superior Quality Flemish String

A plaited loop is twice as thick as an endless-string loop. The plaited loop is almost twice the strength of the main string. For this reasons there is no absolute need to reinforce the loop of a Flemish string.

The timberhitch at the other end is another matter. The main string is diverted around the nock by the hitch and becomes a focal point of strain and abrasion. This is where such strings generally break, unless reinforced. With practice you will be able to anticipate the amount of stretch in a string. It will then be a simple matter to taper in 50 to 100% additional fiber, starting a few inches before where the hitch will be formed.

Until you can predict the amount of stretch a new string will take the timberhitch area can be reinforced after the fact: Once the stretch has left a new string and the string's true length is known untwist the string to a point about eight inches before the nock. When intending to reinforce a timberhitch leave the string a couple of inches longer than needed because thicker strings shorten up

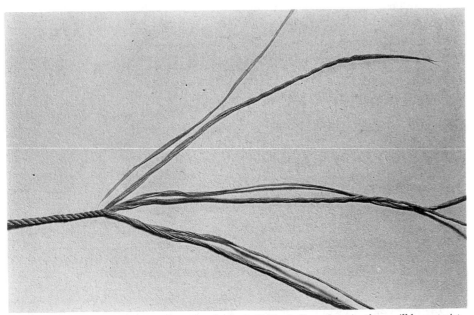

Before laying the reinforcement in place untwist the individual plies, otherwise there will be no twist left in them to accept the reinforcements. Once untwisted wax them fairly heavily. Press the first reinforcement in position; to secure it in place reverse-twist the string for one or two cycles. Repeat with reinforcement number two and three. Continue finger-twist cordage making until finished.

more than thinner strings when twisted. Cut fourteen-inch long reinforcements, each equaling 50 to 100% of existing ply diameter. Taper the last four or five inches of one end of each, as with the plaited loop, and wax fairly heavily. Press the reinforcements into place, then continue standard reverse-twist cordage making.

While it's true that a Flemish loop does not have to be reinforced, occasionally such loops will fray. In addition, uneven pressures and angles strain the loop where it joins the string body. Since there is no measurable loss of performance with increased loop weight it is prudent to add 50 to 100% more fiber to the loop when first making it.

Except for reinforcements being tapered at both ends, the loop is reinforced much like the timberhitch. Let the reinforcements be eight to twelve inches long, including taper, and equal 50 to 100% of existing ply diameter. Center these tapered additions where the top of the loop will be. Wax reinforcers heavily enough so they will press into and hold against the well-waxed main string. Tapered portions should lay down smoothly without frizzy ends. Proceed from here as with an unreinforced loop.

Serving is not needed at either loop or hitch, but is useful at the arrow nock. With a reinforced loop and timberhitch, the nocking area is now the chain's weak link, and should be served with fine, soft thread. Use less serving rather than more, because mass on this portion of the string slows arrow speed as if added to the arrow itself. On strings made from commercial thread it is hardly worth burdening the string maker or the string with serving. String material costs 50 cents and takes fifteen minutes to twist into a string. Such easily made strings can be replaced when even slightly frayed, or otherwise suspicious.

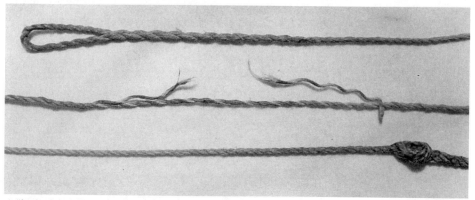

A "lucky break." With both loop and hitch reinforced this string's unserved, unreinforced arrow nocking area became the inevitable point of eventual failure. Signs of wear were ignored on this string. In this case the string did not fail completely, about a one-in-three outcome. It is worth noting that overbuilt, low-set bows are far less likely to break when strings fail.

A superior string can be formed by reinforcing the arrow nock area. As the string is first being twisted, add 20% or 30% more fiber, tapered and waxed, as with loop reinforcements. Although serving helps resist wear, it does not prevent it; and neither does it increase strength, which means the entire string length must be made stronger in anticipation of wear. A reinforced nock area will permit the bulk of the string body to be lighter. A light, soft serving in still used, so that reinforcement bulk can be kept low. Too-thick reinforcements do not twist up smoothly. To keep mass low, reinforcement need only be three or four inches long, each end then tapering off to zero over three inches or so.

Positioning the reinforcement requires forethought and practice. Complete the loop and reverse-twist the string almost to its center. Brace the intended bow with a temporary string. Place the new string over the temporary. Modified by experience, allow about one half inch for final string stretch, then mark the estimated nocking point on the new string. Press the reinforcements in place, and twist into place as with the timberhitch reinforcements. Then finish the string as usual.

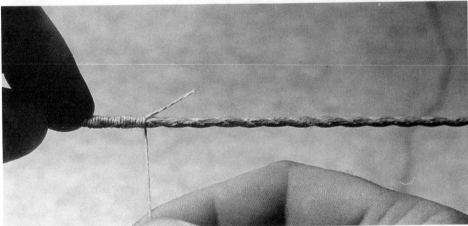

Vibrating strings will untie the most elaborate knots. This ingenious serving is shake-proof. Its long-forgotten inventor deserves much thanks. At the lower end of the area to be served untwist the plies, push an inch or so of serving through, retwist the cord, and begin serving.

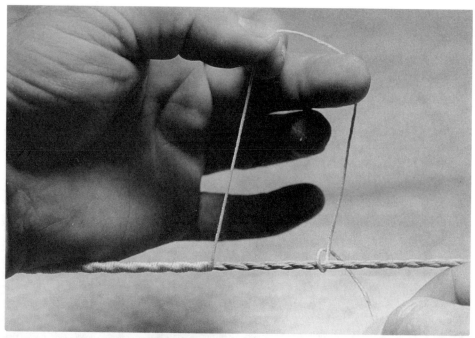

Stop serving about one-quarter inch sooner than intended serving length. Let the serving string rise up into a loop, as shown. Starting just within the right side of this loop, begin serving again, this time serving right to left. Serve about eight or ten turns.

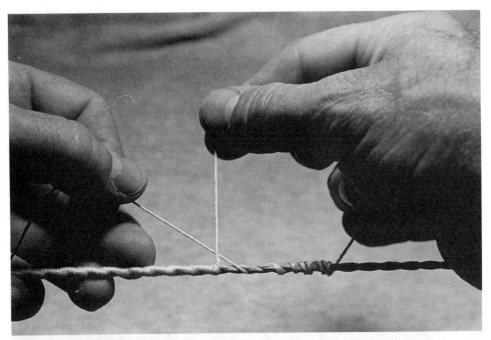

Lay the free end of the serving string horizontally against the bowstring and behind the loop. Using the left side of the loop, continue the original left-to-right serving. You will be encircling the string end just laid behind the loop. Serve this section tightly. Notice that as the serving grows on the left it shrinks on the right.

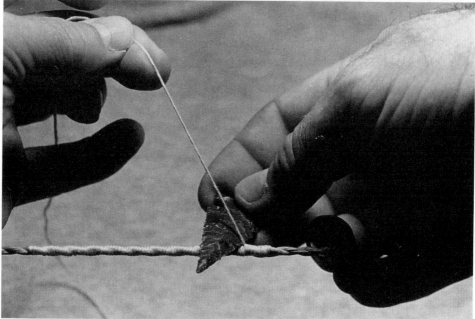

When all eight or ten turns have been used up squeeze the end of the serving and pull the loose end through till taut, then cut it free. Use this serving for endless-string loops, arrow fletching, hafting, and so on.

The Double Loop Flemish

Some archers like a loop on both ends of their Flemish string. Many good arguments are made against this practice but few can be made for it.

Because of the unpredictable string-shortening effects of plaited loop-making, double-loop strings can not be made to exact length. They must be made slightly long, the body then twisted to shorten.

A timberhitch is more convenient than a second loop. It is also easier to make, safer to adjust, and each ply in the string body is equally strained. And strings are more interchangeable.

Before forming the second loop, untwist the twist that has been put into the plies while making the first loop. Untwist more than needed in order to counter whatever twist the second loop will ad. Lay the plies out parallel, making sure they are evenly strained.

While forming the second loop, plies often come into uneven tension, with one ply pulling more than its share of the load. Unless careful attention is paid to this problem, double-loop strings become weaker than those with a single loop.

A New String Design

Made originally due to laziness, this pictured design turned out to be efficient, and quick to make. Strands are wound out endless-string fashion, about eight-inches longer than needed. Starting four inches from one end, serve the loop-to-be for three inches. Fold the serving, forming a loop. Impregnate the four-inch, double-thick area with glue, then serve as with an endless string loop. Brace the bow with a temporary string. Measure second-loop position, and form as above. Allow glue to set before use.

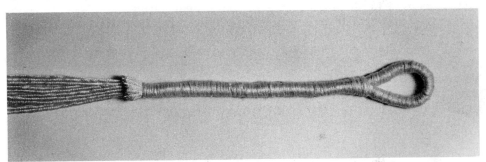

Conventional endless string bodies must be somewhat thicker than needed in order for loops to have sufficient strength to resist abrasion. The loops of this string are twice as thick as those of an endless string, its body can therefore be lighter.

Making the Sinew String

Backstrap or leg sinew from deer, elk, moose, buffalo, cattle, horse, or any hooved animal will make efficient bowstrings. Thick-ply, primitive strings are stronger if made from sinew than from vegetable fiber — despite the fact that vegetable fibers are often stronger than sinew fibers. But how can this be? Why would stronger fibers make weaker strings? Why did Indians prefer sinew when Europeans, shooting far heavier bows, preferred vegetable fibers? Why do current neo-aboriginals report sinew outlasting vegetable fiber bowstrings?

This was a disturbing mystery, but now the answer seems clear. "Primitive" strings are made of two or three thick simple plies. As we have seen, such plies are weaker due to non-uniformity, and having being made thicker to compensate, they now suffer even further from the thicker-is-weaker problem.

"Advanced" strings avoid both problems, being composed of many small threads.

Sinew and other animal fibers, on the other hand, are far less affected by thickness. Their more-strained outer fibers can stretch many times farther than vegetable fibers. Even when strained enough to put inner fibers to work, outer fibers are still stretched below capacity.

In a pinch sinew (also hide and gut) can be obtained from any animal, of any size.

Bird sinew bears investigating. It seems tremendously strong, and might be considerably lighter than that of ground dwellers.

Sinew should be shredded down to fine-diameter fibers. The finer the fiber, the higher the internal friction, the stronger the string. Backstraps shred up quickly, but only the thin, outer portion reduces easily to thread size. The thick, coarser side takes about as much time to reduce as leg sinew.

Leg tendons are tough, but do reduce to fine, more uniform fibers. The smaller tendons on the front of each leg yield finer fibers. Smaller animals yield finer fibers. But larger animals yield longer fibers. For their size buffalo legs yield finer, more easily separated fibers. But this is, literally, splitting hairs. Any sinew will make a good bow string.

The bulk of current opinion says to pound leg tendons to facilitate reduction. This is OK for sinew-backing, but can result in short, broken fibers which must be twisted more tightly. Pristine fibers make stronger strings.

Hupa Indian bowmaker George Blake employes a different method. He uses fresh leg sinews, or soaks dried ones until as soft as if fresh. He cuts the outer sheath open, then pulls fine, full-length, uncrushed fibers free. The string is twisted from these long, fresh fibers, then stretched and dried, resulting in a very smooth, strong string. This technique is reminiscent of the stringmaking method of another California Indian, from 100 miles southeast in space and 76 years in time. Quoting here from a frayed relic, my 1918 first edition of *Yahi Archery* by Saxton Pope:

"... The tendons used in this were of a finer quality than those used before and were obtained from the outer, more slender group of tendons in the deer's shank. These he stripped far up into their origin in the muscle bundles, tearing them free with his teeth.

If fresh, he simply chewed this tissue and teased it apart into threads no larger than floss silk. If dry, he soaked it in warm water before chewing it. He then proceeded to spin a string by fixing one end of a bundle of tendon strips to a stationary point and rolling the other end between his fingers in a single strand. As he progressed down the string he added more threads of tendon to the cord, making a very tight, simple twist one-eighth of an inch thick. When about five feet long, he twisted and secured the proximal end, leaving his twisted cord taut between two points. The last smoothing-up stage he accomplished by applying saliva and rubbing up and down its length. The finished bow string was now permitted to dry. Its final diameter was about three thirty-seconds of an inch ..."

Long sinew fibers can also be pulled from dry leg tendons, sometimes lightly pounded to assist reduction. The string can be twisted dry, or moistened with water or saliva; when wet, sinew is somewhat self-gluing. The strongest sinew strings seem to be made of very fine fibers dampened with saliva, twisted tightly, and dried under tension. If individual fibers have been reduced to properly small diameter, there will be no thick, stubby ends protruding at splice points.

Sinew's natural gluiness can be enhanced. In *Secrets of the Omaha Bow*, Bill Vonderhey describes soaking sinew fibers in hide-glue water before forming the string.

Sinew strings can be made single, double, or triple ply. Fibers can be added as the string progresses, or full-length plies can be assembled first. Loops can be plaited, or tied in later.

Animal strings, being more elastic, might be expected to slow a bow's cast, and they are often reported as doing so. But it's their mass, not their elasticity, which is at fault.

Silk, sinew, rawhide, and gut are quite elastic, as is nylon. But unlike nylon, animal fibers lose this quality once severely stretched. Once strained they take a large, permanent set. By the time an animal-fiber string is broken in, it is quite hard and relatively inelastic. Vegetable fibers behave the same, but less noticeably because they are much less elastic to begin with. Virtually all of an animal-fiber's elasticity can be removed by straining it to near breaking. This will not degrade its strength or durability.

Making the Rawhide String

Rawhide and gut strings will take more abrasion and impact abuse than other natural string materials. Composite bowmaker Jeff Schmidt uses rawhide as a drive belt on his hand-powered wood lathe. Primitive technologist John

An unfinished Walrus rawhide string used for bowstrings by Chinese, Mongols, and Eskimos. The hide is cut, pulled through a round hole while wet, then twisted and smoothed (courtesy Grayson Collection).

233

McPherson reports that when used to spin fire drills, rawhide strings hold up far longer than flax or sinew.

Rawhide is heavier-per-strength than vegetable fibers, cast is therefore slower. Rawhide seems to ascend in strength-per-mass as animal size descends. Deer is stronger than cow, and Al Herrin reports from great experience that squirrel and groundhog strings are stronger than deer. Al describes the Cherokee method of rawhide string making in his book, *Cherokee Bows and Arrows*.

Smaller animals no doubt make stronger strings partially because wider or more numerous strips are needed. Weak spots are therefore more likely averaged out.

Cut an average-thickness test strip and determine average breaking strength. Then do the arithmetic to determine how wide strips need be for a three-ply string of intended strength. If required strip width is too wide use four or more narrower plies instead.

If possible, arrange any visibly narrower, thinner or weaker areas next to strong areas.

Soak the hide until soft and elastic. Tie plies together at one end and secure them to a nail or such. Arrange the plies in uncluttered, parallel lines, and as individually twist-free as possible. Tie a weight on the bottom and twist the plies until a smooth, uniform cylinder results. Keep the weight in place until the string is dry.

A squirrel-hide string. This spiral-cutting method for creating hide strips can be used for deer, cow, and other hides. Thicker hides require narrower cuts.

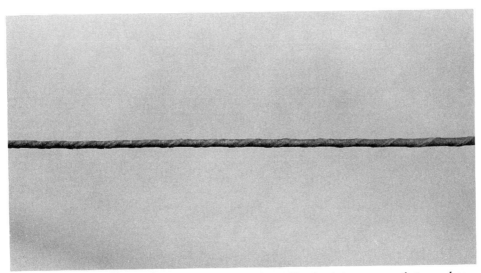

If rawhide plies are uniform in thickness and width they will twists into a near-perfect, seamless cylinder of almost manufactured appearance. Slight rises at the seams can be sanded smooth. The finished string can then be oiled or greased for moisture resistance.

The collagen fibers in rawhide and gut are not parallel, as in sinew. They are arranged randomly, like fibers in paper instead of wood. But when formed into strings they are stronger than their randomness would lead us to expect. Dr. Grayson believes that stretching hide or gut aligns fibers more parallel to the direction of elongation.

Making a Gut String
Gut is the easiest and fastest string to make — if you don't count removing and cleaning the gut. And gut is extremely durable — ask a tennis ball.

To determine the number or strands needed when working with unfamiliar gut it's wise to first measure the strength of one strand, then divide that figure into three times the bow's draw weight. Three times bow weight instead of four because gut is more durable, so less margin of safety is needed.

Gut is naturally very uniform along its length. If you feel your rawhide strips are especially uniform three-times bow weight is also a good design decision.

To test strand strength, twist a short length until the gut's natural lumpiness becomes a smooth, uniform cylinder. Do this while pulling at about half its wet breaking strength. Let it dry while under this twist and tension. When dry, break the strand, using a scale to judge its strength.

To make a bowstring, wind out sufficient gut, endless-string fashion. Twist the wet strands tightly together as with a simple-ply, while stretching as with the test strand. Let the string dry in place. If exact bowstring length is known, loops can be formed at this time, and dried in place. If dried without loops re-wet loop areas, form any of the various loops or hitches, then let dry again before bracing the bow.

Endless type, four-strand gut string. Wrapped with silk string. Silver wire helps hold the loops. From an old hand-forged steel, one-piece bow, likely Persian (courtesy Grayson Collection).

KNOTS

Knots weaken strings. A knot is a bit like a stone thrown into a pond; disruptions flow out from it, slowly dissipating over distance. Knots disrupt the balance of strain in string fibers, causing the string to break, not often precisely at the knot itself, but some distance from it. Knots can safely be put in bow-strings only if the knotted area has been reinforced.

Knots are not as damaging in sinew or other elastic animal fibers, especially if tied before stretching the string, permitting fibers to adjust to uneven tension.

The timber hitch. Under and thru, then thru again. Once tightened, string tension prevents slippage; but with tension removed this knot is easily adjusted.

Once the string has been stretched, adjust the timberhitch for proper brace height. Then cut off the excess, leaving about two-inches to be formed into a "rat tail." Unwind the plies, taper their ends, wax very heavily, then complete a very tight reverse-twisting until the sting is too small to grip. Finish up with a tight twist in the reverse-twist direction. Infinitely more elegant than a knot.

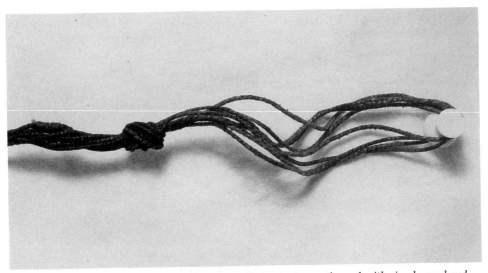

An endless-type gut string from an old bow from India. Loops are formed with simple overhand knots. Additional knots appear near these loop knots, apparently for the sole purpose of shortening the string. Unless seriously thickened, vegetable-fiber strings would not tolerate such knotting (courtesy Grayson Collection).

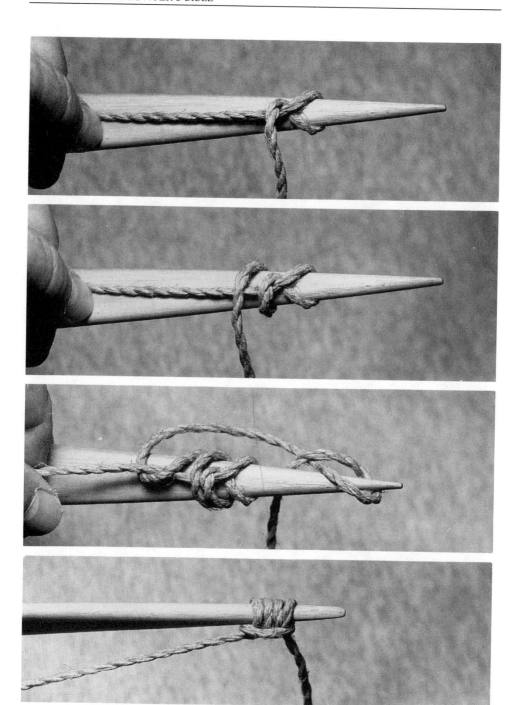

Here are two knots not described in archery texts. This sequence is used for the semi-permanent bottom loop.

This sequence is used when bracing the bow. When making very narrow, low-mass limb tips there may be insufficient width for conventional nocks. One option is tie-on loops. Such loops also let you vary a bow's draw weight by up to 20% or so. Tie loops near the tips for low-weight target shooting, farther down the limbs when hunting. Of course the bow must be designed for the high-weight position.

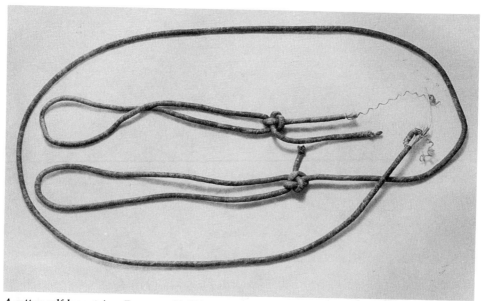

A cotton self-loop string. From an old Chinese bow. Note that the knot is part of the main string itself. Unlike the separate, stronger, more common Oriental knot (courtesy Grayson Collection).

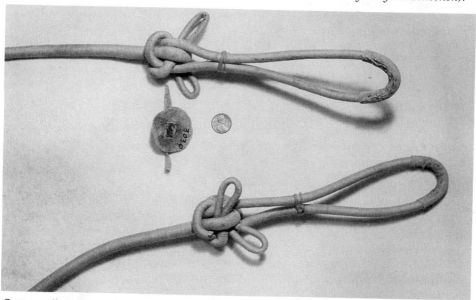

Cotton endless-type mainstring, with separate loops. Pads rest on the bow's string bridges. Loops attached by traditional Oriental knots used from China to Turkey. Such loop knots permit the manufacture of relatively standard string lengths. This particular string is 62" long and weighs 8 oz (3,500-grains) It is from a Tartar bow of great weight, used for exercise, or to demonstrate the archer's strength. Such strings are usually of rawhide strands, the loop formed by a simple knot (courtesy Grayson Collection).

OTHER STRING QUALITIES

Air Resistance — In *Bows and Arrows* Pope, when giving reasons for waxing strings, writes: "...to reduce the diameter, thus cutting down on air friction..."

This is good place to restate the value of *testing*. Theory alone has limited value — even for as keen a mind as Pope's. String diameter has an insignificant effect on performance.

A 50 lb. yew longbow shot a 500-grain arrow 148 fps. One hundred and twenty-five grains of silver wire was wrapped around the string near the arrow nock. The wire was wrapped tightly, drawing its profile down to pre-wrapped diameter. The bow then shot 143 fps.

The silver wire was replaced with 125 grains of tissue paper, loosely taped near the arrow nock. After many shots an additional reduction in cast of less than one fps appeared in the averaging. The tissue's wind profile exceeded that of the entire string, and was concentrated at the fastest moving portion of the string. Yet even under these extremes the arrow was barely slowed.

Because of its high volume per strength, sisal yields about the largest diameter string likely to be put on a bow. When strung with a same-mass sisal string, the test bow and arrow showed less than 1 fps reduction in cast.

Silk also has a high volume per strength, but was used by Turkish flight shooters.

For all reasonable purposes, air resistance due to increased string diameter has no effect on cast.

Durability — Roger Ascham tells us that, "... although apparently a trifle, it is of much importance, as a bad string breaks many a good bow ..."

Even a heavily waxed string can soak up nearly its own weight in water. In *Longbow*, Robert Hardy describes the moments preceding the battle of Crecy in 1346: "As the thunder cracked and rolled and the rain bucketed down, drenching the thousands that had gathered there to fight ... legend tell us the English and Welsh archers unstrung their bows, coiled the strings and popped them under their helmets to keep them dry. Science tells us that a linen string, such as the men would have had at Crecy, can be soaked for days in water without suffering any weakening, or stretching. But almost any archer, in heavy rain, would either shelter his bow, or do as legend says was done at Crecy, even if, scientifically, it were quite unnecessary."

The word "unnecessary" takes on a different cast when outnumbered three to one by crossbow-armed mercenaries and mounted, armored knights. Exactly what benefit might accrue to an archer who keeps his string dry?

A 49 lb. maple longbow carrying a 180-grain waxed linen string shot a 500-grain arrow 150 fps when drawn 28". After soaking in water for fifteen minutes the string's mass rose to 330 grains. The bow was strung, the string twanged a few times, shedding loose water. When reweighed string mass stood at 240 grains. Arrow speed was slowed to 147 fps. During several subsequent releases arrow speed did not rise and string weight did not fall. Apparently the vibrational shock of releasing a full-drawn arrow is no greater than a light twanging.

English war bows of 120 lb. and more, with rain-wet, moderately waxed strings, but shooting arrows not proportionately heavy (likely 800 to 900 grains), would have been slowed by about 4 - 5 fps, costing the war arrow in the neighborhood of six to eight yards of cast. Not a great price in raw distance, but possibly a life-or-death difference in accuracy, especially at distances of over fifty yards.

If these strings had been unwaxed, string mass would have more than doubled; cast would then reduce by about 20 yards. That the English archers covered their strings might indicate they were only lightly, or imperfectly, waxed. There is also some small chance these strings contained animal glue.

Hardy is correct concerning linen's stretch and strength when wet. Brace height drops slightly on just-braced bows but after two hours all movement stops. Once stable, various diameters and configurations of strings were kept dripping wet for several hours. No significant stretching or shrinking occurred.

Break tests showed the strength of linen rising when wet. Linen weakens when very dry. Strings used in low humidities should be slightly thicker. Break-testing fibers before making the string would automatically remove any danger.

Rot — Organic materials decay quickly when exposed to moisture. A damp string's margin of safety can dissipate quickly. Strings are so cheaply and easily made it's wise to replace those which have been in conditions, for example, in which dry food would spoil.

Vegetable fibers vary in their resistance to rot. Linen, hemp and other fibers prepared by retting (a word-cousin of rotting) are obviously more decay-safe. But linen strings left on a damp earth floor, for instance, begin to biodegrade within days. If buried at room temperature, strength falls by one-half in ten days.

If kept dry, year-old linen strings show no measurable loss of strength when tested. Linen strings from forty-year old "Garage sale" bows, stored under unknown conditions, show varying amounts of degradation, some literally falling apart. But even the strongest were noticeably weaker than their estimated original strength. "The Technology of Cordage Fibres and Rope", 1957, report other cellulose-based cordage losing strength at between 1% and 2% per year, if stored cool and dry. Moist, warm conditions would speed strength loss.

Dogbain rabbit nets are reported to have been used for decades by Great Basin hunters. The word among modern "abos" has it that milkweed and nettle fibers decay more easily.

Perfectly sound sinew can be taken from moderately "retted" animals. Even when flesh is quite gamey, sinew is unaffected.

Silk weakens in ultraviolet light. Asiatic composite strings were sometimes wrapped, possibly to screen the sun.

Unless fully encased or saturated, waxed strings are only slightly protected from moisture. Wax combined with a percentage of linseed or tung oil soaks more easily and deeply into string fibers, but this proves little barrier to moisture. Even when saturated with linseed oil, a linen string takes on substantial water weight if wet by rain.

Rainforest Indians of South America often coat vegetable-fiber strings with plant resin, possibly to prevent rot. Osage orange is the most decay-resistant wood in North America. Something in this wood prevents cellulose from rotting. The active ingredient might be extracted and applied to bowstrings. Scores of other plants protect themselves from decay. Some perfect string-preserving fluid may be coursing through the veins of a familiar, nearby plant, just awaiting discovery.

In the past, linen fish nets were sometimes boiled for 12 hours in oak-bark tea, doubling net life.

A bow is worth many strings. It's good economics to discard a string at the first suspicion of its integrity.

Retired strings can spend many happy years on lower weight bows.

Wax — Waxing does not increase string strength. But it is useful in other ways:

1) By holding loose or tapered threads together wax is helpful when plaiting loops. And here it can be used with little cost — string weight near the nocks has an insignificant effect on cast.

2) Wax acts as a lubricant, damping internal friction, and the effects of external abrasion.

3) Waxed strings look better: frizzed surfaces are distracting and unappealing.

4) Wax helps keep strings dry.

During the pre-fiberglass era something of a controversy existed concerning the value of glue in wax (in those days "glue" meant hide glue only). Glue was sometimes added, about one part to four parts wax. Powered glue was sprinkled slowly into stirred, melted wax. When hardened, this mix was applied normally. Gordon complained that the surface of glue-waxed strings tended to crack in dry weather and become sticky with high humidity. Shellacking has been suggested for sealing strings against water. Hard shellac riding on a soft surface of wax would also crack. And strings sealed with shellac alone are too stiff, crimping, and twisting open at bends, exposing unsealed inner fibers.

Gordon preferred wax alone: "Unlike a glue-pot, a block of wax can be carried in the pocket. Warm it a little, and it is ready for use."

Pope said that, "Wax is to an archer what tar is to a sailor; use it often, and always have two strings to your bow."

But strings are sometimes so heavily waxed they could be used as candles. Wax should be used sparingly:

Seven, 110-grain linen bowstrings were waxed in various ways, then soaked in water for 15 minutes. Strings were "twanged" free of loose water, then weighed:

1- Unwaxed,
   110-grains — 280-grains when soaked.

2- Lightly waxed on exterior of string
   130-grains — 270-grains

3- Lightly waxed, heated and rubbed till wax submerged into fibers.
   130-grains — 220-grains

4- Moderately waxed, heated and rubbed, till wax submerged into fibers, lightly rewaxed on surface.
145-grains — 170-grains

5- Heavily waxed, lightly burnished
170-grains — 250-grains

6- Heavily waxed, heated and rubbed till wax submerged into fibers, lightly rewaxed on surface.
180-grains — 200-grains

7- Heavily waxed with 30% corn oil-wax mix, heated and rubbed till wax submerged into fibers, lightly rewaxed on surface.
190-grains — 220

This test certainly shows the folly of mindless, candle-like waxing. #5 For example, would slow cast by 3 fps when dry, and about 7 fps when wet, equaling the performance of about a six-pound lighter bow.

At 110-grains, #1, the unwaxed string would have the best cast — on a dry day. And there is no rule against using a bare string on dry days.

For average day-to-day conditions, #4 is the clear choice, slowing cast by less than 2 fps when dry, and only about 3 fps when soaked.

The key here is to rub the lightly-waxed, semi-taut individual plies vigorously with a patch of leather or cloth. This is more effectively done before the plies have been twisted up as a finished string. Rub until wax and string are hot. When hot enough, the wax dissipates somewhat as it enters interior fibers.

If waxing a finished string, try to apply wax before the string has been pulled to full load, while fibers are more relaxed and open.

Friction-heated wax has the saturation advantages of oil, but once cool and hard, water will not permeate it as it apparently does oil.

Loops can be plaited and strings twisted using hot water instead of wax. Natural pectins in linen fiber surfaces tend to bond fibers together. Highest quality linen thread is always wet spun at 150 to 180 degrees. Wet-twisted bowstrings show less fraying and frizzing, and weighs noticeably less than if waxed. But water-twisted strings proved to be less durable.

Alaskan composite bowmaker Wayne Allex has had considerable experience with natural-fiber strings. He is convinced wax's lubricative action makes strings more durable.

To measure this effect two linen strings of equal strength were tested. One waxed, one unwaxed. Each was sawed back and forth over the slightly rounded edge of a metal bar. Care was taken to apply equal strain to each. The waxed string broke after 51 repetitions, the unwaxed after 32. Variation of this test were repeated with different diameter strings, the waxed strings always showed more durability, at an average ratio of 50 to 29.

High-grade Irish shoemakers' linen averaged 50 repetitions when waxed, but if unwaxed it held up for 40 repetitions, its normal smoothness no doubt reducing friction.

From this it is obvious that a waxed string would be more durable on a bow, especially at the string and arrow nocks where abrasion is greatest. The rest of the string would benefit also, by better resisting general knocking about, and internal abrasions from tightening and loosening with each shot.

No difference in strength was noted when waxed and unwaxed strings of varying diameters and numbers of plies were strained in tension.

The addition of rosin, glue or hardening oils such as linseed and tung will no doubt retard water absorption. But they may be damaging to the string. All stiffen the wax, reducing its lubricative qualities. For longest string life pure beeswax may be best. In colder climates beeswax stiffens considerably; under such conditions adding up to 25% non-hardening oil may be useful.

To add oil to wax first melt the wax in a double boiler (use great care, wax is flammable), pour in the oil, then with heat still on, stir until uniformly mixed. Pour into molds, or such, and let harden. Experiment with different percentages. When melting wax do not use your smoke alarm as a timer. Heat the wax only enough to maintain liquidity.

When replicating small catapults, with engine cords of one-quarter inch diameter, Payne-Gallwey recommends: "... the skein must be thoroughly soaked in neat's-foot oil for some days previously, or it is sure to fray and cut under the friction of being very tightly twisted, Oil will also preserve the skein from damp and decay for many years."

To test Gallwey's procedure the metal-bar-edge test was repeated, all conditions duplicated. This time bare string, and string coated with beeswax, corn oil, and 25% corn oil/beeswax mix were tested. Three tests each. Here are the averaged figures:

Bare string —   31 repetitions

Waxed string —   56

Wax-oil string —   67

Oil soaked —   81

Gallwey was on to something. But these bare figure do not tell the whole story. How important is abrasion resistance vs mass increase anyway? When oiled, string mass exactly doubled, even with all surface oil wiped free. Gallwey's catapult was not slowed by oil-heavy cords, because these cord engines were not accelerated with the arm and projectile, as is a bowstring.

This extra oil mass would slow arrow speed of a 50 lb. bow to about that of a 44 lb. bow.

Beauty

Why did the appreciation for beauty arise in the human species. Homo-Erectus-A, busily about his or her work, would surely have prospered over Homo-Erectus-B, lingering over a gorgeous sunset. And how much trouble have we all gotten into over a pretty face.

And it's the same with bowstrings.

A two-ply string of New Zealand flax. Fibers were pinched free and reverse-twisted with no further preparation. A florist frog, or similar tool, makes quick work of many leaf and bark fibers.

Dogbain, hemp, New Zealand flax, and dozens more can be formed into finished cordage directly from the plant. Or they can be partially processed.

Bark and pulp mixed with the fibers are ragged and uneven — and inefficient. But somehow, against reason, the imperfect perfection of these strings is captivating. They are especially appealing on more "primitive" looking bows.

Glue

At first glance it seems logical to impregnate string fibers with glue. This would keep fibers from slipping, leading to stronger strings. And it would permit less twisting, which would reduce elasticity somewhat. But glue has mass. Strings "improved" with glue invariably slow cast.

Certain aboriginal strings are reported to have been made using animal glue. And the old Flemish also. It seems most likely glue's function was to save labor, not enhance efficiency. Such Flemish strings, even though imported, sold far below domestic twisted strings.

TYPES OF FIBERS

Bowstring quality cordage can be made from a surprisingly large cast of natural fibers, even human hair.

In the ancient Scandinavian tale, "Story of the Burnt Njal," Gunner's bowstring has been cut by his enemy. Gunner says to his wife, Hallgerda:

"Give me two locks of thy hair, and ye two, my mother and thou, twist them together into a bowstring for me."

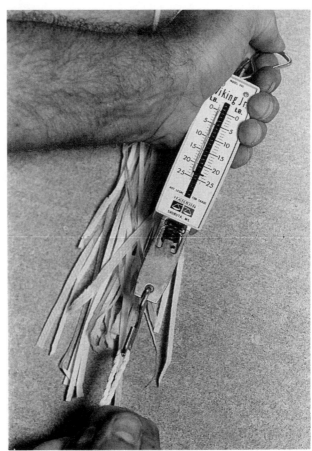

Useable cordage can be made of virtually anything fibrous. Even from the unlikeliest of materials: When cut into narrow strips, to tolerate tight reverse-twisting, even paper towels have useable strength.

Hallgerda, incidentally, declines, reminding Gunner of the time he slapped her face. There are probably several good lessons to be taken from this story, keeping a spare string being only one.

Horse hair, walrus hide, camel hide... even human skin. The old writings list all these materials and more.

Historically there have been three principal bowstring materials: Hemp, flax, and silk.

Sinew, rawhide, and gut, as Elmer saw them, "...are so far inferior to the natural fibers of hemp, and flax that we may lay them aside for examination under the light of history and ethnology."

Reading through the old literature — Western literature that is — reveals preferences for all three fibers, with hemp receiving slightly more press. Here, via Elmer, are some opinions from the past.

1400's, *Le Livre du Roi Modus:* "The string should be made of silk, and nothing else ... because ... it will drive an arrow ... farther than any string made of flax or hemp ..."

1545, *Toxophilus*, Roger Ascham: "Now what a string oughte to be made on, whether of good hempe, as they do nowe a dayes, or of flaxe, or of silke, I leave that to the judgment of stringers, of whom we must buy them,"

1590, *Certen Discourses*, Sir John Smythe, "... and the strings being made of verie good hempe, with a kind of water-glewe to resist wet and moysture; and the same strings being by the Archers themselves with fine thread well whipt, did also verie seldome breake."

1792, William Moseley, "The most general material of which Strings are now made in England, is hemp; of which the Italian answers the best; and this substance possesses many advantages over all other sorts."

1801, *The English Bowman*, Thomas Roberts, "It cannot be collected eithr from record or tradition that any other than hempen strings have been used for English bows.

1833, *The Archer's Guide:* "The material of which strings are now made in England, is hemp; of which the Italian answers the best."

1845, *The Book of Archery*, George Agar Hansard, "I believe few bowstrings are now made in England, the great mart being Flanders, where both materials and workmanship are excellent. Chose such as feel hard and are of a brownish-grey colour."

1854, *Archery*, Horace Alford Ford, "The good ones ... are the product of one particular maker, a Belgian, in whose family the secret of their manufacture is preserved with such jealousy as to cause a fear of its being lost, inasmuch as the present possessor is the last of his race."

1879. *The Witchery of Archery*, J. Maurice Thompson, "Bowstrings are made of hemp or flax; the former is considered the best, and the material is waxed and slack-twisted without doubling. A loop is formed by the manufacturer in one end, and both extremities are trebled in size, forming a three-cord for about ten inches, gradually tapering."

1894, *Archery: Badminton Library*, Col. Walrond, "The string is made of hemp treated in a particular way with some preparation of glue, the composition of which was a secret possessed only by a maker named Mules, who lived in

Belgium, in whose family it had been for generations. He died without revealing the secret; consequently it was lost, and for some years no really good strings have been procurable."

1917, *American Archery*, Robert Elmer, "Until the World War we all used hempen strings from Europe … from that day to this our major dependence has been upon strings made of strands of linen thread."

Much was made of the family of Belgian stringmakers and their secret methods. Thompson's description is the most revealing. And detailed enough to invite experiment. Some of the secret might rest in the glue, possibly water repellent glue. For waterproofing hints, see "Glue," in Volume One.

Describing early twentieth-century Flemish strings, Elmer notes that they were, "… soft and flexible in the eye and tail but hard as bone … in the cord. They are covered with a thin glue."

There is confusion and disagreement over materials used and the precise design of medieval, Flemish, and other historic strings. But don't despair that some magic principle or property has been lost to us. Flax and hemp were no stronger then than now. And with what we now know of principles and properties, getting these fibers to perform their best is simple enough.

The old accounts all agree that flax, hemp, and silk make excellent bowstrings. But many other vegetable fibers are as desirable, once gathered and processed. They have not been domesticated, however, or are labor-expensive to process, and have therefore remained in archery history's shadows.

Ramie is a good example. Ramie, in fact, is nature's strongest fiber, a silk-like material which makes excellent cloth and superior bowstrings. But due to the high labor expense (until recently) of extracting its fibers, few have heard of it.

A new bow can often be made in the time it takes to gather, process, and

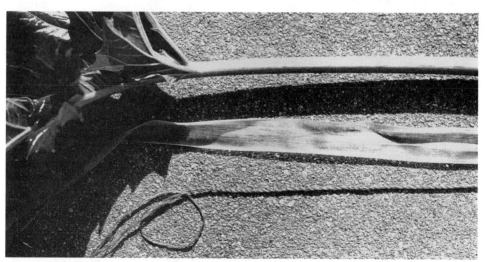

This yet-to-be-identified plant was stumbled across during a recent walk. The stalk's tissue-like outer skin yields a serviceable and attractive string. An equally valuable new string source is possibly hiding behind your neighbor's favorite tulip.

make a decent string from alternative fibers. But making a string from locally gathered material is rewarding.

Bowstring quality cordage can be made from hundreds of species of plants and animals. A suitable source of bowstring quality fiber is only a short walk away from virtually any spot on earth, possibly excepting inland portions of both poles.

Listed later are just some of the more available and familiar, but as you walk through the woods check the fiber characteristics of leaves and stalks of unfamiliar plants. Sooner or later you'll be rewarded.

Strengths of Various Fibers

As with bow woods, fiber strength varies greatly within a species. Conditions of growth, harvesting, and processing can cause greater strength differences within a species than between species. Fibers intended for bowstrings should be very carefully retted (surface bark rotted loose), pounded, scraped, boiled, or otherwise prepared. Some unbleached commercial linen thread, for example, is relatively dark brown and sometimes carries the faint aroma of decomposing vegetation. Such linen was likely excessively dew retted; flax retted in tanks or running streams is lighter colored, smells cleaner, and tests stronger.

Exact relative weight, mass, elasticity, and performance qualities cannot be precisely given here. Large numbers of samples of the various fibers, each produced, collected, and processed under varying conditions, would have to be tested. From my limited testing, I feel safe using only the following broad relative categories:

Linen (flax), best quality	Superior
Hemp, best quality	Superior[1]
Ramie	Superior
Nettles	Good/superior
Linen, normal quality	Good
Hemp, normal quality	Good
Dogbain	Good
Milkweed	Good
Iris	Good
Bromelia	Fair/good
New Zealand flax — fibers only	Fair
Manila hemp (Abaca)	Fair
Palm (tucum) — fibers only	Fair
Yucca	Fair
Bamboo	Fair[2]
Raffia	Fair
Velvet leaf	Fair/poor
Cotton	Poor
New Zealand flax — as is	Poor
Sisal	Poor
Jute	Poor
Palm frond — as is	Poor
Cattail	Poor

Sinew ....Good
Silk ....Good
Gut — highest quality............................Good
Gut — average quality...........................Fair
Rawhide...Fair
Sturgeon skin ....Fair/poor
Hair...Poor
Rattlesnake skin....................................Poor

B-50...Superior
Fast Flight ....Superior-plus
Kevlar..Superior-plus[3]
Nylon...Poor

1 *Best-quality hemp is presently unavailable for testing. A rating of "superior" here is based on opinions expressed in old literature, and the fact that less-than-optimum samples available for testing performed as well as medium-quality flax.*

2 *Bamboo would be listed as good, but is difficult to harness as string.*

3 *Kevlar has the reputation of "breaking after 1,000 shots."*

A 200 lb. test, 63" long string will have about the following mass if made from the following quality fibers:

Poor   = 325-plus grains
Fair   = 225
Good   = 150
Superior   = 90
Superior-plus = 40

Inner Bark Fibers

Listed here are a few of the scores of inner barks suitable for cordage. For a bowstring of normal strength all would be too bulky and heavy for reasonable efficiency, but could be used in an emergency. Each will produce serviceable twine and rope. It is even more important to reduce such weaker fibers to smallest possible diameters, and to twist them into the smallest feasible sub-plies.

Basswood
Red mulberry
Elm
Willow
Mesquite
Cottonwood
Big leaf maple
Cedar
Juniper

Finding Fibers

To locate and identify any of the following fibers in your area, contact your county Dept. of Agriculture, university or city library, park ranger, or horticultural society.

FLAX (linen) — Flax can be grown in your yard (Hemp can be grown in your neighbor's yard).

Flax grows wild in many parts of the continent. Harvest in fall or early winter of its growth year when stalks are dry. Pull from the ground, with roots intact, and lay out flat on open ground.

Retting is completed by dew. Turn every week or so. Take up when stalks are fully brittle, the inner fiber then being easily extracted. Break stalks free and comb fiber clean.

"Line linen": The neatest, longest flax fibers is used for best quality thread. "Tow linen," combings and short ends, is used for lower quality thread. "Flaxen-haired and tow-headed" derive from the linen trade.

If you'd like to grow your own bowstrings, suppliers of unspun flax sometimes carry seed, along with growing, harvesting, and processing instruction. Once gathered and retted, your crop can be safely stored for years. Seed can be saved and pressed for linseed oil, a traditional bow finish. Flax-seed soup is a centuries-old recipe.

Annual fiber plants are usually best picked at year's end, when dead or dying, but in a pinch most can be used when green and immature. Fibers will not be as well developed, and will suffer from the trauma of being scraped clean, but usable string will result.

HEMP (MARIJUANA) — Originated north of Tibet, reached China by 2,800 BC, Europe by the fifth century, and America in 1645. When grown specifically for fiber, hemp is planted very close, like flax. It grows thin-stalked, up to ten or fifteen feet tall and branchless. It would likely be harvested at the moment of optimum strength and retted with great care. When describing hemp string, writers of earlier times often, but not always, reported it superior to linen. In 1515, Michel Noir, of Paris, wrote that strings should be made of "fine female hemp, which is finer than male hemp."

Hemp fibers can easily be as long as a bowstring, therefore needing little twisting. Similar in appearance, flax and hemp are sometimes thought of as little and big brothers. Both are grown, harvested, retted, cleaned and combed in the same manner. Due to its deeper, hardier roots, hemp does not exhaust soil as flax does. Hemp is a distant relative of nettles and ramie.

Lacking the narcotic component of its leaves and blossoms, retted hemp is legal to possess, and can be ordered from suppliers in Spain, Hungary, and elsewhere. Such samples tested so far cost about $12 per lb, but were short, scruffy and poorly retted. With interest growing, a source of bowstring-quality hemp will likely surface soon.

Until WW II hemp was commonly used for rope in this country. Due to drug laws, it was grown and processed primarily in the Philippines. Japan quickly cut off this supply. In 1941, the U.S. Dept. of Agriculture produced a short film on the cultivation and processing of hemp for fiber. It was made widely available to farmers in the hope of stimulating domestic production of this essential war material. Videos of this film are currently available.

RAMIE — In his 1923, *Hunting With the Bow and Arrow,* Pope published the breaking strengths of several fibers:

Horsehair ....breaks at 15 pounds.
Cotton...breaks at 18 pounds.
Catgut...breaks at 20 pounds.
Silk ....breaks at 22 pounds.
Irish linen..breaks at 28 pounds.
Chinese grass fiber ....breaks at 32 pounds.

But what in the world was China grass? No one seemed to know.

Patricia Baines' book, *Linen,* includes an "Appendix of Comparable Fibers." Ramie is listed. The passage begins: "Ramie, know also as 'China Grass' ..."

Baines reports that ramie is cultivated in China and Formosa, is related to stinging nettles, and was grown in North America in the nineteenth century. It is "prohibitively expensive" to process. Recently improved extracting procedures have now made Ramie competitive with flax.

Ramie is white, lustrous and non-elastic. It was once used for fishing nets, so it may be somewhat rot resistant. Ramie needs rich soils and high rainfall. Seed could probably be located with some effort.

High quality combed ramie, ready for spinning, can occasionally be found at yarn and weaving supply shops. Prices roughly parallel those of top-quality combed flax. Ramie, and other fibers, are sold in the form of "top", and "strick." "Top" has been cut to shorter lengths, and formed into finger-thick long hanks — more convenient for spinning. But being shorter, it produces weaker thread. "Strick," or full-length combed fibers, yields superior bowstrings.

DOGBAIN — Distributed spottily from coast to coast, usually confined to wet ground. This fiber is time consuming to process. Like flax, dogbain is harvested in the fall or early winter of its growth year. Stalks should be taken after the plant has died, when red and dry but not yet rotting. Dogbane is not retted. Instead, crack the stalk into long strips, then break the thin stalk strips into short lengths, freeing the paper-like bark. Twist the bark vigorously between the palms to remove the chaff. Dogbain string can have medium to high strength depending on the ratios of pure fiber to bark chaff.

NETTLES — Related to ramie, strongest of all natural fibers. Nettles may be the strongest of all native fibers. Processing is labor-expensive. Harvest when fully grown or dying. Light, careful retting, following by boiling will release the fibers. Or the stalk can be gently wet pounded. Or fiber can simply be pulled from broken sections of stalk: Split the stalk lengthwise into four strips. Bending the strips away from the bark breaks the stalk into short lengths, lifting the fiber-filled bark with each break. Strip bark into fine threads. Strength varies among the several species. Plants grown in sunny, damp conditions are reportedly stronger. Nettle fiber rots fairly easily.

MILKWEED — A fine, white fiber. Labor-expensive. Harvest in late summer or early fall of its growth year. If stalks are dead, try to harvest before the rains. Peel off outer layers, roll between the palms to clean. A net bag of milkweed fibers endured between 6,000 and 9,000 years in a Utah cave.

IRIS — Pull leaves from the plant in the fall when mature and beginning to wilt. Scrape each leaf on both sides, scraping from the middle outward, exposing its white fibers.

YUCCA — More common in dry southern areas, but occasionally grows as far north as Montana. Can be harvested all year. Best fibers are taken from young, green leaves. Strip fibers directly, or for stronger string pound lightly and soak, repeating several times. Recent experimenters report success with tank-retting.

BAMBOO — The very surface layer of bamboo is strongest. This portion of the bamboo is extremely strong, but extremely difficult to adapt for use.

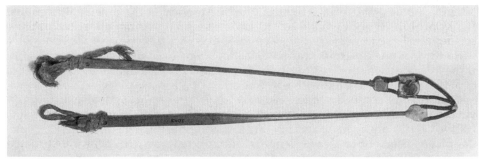

A bamboo bow "string," from a Chinese pellet bow. Bamboo may have been used to prevent string twist, so the pellet would dependably face forward. Its braided loops support this idea: Braid, though weaker, does not twist when strained. (courtesy Grayson Collection)

NEW ZEALAND FLAX: Native to New Zealand, this plant is a widely used ornamental. Leaves grow to eight feet. Cut any time of year. Smaller, one to two year-old leaves yield the finest fibers.

Retting may be possible but would take several months. Maoris scraped the fibers clean with a clam shell, then washed, scraped and washed again.

This fiber, and many other green leaf and stem fibers, are intermixed with pulp. When dried, this pulp adds little mass, and since the multi-color, multi-textured appearance can be so appealing you might be tempted to use the fiber as-is. This is OK if you're interested in looks over performance. The pulp on such plants, however, acts as a spacer between fibers, increasing the string's diameter-per-strength, causing outer fibers to overwork — the thicker-is-weaker problem again. For highest strength, fibers must be as clean as possible. This is true of all plant and animal fibers.

SISAL (agave) — A large green spiked plant native to southern and central areas of the continent. Sometimes called a century plant, it has been widely planted in more temperate areas of the continent. Agave occasionally has a tall central stalk similar to New Zealand flax. Leaves are pounded with a large mallet to expose fibers, then washed and soaked to remove the fleshy pulp. Sisal twine and rope can be found at most hardware stores.

PALM — Brazilian Indians prefer a particular species of palm — tucum — because, once bent, its fibers become exposed and easily removed. Not so with any palm leaf tested here so far. Palm leaves are tough. The varieties tested began to rot before retting. Long, clean fiber can be extracted if the leaves are scraped, soaked, pounded, and washed. If stripped out from leaves and used as-is, palm makes a medium-low strength, but very appealing, string or twine.

ABACA (Manilla hemp) — From the leaves of a tree of the banana family. This fiber it strong enough for medium-quality rope, and much cheaper to grow and process than hemp. For this reason Abaca largely dominates the natural-fiber quality rope market. It is sometimes confused with true hemp, giving true hemp a bad reputation.

BROMELIA — From the leaves of a South American rain forest plant. Some species are grown as ornamentals in North America. Leaves are scraped on both sides exposing fine creamy-white fiber.

RAFFIA — From a South African, and South American palm. Long, clean, fibrous leaves. Makes fast, easy cordage. One of the most convenient fibers for miscellaneous cordage uses. Can be occasionally found in hobby shops.

VELVET LEAF (buttonwood) A sunflower-like plant which grows throughout the mid-west. Medium strength. Fibers are taken from the papery bark.

UNKNOWN VEGETABLE FIBERS — After learning to extract a few known species of fibers, experimentation and common sense will generally lead to success with new specimens.

SINEW — Sinew can be obtained from deer and elk hunters, and butchers. One "abo" couple I know hits the hunting camps, offering to dress out deer in exchange for the hide and sinews. Several small-scale suppliers of deer, elk, buffalo, moose, horse, and cow sinew have already appeared, with more surely to follow. Once you meet a few other wood bowmakers you will become plugged into an informal information network, and a world of natural-material supplies will become available.
Fresh sinew, if kept from hungry dogs, moths, and the like will dry quickly. If stored dry it will keep indefinitely.

RAWHIDE — Same sources as sinew. Tandy, and other leather suppliers also sell rawhide. Smaller hides are better for strings. Rawhide is designated by its ounce weight per square foot. Up to 4 oz. is a good weight for bow backing. Order the lightest in stock for string making.

GUT — The translucent inner lining of the small intestine is used for string making. Sometimes listed in the yellow pages under "Sausage casings." This is a quick, handy source, but Dr. Grayson reports this brine-soaked gut to be inferior, and that properly-prepared gut equals sinew in strength-per-mass. My early tests, done with sausage casings, were repeated using lute strings. Strength nearly doubled. The strength-per-mass of highest-quality gut does compare to sinew, and to silk, and moderate-quality linen. The rare tennis pro can direct you to a source of natural gut. At about $1. per foot, musical instrument strings are too expensive.

SILK — Silk, spun and unspun, natural or bleached, can be found in superior yarn and weaving shops. About ten times the cost of linen.

Why didn't the Turks, and other composite bowmakers, use hemp or linen for strings? Best linen performs better than silk. Wayne Allex has had much experience with linen fish nets. He reports that frequent soaking in copper sulfate solution was needed to prevent decay. Wayne believes the problem of decay may have led to a preference for silk. But why not carry an extra string, as the English did? It's possible archers didn't want to change these hard-to-string bows while on campaign. Or possibly superior silk was available at that time. It remains a mystery.

Silk string with sinew loops. From a small Turkish bow. Signed and dated 1860. Typical Turkish knots. Length: 26"; weight: 72 grains. The sinew loops are considerably heavier-per-length than the main string (courtesy Grayson Collection).

The silk we are most familiar with is the single type spun by mulberry leaf-eating caterpillars. But the engineering demands of a spider's web require several varieties of silk, some far stronger than cocoon silk. The ultimate natural-material bowstring may one day be made of spider silk by some enterprising experimenter.

A.E. Pratt's 1906 edition of *Two Years Among the New Guinea Cannibals* describes an ingenious use of spider silk. Certain spiders were induced to spin six-foot diameter webs across bamboo hoops. These hoops were then used as fishing nets, capable of holding a catch of up to one pound in weight. The strain

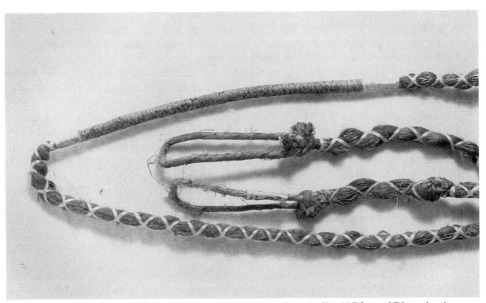

Endless-type silk main string, sinew loops. An old string from India. 40" long, 270-grains in mass. Main string is principally floss silk, mixed with a few silver-wrapped threads (courtesy Grayson Collection).

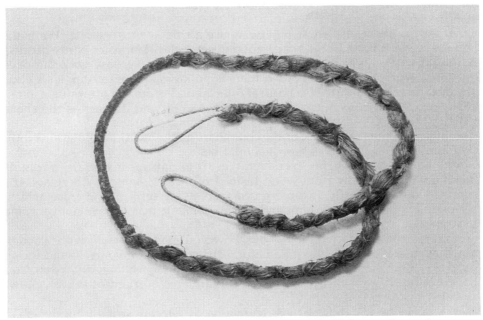

Sind bowstring from N. India. Sinew core and loops, covered with silk floss, endless style (courtesy Grayson Collection).

imparted by this one-pound fish was concentrated in a small area of the net. Should such a web be spun up into a six-foot string it seems reasonable to expect it might hold several pounds. Fifty or so such webs would then yield a full-strength bowstring with a lightness of mass we can only long to know.

The subject of spider-silk strings came up during a recent call. The caller described a particularly large and ugly patch of spiders which cast long, strong webs across the caller's favorite hunting path, a span of about six to eight feet. The caller agreed to gather this silk. With the help of a friend, each on opposite sides of the path, the caller spent several hours lifting strands free of their moorings, combining the strands into a thread. He reported shortly after this experiment, sounding harried, complaining that his hair, face, and upper body orifices were congested with spider silk. The caller claimed it would take days to gather sufficient silk, then expressed the opinion that anyone who suggested making a bowstring of spider silk was crazy.

Inducing spiders to weave webs over rectangular hoops might be a better approach.

A little neighborhood girl was recently learning to make a bowstring for her 14 lb. bow. Raw linen was used for the lesson. When ready to start on her own, I handed her a roll of B-50 Dacron. She frowned, and asked for the linen, "Not the *boring* string."

Archery is more satisfying if every atom of gear comes from natural materials. This sounds like an arbitrary, unsupportable bias, but I believe it is a reasonable stance:

Archery is about challenge, otherwise use a rifle — or dynamite! We make and use wooden bows instead of compounds and glass-laminates partly because of the satisfaction which comes from shunning the simple, easy way. But once one jot of synthetic material is used there is no logical place to stop; it's a clear slide to the compound. The natural/synthetic boundary offers us a most conspicuous and convenient place to stop. As real and distinct as the shore meeting the sea.

Reinforcing the soundness of this boundary is the wild, non-logical, subtly profound sense that, "this-is-how-it-should-be."

Making your own string from scratch, from natural materials, parallels making your own bow from wood instead of factory-stamped fiberglass. It's simply a more complexly textured process, involving subtlety and grace, which, sorrowfully for them, the compounders and laminate people have not yet come to appreciate.

Step into the woods with a wooden bow you made yourself, with wooden arrows you made yourself, with a natural string you spun yourself, and for all purposes of the moment you have stepped back in time ten thousand years. You have voluntarily given up the unfair advantages accrued of wheel, plow, alphabet, and forge.

When once by wit and craft you tease a hardy, elegant string from the grasp of nature, it will be quite a tedious and deflating exercise spooling out soul-less strands of Dacron.

HELPFUL HINTS AND SHORTCUTS

Jay Massey

TIPS FOR BEGINNING BOWYERS

For splitting out staves & billets:
When splitting wood, especially "snarly" wood with interlocking fibers such as Osage or elm, you may find yourself running short of wedges. If you have a bandsaw you can quickly fashion a makeshift wedge from scrap wood. These wooden wedges are fairly durable and won't gouge an ax blade as will a steel wedge. — *Jim Hamm*

On using various woods for bows:
John Strunk, who recently has been building some great shooting bows from Oregon vine maple and Cascara, says: "Experiment with the woods which grow in your particular area. There are lots of good bow woods out there!"

How to get square cuts with narrow billets:
If you're splicing narrow or thin billets which don't have enough surface area to keep them square on the sawing surface, just clamp on a short length of 1" thick wood with C-clamps. This will keep them square and at 90-degrees to the bandsaw blade. — *Tim Baker*

Advice for preventing limb twist:
When you're roughing out a bow which you suspect might develop limb twist, leave it real wide at the tips. If twist develops, the offending side can be reduced, bringing the string back true to center. — *Tim Baker*

TIPS FOR USING LESS-THAN-PERFECT WOOD

To lay out your bow straight:
The centerline of a stave which is severely reflexed or set back in the handle can sometimes be hard to determine. To mark out the centerline of such a stave, you can stretch a string between the two ends and then put the stave under a light source (either the sun or an artificial lamp will do) and mark where the shadow of the string bisects the stave down the center. — *Jay Massey*

For better limb tiller:

If one limb of your bow stave has more natural deflex than the other, and if the limbs are of equal length, make the limb with the greater deflex the bottom limb. Failure to do this could cause the lower limb — which is under greater stress — to bend too much once the bow is broken in. This problem is more pronounced with wide-limbed bows. This is less of a danger with English-style bows, which have longer upper limbs. — *Paul Comstock*

How to conceal cracks and other imperfections:

Use super glue to seal cracks in the limb, especially any which run off the side of a self bow. Not totally traditional, but it can spell the difference between a functional, durable bow and firewood. — *Jim Hamm*

Heated epoxy works okay too — it becomes thin at higher temperatures and "flows" into the crack. -*Jay Massey*

To avoid over-stressing a reflexed stave

A bow made from a stave with a severe reflex (more than 2" of reflex or set-back) will be under severe stress when it is first strung. To lessen the chance of breakage, first back it with a thin layer of sinew. The sinew can always be removed later if you want an unbacked bow. — *Jay Massey*

How to keep the tips straight on a reflexed stave:

Limb twist can be a problem with severely-reflexed staves. On such staves, leave the tips extra-wide when roughing out the bow. The more reflex the stave has, the more a bow will tend to have limb-twist. You can narrow the tips as you work the bow to its final shape. — *Jay Massey*

Working with staves that have natural string-follow:

A stave with severe string-follow will suffer from a loss of cast. However, the string-follow can be corrected by steam-bending. First reduce the stave to nearly its final dimensions, then steam the to be bent portion for 20-minutes and clamp down to a form. Let dry for several days before attempting to tiller it. — *Tim Baker*

Tips for working around knots:

"When you're working around a knot in a limb, don't attack it just from one direction, otherwise you'll likely gouge and tear the wood around the knot. Instead, rasp or shave off the wood from the center of the knot, working "downhill" or outward from it." — *Tim Baker*

Knots can weaken a limb. Some can be strengthened by leaving them "proud," but others should be dug out and filled. Dig the knot out to the healthy wood and then rough up the surface of the wood inside the knot and fill it with bits of chopped sinew and hide glue. That's the way the Turks did it. With extra-large knotholes, you can stuff strands of sinew completely through the hole and smooth it out flat on the back side. This method works much better than putting in a "Dutchman," which can sometimes crack out. — *Jay Massey*

Another good method of dealing with knots, says John Strunk, is to use wood scrapings, sanding dust and glue to fill the hole. Tamp this material down into the knot hole and then apply some Locktite 420 to make it solid. Let it dry and then sand the area down before finishing.

Strunk sometimes digs out the punky center of a knot and fills it with Locktite 420, one of his favorite glues.

For a number of reasons, Paul Comstock says, a wooden bow may have a small working crack in the wood that seems to have no effect on the bow's performance or durability. Such cracks will flex or open tiny amounts as the bow is used. Examples can include areas around a knot or pin on the back, a fret on the belly, or a small crack on the side of the limb. It is particularly risky when water works its way into such a crack. Bending the bow in such condition can create significant damage where none existed before. The crack can enlarge and threaten to destroy the bow. To fight this danger, the archer can religiously keep such spots heavily waxed or greased when wet conditions are anticipated. Another option could be to use such a bow only in dry weather. Drying checks in the wood usually pose no danger in such circumstances. The wood fibers around a drying check are perfectly intact (as long as the check does not run off the side of the limb). The check was created when the fibers moved. Even though they moved they have not been ruptured, which is the case with a working crack. It is the combination of ruptured fibers, water, and bending that can cause significant damage.

SHORTCUTS DEPT.

A quick way to follow the grain on the back:
A quick way to follow a single growth ring on the back of a bow is to sandblast it. Sandblasting works well when there are knots on the back, which would make it difficult to use a scraper, rasp or drawknife to follow the grain. — *John Strunk*

For quick drying of white woods:
Much of the U.S. is fairly humid, and any wood left outdoors or in a shed is usually too wet to make a bow. The difference between 12 percent moisture and 9 percent can be the difference between three inches or one inch of string-follow. Before building a bow from white woods stored outside, bring the wood inside. Put the wood in a box of stovepipe dryer or put it in a closet with an electric lamp. You could also dry the wood by putting it in the kitchen (usually the warmest room in the house), or even put is under the bed; anything is preferable to leaving white woods outside. — *Paul Comstock.*

From living tree to finished bow in six days:
Floor tiller the green wood until it will bend about five inches. Being so thin it will now dry in about three weeks. Or six days at 100 degrees and 50% humidity. To prevent twist while drying leave the stave full width its entire length. Narrow during final tillering. — *Tim Baker*

WORKING WITH SINEW-BACKED BOWS

How to avoid belly checks:
Really old, well-seasoned Osage is often apt to develop longitudinal belly cracks after it has been backed with sinew. Sealing the belly of old Osage with a waterproof tape before the sinew is applied will usually eliminate the checking. — *Jay Massey*

Protecting the sinew backing from string chafe:
Sinew-backed bows in which the sinew extends completely over the end of the bow nock will expose it to moisture because the bowstring rubs and chafes it at that point. Best to cut through the sinew and taper it down to bare wood below the nock and then wrap the sinew completely around the bow limb at that point to hold it down. — *Jay Massey*

Or you can glue on horn overlays at the bow tips and cut the string grooves in these. This eliminates the need for wrapping the limb with sinew. — *John Strunk*

For faster sinewing:
Bowyers who use sinew for the first time invariably find it a tedious affair. It needn't be. Follow the example of the Asiatic composite bow makers, who used to comb their sinew out before laying it onto the bow. This way you can apply a bundle of 50 or 100 sinews down at once. The sinews are first saturated in warm hide glue and then placed down on a flat board and combed out straight with a coarse-toothed metal comb, or even a plastic hair comb. With this method, a bow can almost always be sinewed in less than an hour — sometimes as little as 20 minutes. — *Jay Massey*

Avoid using too much glue:
Another tip with sinew: hide glue should be thinner than table syrup and should be lightly "squeegeed" out of the sinew fibers before being laid down on the bow. The ominous-sounding "crack" sometimes heard in some sinew-backed bows is caused by using too much hide glue. — *Jay Massey*

How to "quick-cure" sinew:
A tip from Ron Hardcastle for "quick-curing" sinew during the summer, when humidity is often high: After applying the sinew to the back of the bow, put the bow in a cold air-conditioned room. The cold causes the glue to jell quickly, and the low humidity of the air-conditioned atmosphere causes the water in the sinew and glue to diffuse out very quickly. This approach, Hardcastle says, cuts in half the time required to cure a summer sinew job in his native Texas, where the humidity is rather high.

Notes on degreasing the back before sinewing:
Ron Hardcastle's thoughts on degreasing the back of a bow before applying sinew backing: "Since all soaps, cleansers and detergents are strongly alkaline, I have found them all equally effective as dilute lye is in degreasing Osage and

other woods before the sinewing process. Fels-Naptha, a kind of granny's lye soap, is as good as any, and very easy to work with. Moistened with warm water and applied vigorously with a toothbrush, it causes Osage's yellow, oily pigment to rush out of the wood with a will. Rinsing need not be with harsh (and possibly weakening) boiling water; lots and lots of very warm water, such as from a shower, will suffice. Rinse not just until the yellow color stops flowing, but until the treated surface no longer feels slick and slimy.

Avoiding problems with humidity & moisture:
To prevent sinew-backed bows from picking up moisture in humid conditions, use a product called End-Damp (available at bigger hardware stores). Put some in a cloth bag and leave it in your bow tube with your bows. It will drop the humidity to 30% or less. — *Tim Baker*

SALVAGING BOWS FROM THE JUNK PILE

How to strengthen a weak limb:
You can build up a hinged portion of a limb with either linen or flax (either linen string material or raw flax fibers), set in glue — *Tim Baker*

How to repair splinters on the back of a bow:
For transverse tension cracks on the back of a bow, use a linen patch about 1/8" thick and taper it on either side of the crack, Set it in hide glue or other glues. "It's a last-gasp way to save a bow." — *Tim Baker*

If your bow starts to develop a splinter or tension crack, you can wrap completely around the limb at that point with sinew. First saturate the sinew in hide glue then wrap on. After drying, the area should be waterproofed. — *Jay Massey*

Al Herrin's method of repairing a splinter on the back of a bow is to cut a patch of rawhide to go completely around the bow limb. First wet the rawhide and then sew it up tightly on the belly side. Slip the rawhide down and then coat the entire area with Elmer's glue and slip it back up. When the rawhide shrinks it tightens up and makes a very strong patch.

If you ruin a good stave:
Beginning bowyers will often chrysal a limb or will weaken it too much in one spot. If this happens, you can always cut the bow in half and make a take-down, fitting that limb with another one. You can even conceivably splice a yew/Osage combo or even an American Flatbow/Longbow design together! — *John Strunk*

BACKINGS & FINISHES

New glue for applying backings:
Franklin glues has come out with a marvelous new and convenient water-proof glue for any wood-wood or wood-snake or wood-rawhide bond. It comes

in a squeeze bottle and is a one-part glue which looks like plain old yellow carpenter's glue and is water-soluble until it sets up. It's called Franklin Titebond II. — *Ron Hardcastle*

Getting rid of air bubbles:

Sometimes when you glue on a thin skin, such as snake, you'll get an air bubble. Use an Exacto™ knife, make an incision and flow some Locktite (other glues won't penetrate as well). Or, if the edge of the skin begins to raise up in damp weather, use a few drops of Loktite™ — it works quick. — *John Strunk*

Tips for making homemade finishes:

When making homemade varnish (described fully in the Handles and Finishes chapter in Vol. I), the turpentine/pine pitch solution can be strained through an old T-shirt to remove the big particles, then poured through a coffee filter to leave a pure amber varnish which works as well as anything you buy. — *Jim Hamm*

TIPS FOR BETTER TILLERING

Use a mirror to find the problem:

Having tillering problems? Can't see what's wrong? Look in the mirror — not at yourself, but at the bow. The human eye has a natural inclination to "correct" things — to put them in proper balance. To see the imbalances, turn the bow around, with the upper limb to your left, and watch while you draw it in front of a mirror. — *Jay Massey*

Or use the "strobe effect:"

Tim Baker's method: String the bow and from the side-view hold it vertically at arm's length away from you so you can see the curve in the limbs. Flip the bow suddenly by rotating your wrist, so that the uppermost limb is now on the bottom. Flip the bow quickly again and again, thus creating a "strobe effect" which makes any discrepancies in the limbs jump right out at you.

Emerging limb set can point out weaknesses:

Another tip from Tim Baker on tillering: After you've first strung the bow and drawn it a few inches, unstring it and examine closely any set the limbs might have taken. The amount of set — and the location of the set — will tell you which parts are too weak. Baker often uses the shape of the emerging set as a tillering guide.

For final tillering:

During final tillering, it works well to first make one wood-removing pass with a fine rasp (sometimes called a cabinetmaker's rasp), check the weight, then make the next pass with a scraper or a pocketknife. Alternating the tools this way leaves the belly of the bow perfectly flat, with no washboards or crown — thus making for more even limb tiller and less string-follow, which yields a faster bow (see also Tools, Vol. 3). — *Jim Hamm*

If you get carried away:
One of the most common mistakes made by novice bowyers is to scrape off too much wood and end up with a bow which is too light. In building your first few bows, it's best to start out with a stave several inches longer than your desired length. Later, you can reduce the length and increase the poundage. — *Jay Massey*

VISUAL BLEMISHES

To prevent chrysalling in the bow's belly:
If a scraper or other tool leaves faint ripples in a bow's belly, these ripples can eventually create chrysalls (small frets or compression fractures) if the belly is highly stressed or if the wood is somewhat damp. The answer is to sand the ripples smooth once the bow is otherwise finished. First polish the belly with steel wool. Look down the belly with the limb tip pointed at a light source. This makes the ripples much easier to locate. Wrap some 60-grit sandpaper on a sanding block and the ripples can usually be removed with no loss of draw weight or change of tiller. — *Paul Comstock*

To remove minor blemishes:
John Strunk offers this tip for removing minor scratches and dents from soft woods such as yew, juniper or Cascara: "Use the smooth bottom of a spoon to burnish the area. This lifts out the scratch without disturbing the finish, thus no sanding or refinishing is needed."

USING OLD BOWS

Paul Comstock's comments on this subject:
Increasing interest in wooden bows has led a number of archers to attempt to use wooden bows that are at least 40 years old. If a wooden bow has not been used for 30 or 40 years, stringing it and immediately pulling it to full draw can easily make the bow explode into several pieces. I have examined the wreckage of two such attempts. Such disasters are particularly sad because an artifact from the pre-fiberglass era — an artifact that cannot be replaced — is destroyed.

Old lemonwood bows are the type most likely to break this way, even if they are backed. Old Osage orange self bows are perhaps a bit tougher, but they too can be damaged. The first full draw in 40 or 50 years can crack or splinter the back around a knot or pin.

A really good wooden bow is one that performs well when it is thoroughly broken in. Strain in the back of such a bow is reduced because the compacted wood of the belly provides nominal resistance. When a wooden bow sits unused for 30 or 40 years, much of the natural compaction of the belly has been lost. This means the wood in the belly is providing a proportionately higher level of resistance. This greatly increases strain on the back, increasing the odds of damage or fracture.

It is possible to return an old wooden bow to service. First examine it carefully. See that the backing, if any, is in good shape and has no loose or missing spots. If the bow has a handle riser, examine it to make sure the glue lines are still solid. If the bow is unbacked, examine the back for cracks or other signs of damage.

If the old bow is in excellent condition, string it about 5 or 6 inches high. Once the old bow is strung, let it sit strung for six to eight hours. Then unstring it. Repeat the process a second and third day. String it a fourth day and pull it to half-draw 100 or 200 times. Then gradually increase the draw.

During this process, constantly check the old bow for any signs of damage, and listen for cracking noises. If there is no damage or cracking noise, odds are high the old bow can be confidently used.

This process can gradually and safely return the normal level of compaction to the bow's belly. If this is done, the belly is providing a safe level of resistance and strain on the back is greatly reduced. The danger of fracture or back damage falls dramatically.

The finish on many old bows will be in bad shape. The bow's historical value will be reduced if it is sanded clean and refinished. If the bow is not to be refinished, the safest practice would be to keep the old bow waxed and never use it in wet weather.

GENERAL BOW-MAKING TIPS

When steam-bending bow tips:
Tim Baker advises leaving the bow tips extra-wide during the steam-bending, because some twisting usually occurs even when you do it carefully. If you've already narrowed down the tips, it will be hard to remove any limb twist resulting from the steam-bending.

Building a primitive take-down bow:
Tim Baker's tip for making a quicky, primitive-style "take-down" bow: Make the splices 6" long and blunt ended (you can splice side-to-side or back-to-belly), and then wrap with strong line, an extra bowstring or sinew. Such wrapped splices are strong and according to Baker, "They shoot just fine."

STEEL POINTS

Glenn Parker

Years ago, it was common for bowhunters to make their own broadheads; after all, there were few broadheads commercially available. In this modern age, it may seem impractical to make your own points since many good ones can be purchased for only a few dollars. However, the process of construction is not difficult, and there is an added feeling of accomplishment when hunting with equipment made entirely from scratch.

Choosing a particular broadhead shape depends on a number of factors, but a properly designed point is vastly superior, in both penetration and durability, to a poorly designed one. I believe the following historical information from Forrest Nagler, Roy Case, and E. F. Pope is important background material which will assist in the correct design of a broadhead.

Forrest Nagler was an engineer concerned not only with points but also with the construction and function of self bows. In 1933, he gave his thoughts about broadhead design:

"The length need not be over 2 inches and might possibly be shorter without involving too steep a cutting angle ... the width should not be over 1 1/8 inch for heavy game but could be wider for deer, bear or mountain lion, though greater width is hardly necessary." He felt the total broadhead weight should be around 90 grains with as short a ferrule as possible, around an inch, because a longer ferrule tends to break the shaft just behind the head. The unsupported head (beyond the end of the ferrule) should be less than an inch long to increase strength and prevent bending. Ideal thicknesses, said Nagler, were .050 for mild spring steel and .035 for very hard steel.

As to specific heads (next page), Nagler liked head No. 4 but disliked No. 2, as it was too wide and too weak unless its thickness, and weight, was excessive. He felt No. 4 or a cross between No. 3, 4, and 5, was an ideal point.

The late Roy Case, of Case Broadheads, proved several years ago that longer blade designs did not necessarily yield the greatest penetration, thus backing Forrest Nagler's claim as to broadhead shape. The heads of today, such as Zwickey, Bear Razorhead, and others fit this basic design group.

In an article entitled "Broadheads," which appeared in *Archery*, April, 1958, Case explained how the publication of Howard Hill's book, *Hunting the Hard Way*, brought about, in Case's words, "a spate of broadheads." In his book, Hill maintained that a broadhead should be at least three times as long as it is wide.

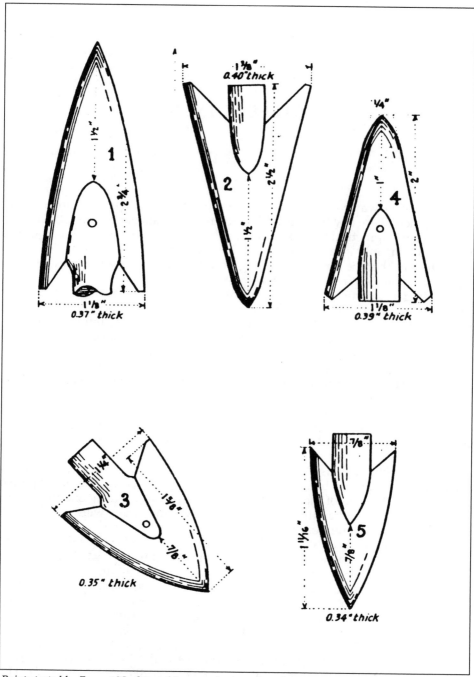

Points tested by Forrest Nagler on big game during a hunting trip to Canada in 1931. Shown actual size. (The Archery Review, Feb., 1933)

Case Konvertible.

Case Korrek, circa. 1936.

This, Case wrote, was "in spite of the fact that thousands of deer, at least, and many larger animals were being taken with the much shorter heads."

Case went on to explain how he, as well as several other bowhunters, went to great lengths to test several different sizes, makes, and shapes of heads for penetration. Of the broadheads he made himself, he expected the Keen, a broadhead with a long slim dagger point, to lead the list. But his shorter curved-blade Korreck won out. Shortly after these tests, Case discontinued making the Keen.

Case Keen, circa. 1940.

Case stated in his article, "I wanted to know whether length of blade for a given width affected penetration so I made a broadhead exactly like the Case head (same steel) with ferrule well to the rear of the blade, but three times as long as it was wide. This head I could sharpen as easily as the regular Case head. I tested them. The shorter head still penetrated better."

Again, Case's best performing broadhead was a shape following the concepts laid out by Forrest Nagler.

E. F. Pope was another highly respected bowyer and broadhead manufacturer whose basic blade design also fit this criteria. Pope was internationally known for his quality arrows and broadheads. The famous bowhunter, Art Young, purchased his Osage staves from Pope (no relation to Saxton Pope) for use on his hunts in Alaska, Greenland, and Africa. Pope's first advertisement for his Osage bows and staves appeared in the September, 1927, issue of *Ye Sylvan Archer*. Pope's Yorkshire Broadhead had a wide enough blade to clear a track for its shaft and give deep penetration without setting up too much friction on the cutting surfaces for maximum penetration. His ferrule was the lightest on the market yet was fully reliable in strength.

These concepts of shape and design, as first written by Forrest Nagler in 1933, still hold true today. Jay Massey, well-known traditional bowhunter and author, makes and uses a head of this type. The broadhead is triangular, 1 1/4" wide X 2" long with a turned target tip for a ferrule. In a personal conversation with Jay (June 1992), he informed me that this head has been proven on the largest of big game animals, including moose.

Yorkshire Hunting Head, 1929, by E. F. Pope, 130 grains. Pope believed in the longer ferrule, but basic blade design and supportive tip still fit Nagler's criteria.

Jay Massey's "Half-fast" Moose John Special.

Howard Hill style broadhead, with concave edges and 3 to 1 length to width ratio.

Ben Pearson Deadhead, 1965.

The main blade edge may be concave, straight, or convex. Howard Hill believed that the concave blade design and the 3 to 1 length added to penetration. However, the concave design so close to the ferrule is difficult to sharpen and the 3 to 1 ratio, as later tests have proven, does not aid penetration. The straight edge is obviously the easiest to make and sharpen as well as yielding the most blades for your material. The convex edge or rounded edge was the type on the old Ben Pearson Deadhead™. When Roger Rothaar first made the Biscuit Cutter™, he used the blades from the Ben Pearson heads. He felt there was a lack of penetration in this design, and this later led to the development of the straight edged Snuffer™ broadhead. This point has shown good results on all big game animals.

Before undertaking the project of making your own broadheads, remember to exercise all safety precautions, such as the use of eye protection, gloves, and adequate ventilation.

Today, there is a wide choice of steel for use on broadheads, such as 1040 to 1095 annealed spring steel. What is the difference between 1040 and 1095? The last two numbers denote the carbon content of the steel; i.e., the 1095 has over twice the carbon content of 1040 and should hold a keener edge. Blades can be made from banding steel two inches wide and .050 or .044 inches thick, from old saw blades, large band saw blades, spring steel, or various types of annealed spring steels, and stainless. 440C annealed stainless steel, .062 inches thick, can be purchased from a knife maker supply to use as blade material. A thinner stainless would be preferable but is not readily available. The annealed type

Three blade Biscuit Cutter based on the Deadhead design, 1968.

Improved three blade Snuffer, 1981.

steels, which are softer, are much easier to shape and fit to a ferrule and to fashion as a tie-on type broadhead. A large hand-operated shear can be used to cut the material, and will handle even the hardest steel. After cutting the steel with a hand shear, you will have material which is concave on one edge and convex on the other. This is the reason for using a 2.5 inch layout for 2 inch material as illustrated: up to a twenty percent loss of the blade occurs during straightening,

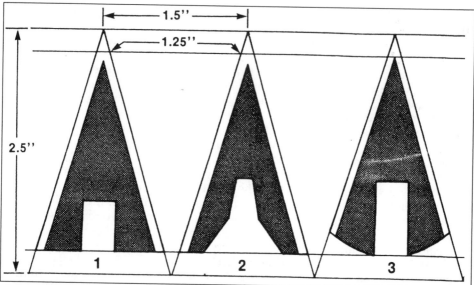

Full-size template for cutting various designs from steel stock.

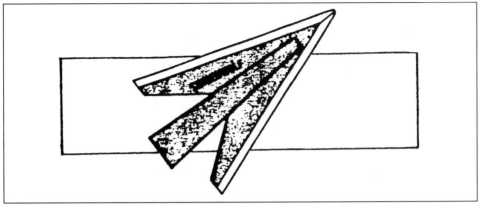

A blade design similar to No. 2 on one of the author's Timberwolf ferrules.

heat treating, and shaping the broadhead to a point. A standard benchgrinder and file may be employed to shape the blank and bevel the edge.

The style of the very tip is optional: the sharp point (which I prefer), or the chisel or rounded tip. There are advantages and disadvantages to each. The sharp point penetrates better and has less tendency to glance off and change the arrow's direction, but it also may bend, causing the blade to fold at the tip. The chisel point's primary advantage is its ability to glance around bone and penetrate without losing all of the arrow's energy, but this style does impede penetration to some degree.

The purpose of a barbed design is to reduce weight while maintaining the same amount of cutting edge. Pointed barbs may tend to snag quivers and hands and should be squared off as shown. Some states do not allow barbed heads for hunting, so research game laws before choosing this design.

Various barbed points with the tips of the barbs cut off to prevent snagging and reduce weight.

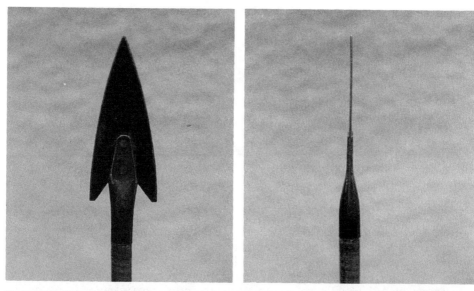

California By-products broadhead with two rivets, on one of Saxton Pope's arrows circa 1925. Of note is a small brass tack, set just below the nock, to allow proper alignment of the arrow on the string by feel alone.

When making your blades, be sure all shaping and beveling is totally finished before heat treating. After shaping the blade, use a torch to heat the material to an orange color, applying heat to both sides to help prevent warping. Quench the blade immediately in heat-treating oil such as used motor oil. A temperature of 1900 degrees is needed to heat-treat; if carbon steel sparks, you are over-heating the material and exceeding 1900 degrees. Once treated, the steel will be very hard, but this hardness will be reduced somewhat when the blade is sol-dered to the ferrule. Use a file to cut across the edge of the point and gauge the temper of the steel. If the file will not cut, the point may be too hard and brittle. The broadhead can be annealed, or softened, by heating to an orange color and air-cooled. If it won't be soldered, heat it a second time to approximately 500 degrees in an oven for two hours, air-cool it, and the temper should be fine.

Many of the old bowhunters used brass, copper, steel, and aluminum to fashion the ferrules. At first, ferrules were made of tubing pinned to the blade and, for added strength, soldered. Then bullet ferrules from ammunition suppliers or target tips were used as ferrules. Later, pre-slotted manufactured ferrules changed the art of making broadheads as only the shaping of the blade and fitting to the slot was necessary to construct a nice head of individual design.

Ferrules can be purchased from manufacturers such as Howard Hill Archery, Delta, and others, or made from tubing or field tips with five degree tapers for

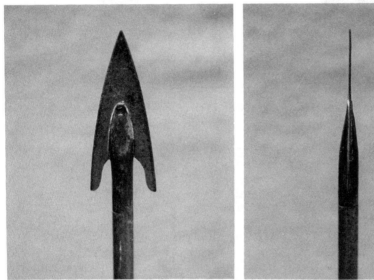

One of the arrows Art Young carried on his Yellowstone hunt in 1923. The point is brazed to the ferrule. The feathers are glued and the ends wrapped with sinew, which is heavily waxed for waterproofing.

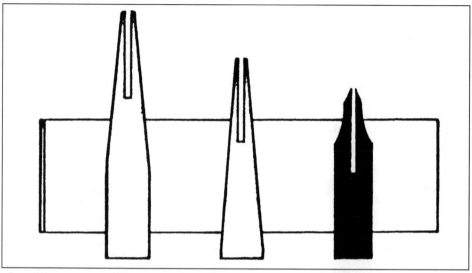

Three types of ferrules: Howard Hill, Glenn Parker, and a slotted field tip.

the shaft. To make a field tip ferrule, you will first need to slot the end for approximately 5/8 inches to accept the head. Secure the tip in a vise between two blocks of wood. To better secure the point, it may be necessary to cut a half-circle in the edge of each piece of wood, smaller than the outside diameter of the target tip. Use a file to flatten the tip and then a hacksaw blade to cut the slot. A power hacksaw blade with the greatest number of teeth per inch works for a wider slot, or two thin hacksaw blades can be taped together. Next, the ferrule is tapered. In order to achieve the best penetration the ferrule should be as stream-lined as possible, so it will not hang on tissue and hinder penetration. For this tapering, I use a broadhead screw-in adapter mounted in a drill, which holds the slotted field tip in place while allowing it to spin. With the drill turning, the point can be held against a power grinder until it reaches the desired shape. This results in a streamlined ferrule as well as a decrease in the weight.

The blades should be carefully straightened before heat-treating and again before insertion into the ferrule. If the point will be held in place with a pin, drill the hole before heat-treating. If you prefer solder, there are two types which work well. The Welco 5A 1/16 inch is a silver base solder, available at the knife supply house. A propane torch is employed with the Welco 5A. The other is Stay Silv No. 45. It is much more expensive but has the greatest strength; it requires a special flux and has a melting point of about 1400 degrees. Stay Silv No. 45 requires an oxy-acetylene rig with a brazing tip. The greater surface area of blade to ferrule gives the strongest bond when using Welco 5A, which also works on stainless steel. The blade and ferrule must be free of dirt, rust, and oil before applying flux and solder. The flux acts as a scrubber which cleans the material so the solder will bond to the materials. If the flux is used up by too much heat, the material oxidizes and the solder will not stick. A muriatic acid bath cleans the material of rust and oil, but caution must be used with all flux and acids regarding proper ventilation. Sandpaper can also be used to clean

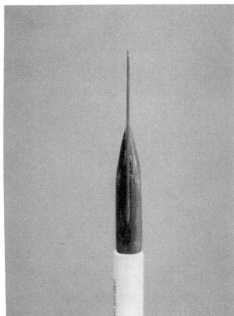

Fal-con Four with rounded shoulders, 1949.

Ace broadhead, circa 1950.

Ben Pearson skeleton ferrule, 1939.

Ex-calibre 45, circa 1950.

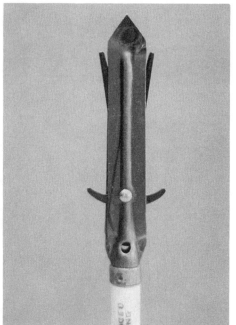

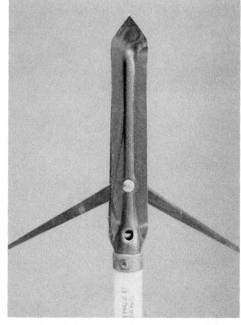

The Hinged Fang, from 1948, a mechanical-type of broadhead which opened on impact with the target. These styles of points greatly impede penetration.

Red Bow Co. Star point, 1953, another mechanical head.

metal for flux and soldering in place of the more dangerous acid. When the solder job is complete, water will clean away the flux. If soldered correctly, you will not have excess solder to remove with a file.

If you prefer not to use a ferrule, another option is that of a tie-on style head. Tie-on broadheads are ones which, in most cases, require a tang, or extension, to secure the head to the shaft. These heads offer little support to the main portion of the blade, unless they are made of extremely heavy blade stock. An example of a long-bladed design is the Indian tie-on design that often folded over or would even bend around a bone between the periosteum and bone

Pioneer Game Tamer, from 1970. The wheel spins and is sharpened around its entire edge.

Homemade tie-on head whose length makes the tip susceptible to folding over if bone is struck.

Tie-on broadhead of correct design.

Broadhead by Andy Vail with serrations in the tang to allow better grip by the sinew wrapping.

A well-designed broadhead by Bill Schram, glued to the shaft. Wrapping the shaft behind the point with wire or sinew would make it even more secure.

("Peri" means "around", thus "Periosteum" is literally "tissue which surrounds the bone"). The shorter tanged heads, such as Ishi's, made for a much stronger head. I personally would not consider a 3 to 1 ratio in a tie-on design head due to the lack of support of the main blade. Tie-on broadheads need to be of at least .050 material for strength as there is no ferrule for support.

Secure the tie-on head's tang to the shaft using sinew, wire, or tubing to help support the shaft and prevent it from splitting. The strongest method is tubing or wire and a liberal amount of epoxy. Steel or aluminum (which is lighter) gasoline line in 3/8" from an auto supply store works perfectly for the tubing, and once I even salvaged an old TV antenna and used the hollow aluminum to mount dozens of broadheads. Pistol cases in .357 work, too, though they take a bit more fitting since the case is thicker toward the base. The tubing should be about an inch long and no larger than the outside diameter of the shaft. Cut the slot for the broadhead in the end of the shaft, then use a fine rasp or a scraper to shape the wood so the tubing slides over the shaft and fits flush at the very base.

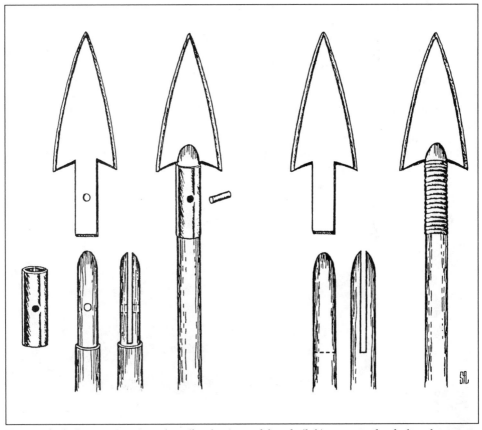

Two methods for securing tie-on broadheads. A metal ferrule (left) supports the shaft and prevents splitting upon impact. Wrapping the point's tang with wire (right) serves the same purpose.

Saxton Pope's early tie-on broadhead. Note brass wire wrapping on shaft.

If the tube and broadhead tang are to be pinned, which I recommend, the hole should be drilled before gluing. Be sure to carefully taper the wood from the leading edge of the tube so it will be as streamlined as possible from the side view and thus not impede penetration. When the parts fit well, use epoxy (or casein or hide glue for the strictly orthodox) to mount the broadhead and secure the pin. After the glue is dry, file any protrusions of the pin flush with the tube.

No matter which style of broadhead or mounting system you choose to employ, once the point is in place on the arrow it must be sharpened. As with most areas of traditional archery, there is a great deal of mystic surrounding the process of sharpening a point. Many old-timers used a fine file which resulted in a somewhat ragged, though razor-sharp edge, which they claimed stayed sharp better if it struck a bone. Thousands of game animals were, and still are today, taken with points sharpened in this way, so the method clearly works. But from

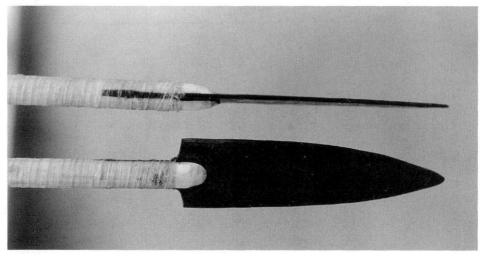

With a tie-on point, always taper the leading edge of the shaft so penetration will not be hindered.

Modern tanged broadhead with aluminum tubing used as ferrule. Note taper of shaft at its leading edge to aid penetration.

a medical standpoint, a smooth-edged, razor-sharp instrument cuts more easily. For instance, obsidian, which under a microscope has an edge smoother than any steel scalpel, is sometimes employed in eye surgery and heart surgery due to the clean cut it makes. From a hunter's standpoint, a smooth edge promotes more bleeding and longer lasting bleeding than any other.

Even if you intend to place a smooth edge on a point, when it is first made it still requires file sharpening with a small bastard file. Support the broadhead and smoothly file into the edge of the blade with even strokes. Work from the back of the blade toward the tip. Flip the point over and file the other side. There are four surfaces being worked to produce a bevel, so you'll have to change hands to sharpen the remaining two sides. It takes a bit of practice, but with the file alone an edge can be produced which is uncannily sharp.

If you wish a smoother edge, the broadhead can be polished to remove rough places. A quick field method involves honing the freshly filed point on a round diamond steel, which fits nicely in a pocket on the quiver. A smoother, sharper edge may be obtained by using finer and finer stones, such as Arkansas whetstones. After this, broadheads can even be stropped with a razor strap, yielding an edge sharp and smooth enough for shaving. A paper wheel mounted on a bench-top grinder can also be employed. These are normally used for sharpening knives, but will place a spectacular smooth edge on a broadhead. A polishing compound is applied to the wheel, then all four bevels of the broadhead are smoothed with it; just remember to hold the arrow so the wheel is not buffing *into* an edge, but *away* from it.

No matter which method you use for sharpening broadheads, the points must be *kept* razor sharp. Experienced hunters check their broadheads every day in the field to ensure that they remain as sharp, and effective, as possible. Remember, if you are not afraid of the edge, then it is not sharp enough! A pleasant ritual for traditional archers is sitting around the fire in the evenings, after the day's hunt is over, and sharpening broadheads while swapping stories.

No matter how well you design your broadheads, how precisely you mount them on the arrow, or how sharp they are, if you do not have perfect arrow flight both accuracy and penetration suffer. Like driving a nail with a hammer, if the blow is "off", the nail goes sideways or bends, but little penetration is accomplished. The same applies to the arrow.

There are many variables in controlling arrow flight. Remember, three small feathers will not spin a fence post! The spine of the arrow must increase to accommodate heavier broadheads. Also, when using heavier shafts and heads, sometimes the number of feathers, i.e., four fletch, or the amount of helical, must be increased for better stabilization. There is also a difference in how center-shot the bow is, or how close to the center of the bow the arrow passes. The right arrow may be different from one bowhunter to the next, even with the same draw length in the same bow. You have to find what works best for your particular style of shooting, as well as the weight broadhead which you intend to use.

The old adage about using ten grains of arrow weight for each pound of bow weight is a good one. A 600 grain arrow is the perfect match for a 60 pound bow. Everything else being equal, a heavy arrow penetrates better than a lighter arrow when shot from the same bow. As an example, a 55 pound recurve shot a 500 grain arrow 182 feet per second. The same bow shot a 600 grain arrow 172 feet per second. Using the formula of arrow speed x arrow speed x arrow weight/450,240 = kinetic energy in foot pounds, it is shown that the lighter arrow yields 36.78 foot pounds of energy while the heavier arrow yields 39.42 foot pounds. At normal traditional hunting ranges of 25 yards and less, the slightly slower speed of the 600 grain arrow will scarcely be noticed, while the energy, and penetration, is significantly enhanced. This added penetration from a heavier arrow can well make the difference between cleanly killing a game animal and being unable to track and find one which is mortally wounded. Again, you won't be disappointed by using ten grains of arrow weight for each pound of bow weight.

Though it is far easier to purchase your hunting points, taking game with equipment you have designed and made yourself, from the bow to the string to the broadhead, holds a special joy and satisfaction, a satisfaction which can be savored by every traditional archer.

IMPROVING ACCURACY

G. Fred Asbell

A bow without an arrow is a bent stick, secured in an arc-sort-of-shape. It is unrequited love, unfulfilled potential. Without an arrow, the bow can never fulfill its life's mission ... it is the proverbial half-filled water glass. It is only a shaped and bent stick until the first arrow leaps from the string, and then it is a bow.

And, as in life, once the joy of that union has been experienced, and passed ... once the marriage is made ... expectations beyond exhilaration begin to surface. The blessed thing is supposed to go where you aim it!!! Herein lies the stuff of this chapter.

The marriage of the bow with the arrow is not completely unlike romantic marriage. It is dependent on the right matchup, upon understanding the idiosyncrasies of one the other, and of working together to create the desired effect. Matching the bow and the arrow together, so they function as a single cohesive unit, is the beginning and end of accuracy with all types of archery equipment. Unfortunately, traditionalists sometimes walk right by that. Sometimes accidentally, because it is not always understood. But probably more often it is our need to escape the trappings of modern equipment and technology which causes us to also reject anything that smells of precision and observation. That is a mistake.

I often hear fellas say "... that's why I quit shooting all that other junk, 'cause I didn't wanna do all that crap." I understand all of that, believe me I do. It is such a common feeling among those who have chosen the traditional way. But, when you step into the woods with a bow and arrow in your hand in pursuit of an animal, regardless of whether you are shooting the most primitive bow ever built or the most modern piece of high-tech machinery, you have the responsibility to kill that animal quickly and cleanly ... and nothing else is acceptable, under any circumstances.

Part of the added challenge of traditional equipment, part of the fun, is in learning to shoot the equipment well ... to make the arrows go where you point them.

As a group, we bowhunters have always been preoccupied with the bow itself. I think that is particularly true with traditional bowhunters. For the most part, our bows are what set us apart from other archers. The arrows can also be very different, but they are not the thing that identifies the traditionalist. Even though we've heard it hundreds of times, it bears repeating, because it is one of those things that is often said, sometimes heard, and rarely soaked up ... the arrow is the most important part of the bow and arrow shooting equation. The finest bow in the world will shoot very inaccurately with unmatched, cheap arrows. On the other hand, a bent willow stick fresh from the river bank, with a piece of binder's twine for a string, will shoot precisely if it is matched with a good, straight, precision arrow.

IT ALL STARTS WITH THE ARROW

Matching the arrow to the bow is more difficult with the self-bow. It is more difficult than matching arrows to modern composite longbows with an arrow shelf cut-out, which in turn is more difficult than recurves. It all has to do with the degree to which the bow is centershot. The more centershot, the more simple is the arrow matchup. The less centershot the bow, the more difficult arrow matchup becomes, and the more important it is to accuracy.

When we say a bow is centershot, or not centershot, we are talking about whether the bow is cut in far enough at the arrow rest to allow the arrow, when

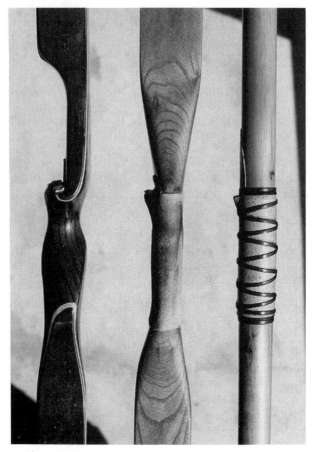

The bow on the left, a modern fiberglass recurve, is centershot; the other two are not. The Osage bow in the middle has a narrow, deep handle, in part so the arrow can pass closer to the center of the bow. The widest part of the yew longbow, at right, is at the handle. With properly matched arrows, all three can shoot with precision.

shot, to pass the bow at about its left to right center, (making it center shot), or to the left of center (non-centershot). This is assuming a right-handed shooter. In general, self bows do not have a sight window cut-out and are not centershot. Because of this, the self bow is more difficult and more critical of bow and arrow matchup than any other type bow. But, I would add here for clarification that this difficulty has only to do with the centershot feature. A compound bow without any sight window cut-out would be every bit as difficult to set up ... probably much more so.

When an arrow is shot, it goes through what is known as the archer's paradox. Here's what happens: the force of the string upon release begins driving the arrow forward. That force (the poundage of the bow) causes the arrow to first bend inward against the side of the bow, then the arrow flexes back in the opposite direction, then back to the original bend, and so on. It is a left to right fish-tailing that takes place every time an arrow is shot from any bow. An arrow shot from a centershot bow does much less of this fish-tailing business than does a bow which is non-centershot (your bow, for example). The reason for this is that the string is basically pushing the arrow straight forward from a centershot bow, and since the arrow is straight in front of the string, there is minimum contact with the inside of the sight window, although there is some. With the non-centershot bow, the arrow is not fully lined up ahead of the string, but is pointing off to the left (for right handed shooters). The string drives straight forward upon release, shoving the arrow into the side of the bow. The side of the bow (from where the arrow is touching) prevents the arrow from going straight ahead, and thus the arrow flexes considerably more to get past this obstruction.

This is why the non-centershot bow is more critical on arrow matchup. When you shoot such a bow, your arrow must go through considerably more acrobatics than does an arrow from a bow with more centershot, such as a modern fiberglass longbow, a recurve, or a compound. And because of this, your arrows must be matched to the bow as closely as possible before you can develop any level of consistency and accuracy.

The critical thing to understand here is that if the correctly spined arrow is used in this non-centershot bow, the arrow will actually bend around the bow and go straight ahead, just as though the bow were actually centershot. You may want to read through the above again, because what it says is that *if you shoot the correctly spined arrow from your self bow, it will shoot just as true and straight at where you are looking as it will from any fancy centershot bow.*

As I said earlier, the tendency is for traditional archers to want to pay less attention to doing things just right, when in fact, they really do need to pay more attention to it all. Sorry.

Without exception, you will need to shoot a *lighter* spined arrow from a non-centershot bow. And I know that you often hear you should shoot a heavier spined arrow from a non-centershot bow. Trust me. Lighter spined is the correct choice (I said lighter *spined*, not lighter physical weight). Again, this is because the non-centershot bow forces the arrow to go through the bending of paradox to a much greater degree. And this means that a lighter spined arrow is required to allow the additional bending. If we consider the modern composite longbow, which has some sight window cut out, and is more centershot ... more that a self bow, and less than a centershot bow ... we see that it will have different spine requirements than will the self bow, because it is "more centershot." You match the spine of the arrow to (1) the weight of the bow, (2) the weight of the arrowhead. These two in combination determine the correct arrow for your bow.

Consider this: if your self bow is 3/4 inch wide at the handle, and mine is 1 inch wide, we will need different arrows, even though our bows are the same weight. This is because my wider handle is forcing the arrow to move farther from the vertical center line of the bow and the thrust of the string than your narrower handle. It would not surprise me if the popularity of the stacked limb longbow over the flatbow was partially a product of its narrower handle section.

There is no magic formula for determining what arrow is correct for your bow. It can only be done by going out and shooting and watching to see what happens. You might find an arrow shoots perfectly from a given bow, and I might not be able to shoot the same arrow from that bow for love nor money. Sometimes having a friend stand behind you to watch your arrow in flight is a help. I stand up on a chair, slightly above and behind the shooter, and that gives me a perfect view of the arrow in flight.

Continuing with this arrow thing; you also need to consider that because your bow is non-centershot, and thusly your arrows are going through more paradox, arrow straightness is more important than it is with other bows. And I know you probably didn't want to hear that either. I am convinced that a handful of somewhat crooked arrows will shoot a baseball-sized group from a centershot bow, and a dinner plate-sized group from a non-centershot bow. Your arrow is flexing and whipping left to right as it comes from your non-centershot bow to a much greater degree than it is with a centershot bow. Any imperfection in the arrow itself will be magnified by this exaggerated motion. This is why broadhead selection is more critical with longbows and self bows ... an air foil is created on the end of the arrow by the broadhead itself. This over-sized object out on the end of the arrow multiplies the effect of the arrow paradox and can possibly even cause the arrow to go careening off in a wind plane.

Sometimes just the additional weight of the broadhead on the end of the arrow messes things up. That weight on the very tip of the shaft serves to magnify the left to right action of the arrow. A 125 grain broadhead might shoot fine, but a 165 grain head in the same design might cause your arrow to do all kinds of crazy things.

This whole non-centershot, additional flexing, arrow straightness thing is why traditional archers typically must shoot bigger feathers. The bigger the feather, the more air it grabs, and the quicker the arrow stabilizes and goes straight forward. Big, helically applied feathers will cure lots of ills in arrow matchup. And if you don't want to use helical fletching, then angle them slightly. The idea is to get the arrow spinning as quickly as possible, and either helical or angled feathers will do that better than will a straight fletch. The formula is based on total feather surface. So look at how much actual feather ... length and height ... you have to determine what is best. Three 5 inch die-cut feathers, 5/8 inch high, are not going to stabilize like three trimmed or burned feathers, 5 1/2 inches long by 3/4 inch high. The 5 1/2 x 3/4 inch, which is what I use, has almost 3 1/2 square inches more surface area. In general, feather height is more important than length. I feel that each 1/8 inch difference in height in the equivalent to at least 1/2 inch in length. It doesn't actually need to be mathematically figured. Just use the amount of feather required to straighten up your arrow. I would add, however, that I've yet to see anyone who was getting decent arrow flight from a self bow with three 5 inch die-cuts.

You must test shoot each arrow from your self bow. This applies even if you are using the finest store-bought arrows available, built by the world's finest fletcher. If you are hand-spining your arrows by feel, you should most definitely test shoot each arrow repeatedly. The same is true tenfold with broadheads. Each arrow should be shot several times, and only those which shoot consistently should be considered as acceptable for taking to the deer woods.

BRACE HEIGHT

Brace height is the distance from the string to the belly of the bow. It is an important factor in arrow flight. The brace height of your bow determines how long the string stays with the arrow, pushing it forward. And it determines how much the limbs are being flexed, and how far back to their natural shape they are allowed to go when the bow is shot.

The brace height is where the string stops when the bow is shot. So it is also the place at which the arrow leaves the string and becomes a free flying object. If the brace height is too low ... too close to the belly of the bow ... then the string and the nock are still together when the arrow begins to bend around the bow. This causes all kinds of interference and is usually obvious because the arrow will "whack" loudly off the side of the bow, and typically wigwag and flop around in flight. There will also usually be a lot more hand shock present in the bow. This is because the tips of the limbs are allowed to travel too far forward. The lower brace height gives you more speed from your bow, and will probably prolong its life somewhat, but if you go too low, then it doesn't work well. My rule of thumb is to shoot all bows at the lowest point where they feel good and shoot well.

Twist the string to shorten its length. This will raise the brace height. Untwist it (or go to a longer string) to lengthen the string. This will lower the brace height. Or adjust the timberhitch. As in so much of shooting the bow, what works for you may not be right for me. So it's trial and error, and observation, to find what functions best.

NOCK POINT

The nock point locates the arrow nock on the string in the same place for each shot. Without a consistent nock point, no degree of consistency can be expected.

The specific location of your nock point is determined by your individual shooting style, draw length, bow design, hand placement on the bow, and many other things. Again, each shooter will need something a little different, but most people locate their nock points someplace between 3/8 and 3/4 inches above 90 degrees (this is for placing the arrow below the nock point). The idea is to find what works for you. Don't worry if you need something a bit higher or lower than someone else. That is very common and shouldn't be given a second thought.

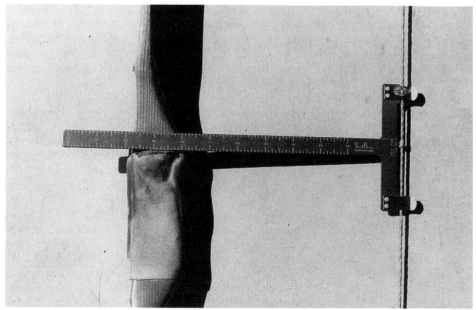

A bow square, used to gauge the arrow's nocking point on the string.

What you are looking for is clean arrow flight. An incorrect nocking point will manifest itself in an up and down porpoising motion. The arrow will visibly flip, maybe seesawing up and down for several feet after it comes out of the bow. Sometimes, if the location isn't terribly off, you'll note that the back of the arrow is simply flying a little high. Typically a nock point too low is much more problematic than a nock point too high. A nock point too low will always cause the arrow to porpoise, where a nock point too high will normally only make the arrow impact a bit lower, unless it gets much too high, and then it, too, will cause porpoising. When the nock point location is correct, the arrow comes out of the bow in a level attitude and flies toward the target in the same manner.

Left to right motion is not a nock point problem, only up and down motion.

HAND PLACEMENT

Just a moment ago, I mentioned hand placement on the bow as a factor in nock point location. Hand placement can be a big factor in arrow flight from your bow. How you put your hand, and where you put your hand on your bow, is very important.

Observe how you place your hand on your bow. Shoot a few arrows with that hand position. Now change the hand position by either moving the heel of the hand farther in, or farther out, on the handle ... first at the heel of the hand, and then up near the "V" between thumb and forefinger, and then both. You should see a number of things happening, sometimes with each different hand location. The handle on a bow does not act independently from the rest of the bow. That is particularly, and specifically, true with a self bow. The handle is somewhat stiffer than the limbs on many self bows, but it is simply a place near the center of limbs from which the bow is bent. The hand pressure which you put in that place (handle) is a factor in how the limbs on each end of the bow bend.

Be aware of a tendency to put too much heel onto the handle. The longbow style bow is shot with the heel of the hand placed firmly down on the bow handle. The bows are built to be shot in that manner. But, if you place the heel of your hand "too far into" the grip, or you exaggerate the pressure of the heel, you will see repercussions in poor arrow flight and inaccuracy.

The pressure of the hand on the bow should be firm and equal the full length of the handle, and it should be basically along the vertical center of the bow, or to the left of center (right-handed shooter). Placing your hand and your hand pressure "too far into", or too far to the right on the handle, causes the bow to torque, or twist, in the hand as the shot is made. This is usually characterized by the arrow "whacking" the side of the bow and erratic arrow flight for the first 10 to 20 feet. I see as many people making this mistake with a self bow, and a longbow, as I do all other errors combined. The smaller handle of the self bow makes it particularly susceptible to too much hand on the bow handle.

If you will stand really close to a target butt or a dirt bank, and forget completely about where your arrow is going, and simply move the hand pressure around the bow to the left on each shot, you will find a place where the arrows shoot soundlessly and cleanly.

Hand pressure on your self bow has a lot to do with arrow flight and with how well and how accurately you shoot.

UP AND DOWN IS IMPORTANT TOO

I like an arrow rest on my self bow, and I think if you don't use one you should give it consideration. Not because I need something to hold my arrow, but because the arrow rest (or facsimile thereof) serves as a locator for the hand on the bow. My arrow rest is simply a piece of leather shoved down into the top of the handle wrap, so a bump is created, with a piece of soft leather on the inside of the sight window for the arrow to pass across. You can't be moving the hand up and down on the handle and expect consistency. The placement of the hand, up and down, on the handle is almost as critical as the left to right placement we just talked about.

Or, if you prefer not to have an arrow rest, anything which gives you a reference to bring your hand back to a consistent place on each shot. The point being that you need something that will remind you of how and where your hand goes on each and every shot from your bow. If your hand is in a different place, either up and down, or right and left on every shot, the arrow will go to a different place every shot. Promise.

This covers most of the things you are going to come up against when shooting your self bow. I suppose I've made it sound complex, but don't let that concern you. It only sounds complex. My desire is to give you enough information on how and why bows work that you will be able to solve any arrow flight problem you encounter. And that if one particular shot goes off the mark, you can say, "Oh, yeah, I ... (your choice) on that shot", and correct it on the next one.

And, I know I've said this before, but it bears repeating: it's fine to reject everything that has to do with modern equipment and modern archery, but do not get caught in the idea of embracing inaccuracy and poor shooting as acceptable, just because you are shooting primitive equipment. Your primitive equipment can be shot as well as any other type of archery gear. You must know your tackle, how to shoot it, its limitations (if, indeed, any exist), and your limitations. When you go to the deer woods, responsibility goes with you, always.

QUIVERS & OTHER GEAR

Jay Massey

No archer's gear is complete without certain sundry items, namely a quiver to hold arrows, a bracer or armguard to prevent the bowstring from slapping your forearm, and a glove or tab to protect your fingertips while shooting. The selection of these items can have a profound effect on the outcome of an archery hunt.

QUIVERS

The ideal quiver, I feel, should hold at least eight arrows. It should be lightweight and quiet and it should provide both protection for, and easy access to, your arrows. It should allow you to sneak quietly through brushy terrain without hanging up. Most importantly, the ideal quiver should be completely non-obtrusive — it should do its duty without getting in your way or interfering with your actions. In other words, you should be able to carry a quiver without being constantly reminded of its presence.

I doubt that the perfect quiver has ever been built. If it has, I certainly haven't heard about it. Over the years I've tried numerous types and found all of them to have certain strengths and weaknesses.

Let's take a look at some of the popular quivers in use today:

Back Quiver

This type of quiver literally emanates traditionalism. It looks great. It projects images of Robin Hood and of archery adventures in distant, shady glens — even though historical records indicate that the medieval English archer carried his arrows not on his back, but at his belt. The back quiver also reminds us of the great Howard Hill, for it was his favorite type.

I've never understood why Hill preferred it, except perhaps that as a realist, Hill simply accepted the back quiver in spite of its shortcomings. It has plenty of them.

I used a back quiver for my entire first archery hunting season and then over the years tried it again from time to time. Each time I tried a back quiver I would remember all the reasons I gave it up in the first place. It wasn't that I tried only one or two different quivers; I tried eight or ten different models, both home-made and "store boughten." Most did the job, but none of them worked to my complete satisfaction.

Mind you, I'm not criticizing the back quiver for field archery and roving. It

The back quiver is fast, and looks traditional, but the over-the-shoulder movement in withdrawing an arrow can "flag" game.

works admirably for those purposes. And it does carry plenty of arrows, with room left over for miscellaneous gear and even your lunch. And it is fast; you can grab an arrow from a back quiver and have it on the string in an instant.

However, for hunting you need a quiver which lets you withdraw an arrow not only quickly but silently, with a minimum of motion. And in this regard, the back quiver falls woefully short. I'm assuming, of course, that the archer doesn't actually carry a broadhead arrow in his hand or nocked on the bowstring while moving through the woods. If a person carries an arrow at the ready, then I suppose that eliminates my first objection to the back quiver, which is that the over-the-shoulder motion "flags" game.

However, let me say this on the subject of carrying a nocked broadhead arrow: it's a very dangerous practice. During my early bowhunting days I did it all the time — until the day I was hunting mule deer near the Three Sisters wilderness in central Oregon and tripped over a log and rammed a razor-sharp Zwickey "Delta" broadhead deep into my calf. A friend of mine had an even closer shave — if you'll excuse the pun — as he chased a bull caribou over a ridge up in Alaska's Nelchina country. As he sprinted around the ridge to head the bull off, he tripped over a hummock and fell forward. He threw both the bow and the arrow away from him, but unfortunately the shaft landed on its nock end with the deadly broadhead pointed straight at him. As my friend fell forward he twisted his body at the last moment and the broadhead barely skimmed his left shoulder, missing his heart by inches.

Such a scenario can give an archer nightmares, for we know the cold efficiency of a sharp broadhead. I'm always extra careful with my arrows, and because of this I've missed out on a few shots at game by not always having an arrow nocked and ready. Perhaps I've been too conservative when it comes time to draw an arrow, but the sight of your leg sliced open like a slab of bacon gives you a harsh glimpse at reality (not to mention mortality!). A broadhead arrow is a deadly thing; we should never become too comfortable with it.

I never nock a broadhead arrow except when I'm closing in during the final stalk, and my conservatism has cost me several shots at big game — at least when I was carrying a back quiver. Like the time I got a nice buck deer out of his bed when hunting Green Island in Alaska's Prince William Sound. It was a quiet, rainy morning and the buck had stood up slowly, not really alerted even though he had already seen my movement. Had I been using another type of quiver I might have been able to get an arrow out undetected. But the over-the-shoulder movement — together with the scraping sound of the arrow being withdrawn from the latigo leather back quiver — was enough to send the buck on his way.

Indeed, noise is one of my other objections to the back quiver. Most of them will produce a faint rustle — or a loud rattle — as you move through the brush. Of course, the quiver can be quietened by placing a handful of grass in the bottom. So the noise problem can be overcome.

Another problem is that broadheads tend to rub against each other in the back quiver and become dulled. A good friend of mine, who always uses a back quiver and swears by it, simply sharpens his broadheads each night after hunting all day. After a week-long hunt his inch-wide broadheads have become filed down below the 7/8-inch minimum. He buys a lot of broadheads.

Back quivers with pockets for extra strings, sharpening file, matches, and compass.

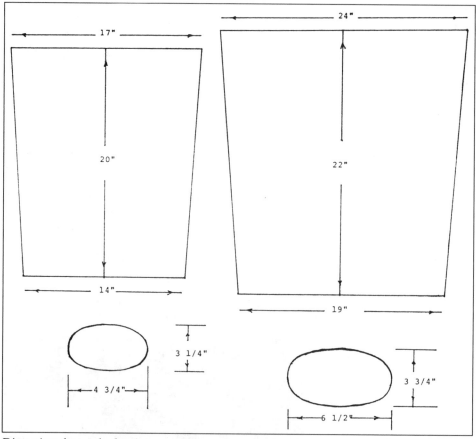

Dimensions for two back quivers.

Some archers get around this problem by adding a special insert in the bottom of the quiver, into which they jam the broadheads to keep them from making contact with one another. I've tried this solution but didn't like it because it made the arrows stand up straight and rigid and didn't let them lie flat as a bundle. It kept the heads sharp but made the quiver noisier. My own solution to the dull broadhead problem is to make loose-fitting "booties" for my broadheads. As you withdraw an arrow, the "bootie" simply falls off into the bottom of the quiver.

So, the back quiver can be modified to be quieter and to keep your broadheads sharp, but that still leaves the problem of flagging game. My final reason for disliking the back quiver for hunting is that they're a problem in brushy country. I'm talking of truly thick brush, like the nearly-impenetrable tag-alders which grow on Kodiak Island. You can negotiate the brush a little better by folding your back quiver under your left arm, the way Howard Hill did, but this puts your quiver in a more or less horizontal position and makes it easy for the arrows to fall to the ground or be pulled out. The last time I hunted on Kodiak

Island with a back quiver was the day I came back to camp minus half a dozen arrows — and I hadn't loosed a single one at game. They'd all been pulled from my quiver in thick brush.

So I'll pass when it comes to using a back quiver for hunting, though I prefer them over all other types for field shooting and roving. They hold plenty of arrows and a good back quiver is so comfortable you tend to forget it's even there. And they look great with a traditional bow.

Modified Back Quivers

Now that I think about it, there's one other problem with the back quiver: your fletching gets wet in rainy weather. Which is why some archers in the Pacific Northwest prefer a modified back quiver such as the St. Charles quiver — a type which was originated by old-time Seattle archer Glenn St. Charles. Several variations of the St. Charles quiver are produced commercially, and many archers make their own. I used to make mine from six-inch aluminum irrigation pipe, flattened to an oval shape and covered with thin leather to deaden the sound.

The St. Charles-type quiver generally rides at the center of your back, with straps going over each shoulder. The upper part of the quiver is completely enclosed and the lower part is partly open. The arrows are "spring-loaded" and

Massey made this St. Charles-type quiver from irrigation pipe for his first year of bowhunting in the rain forest of western Oregon (photo by Ted Kramer).

are secured with the nocks being pushed against a layer of foam rubber; the broadheads are often embedded slightly in soft wood or rubber at the bottom.

This type of quiver is unbeatable for hunting in the rain forest of the Pacific Northwest, for it keeps your arrows dry and your broadheads sharp. There's no flagging of game with the St. Charles quiver; to reach an arrow, you simply reach behind your waist. And the arrows do not rattle.

The only objections I have to this quiver is that it's a bit awkward when crawling through thick brush and its appearance isn't quite as traditional as I would like.

The Hip or Belt Quiver

The belt-style quiver has a rich history, much more so than the back quiver, which seems to have taken over as the quiver of choice for archery traditionalists. As the old English saying went, "Every English archer carries twenty four Scots under his belt." The belt-type quiver was the choice of Saxton Pope and Art Young. And all those Asiatic horse-archers? — they carried their arrows not on their back, but in side quivers, usually made of heavy leather. Many of them used a combination quiver, known as a gorytus, which would accommodate not only a couple dozen shafts, but even a short composite bow in the strung position.

I've made six or eight belt-type quivers and used them for both field archery and hunting. My general observation is that they get in your way a bit. Also, drawing an arrow from one is considerably slower than from a back quiver. They have some of the same problems as the back quiver — being somewhat noisy and tending to dull your broadheads — but at least they don't "flag" game. And unless it is made to ride just so, the belt-type quiver will swing about and hit your legs with annoying frequency.

To be honest I haven't used a belt-type quiver all that much for hunting, though I like them for field archery. I do recall one memorable hunt for Dall sheep in Alaska's Brooks Range when my unfamiliarity with my belt quiver cost me a nice full-curl ram. I was using a side quiver patterned after one described in Saxton Pope's classic, *Hunting With The Bow & Arrow*. This was in my "pre-bootie" days — before I started using leather broadhead covers to keep my heads sharp. On that particular hunt I had loosely wrapped duct tape over my heads to keep them from rattling and becoming dull in the belt quiver. This was not a smart thing to do, as I was to discover.

I'd glassed a big ram on a distant ridge and a two-hour climb and stalk had put me within 50 yards of him. However, the sheep spotted me and began walking away in the characteristic stiff-legged "alert" posture. It was a long shot, but my only hope, so I took it. The arrow zinged off the rocks beneath his belly and the ram hightailed it down the ridge. Knowing that with wide-open terrain below him the ram would try to circle and get above me, I ducked behind a rocky outcropping and ran perpendicular to his line of travel. I sprinted for 75 yards and then cut sharply downhill, grabbing an arrow on the run. I topped the rocky rise and there was the ram, coming hell-bent-for-leather up the hill straight at me, only 20 yards away. By the time I got an arrow nocked the ram had put on the brakes, a shocked look on his face. He couldn't have been more than 15 feet away.

The belt-type quiver is handy for both field archery and hunting, but unless it hangs correctly it will hit your legs when walking.

I quickly drew the string but the sight of that gray wad of tape covering the broadhead completely blew my concentration. I let down and jerked the tape off in a quick motion which couldn't have taken half a second. It was all the time the ram needed. Frozen in time for a millisecond, he swapped ends and showered me with shale as he threw it in high gear. I was still fumbling around in first when he blasted through the sound barrier at the quarter-mile marker.

If that sheep'd had a voice, I'm sure he would have given me the horse laugh. I felt like an idiot. Why hadn't I simply shot the razor-sharp broadhead right through the tape! Of course, in such moments one doesn't stop to reason, but acts instinctively. The incident truly stands out as one of my dumbest moments in hunting.

I learned a lot about arrow quivers while hunting Dall sheep. I learned that a large, open back quiver can be dangerous if you should fall on steep terrain. I learned that a belt quiver, like the one described above, can be a nuisance when traversing a steep slope or crossing rockslides because it often touches the ground. At one point, I thought I had discovered the secret to hunting sheep in wide open country: simply carry a dozen broadheads and "keep some wood in the air" until you connect. I had always felt that I could go anywhere a sheep could go, and that all I had to do was get an arrow in one and then track him down.

I was badly mistaken on the first count, and in time I came to realize that taking long shots with a bow is inexcusable and not in the best interests of archery hunting, which should place a premium on fair chase and sportsmanship. I later read an article by Howard Hill where he admitted to once having taken many long shots at game but gave it up because he had hit and lost a few. I too abandoned the idea of carrying 18 broadheads and "keeping some wood in the air."

The Bow Quiver

After that sheep hunting season I put aside my roomy back quiver and designed a tiny, super-light bow quiver which would hold only three broadheads. From one extreme, I would go to the other. There would be no more 50-yard plus shots at sheep or any other game. I would go light and carry three arrows. If I couldn't get within 25 yards of a sheep I simply would not shoot.

It worked — at least on my next sheep hunt. After switching to the new approach I killed an old ram with huge horns. However, my three-arrow quiver did give me some anxious moments.

I had sneaked to within 18 paces of the feeding ram and had taken a quartering-on shot, aiming carefully to place the arrow tight behind his sheep's foreleg in order to hit the lungs. But my aim had been off by a few inches and the shaft had struck the ram in front of his foreleg, with nearly half of its length sticking out. He fell to the ground and then reared up and fell again. From the angle of the shaft I thought I'd hit him in the leg. Thinking the ram was about to get away, I grabbed my second broadhead arrow, rushed it and shot too high. The broadhead barely skimmed the hair on his back.

As the sheep reared up again I grabbed my third — and last — arrow and sprinted forward, intending to shoot him in the lungs at point-blank range. But in a heartbeat the ram reared straight up, went over backwards and went tumbling, and then bouncing, down the steep mountainside. My first arrow, as it turned out, had taken him squarely through the heart.

The concept of carrying but two or three arrows still appeals to me, but I'll never forget that sheep hunt — the time when I was close to needing more than three arrows. A big disadvantage to the one-arrow-one-buck school of archery hunting is that it leaves you with few or no practice arrows. I like to stump shoot frequently while on a hunt — it's part of the fun of hunting with the bow and arrow and one of the reasons it's so much more enjoyable than gun hunting. How many rifle hunters do you know who get to target practice all day while they're out in the field?

I have made and used various types of bow quivers on both longbows, flatbows and recurves. From a practical point of view, the bow quiver has everything going for it: the arrows make no noise and they are close at hand, easy to reach and do not rub against each other to become dull.

However, the bow quiver — any bow quiver — is an ugly affair; it mars the lines of a beautiful bow. Plus, it adds weight to the bow, making it feel awkward and out-of-balance. It can throw off your shooting.

To many traditional archers, the bow quiver may seem like the perfect solution. I've used several types of bow quivers on both my laminated recurves and longbows, but could never resolve putting one on a wooden bow. The bow quiver may be practical, but it has absolutely no aesthetic appeal and it looks awful on a traditional bow.

Massey used a yew longbow and a three-arrow bow quiver to take this 11-year old Dall ram ...

... and a five arrow bow quiver to take this Sitka blacktail buck. Although the bow quiver is efficient, Massey feels it mars the appearance of a traditional bow. This lightweight recurve is of laminated Osage orange.

If, however, you are one of those archers who likes the bow quiver, here's some advice: always make sure your broadheads are covered and protected by some sort of hood. This is not so much to protect your broadheads as it is to protect your own health. Back in the '60's it was common to see bowhunters walking around with those cheapie bow quivers which left the broadheads exposed. The sight of those quicky quivers used to make me nervous because a good friend in Oregon had an extremely close shave (another bad pun!) with one. Seems he was crawling through some alders, his bow in his left hand and a broadhead arrow in his right. He became careless and allowed the broadhead to nick the bowstring, cutting it so far that the bow unstrung itself with a loud "Whang"! The bow limbs leaped forward and sent four of the deadly broadheads skimming through the flesh of his forearm about a quarter-inch deep.

The only near miss I ever had with a bow quiver happened during an airplane crash in Alaska, when I had my recurve bow and attached quiver in the cargo space behind the seats. The aircraft, a Cessna on floats, lost power on takeoff, and we'd been forced to go down through the trees, finally crashing upside-down. Somehow we made it through the crash with only minor injuries, but later I was shocked to discover eight deadly broadheads lying scattered about the cockpit.

I doubt that the arrows would have come out of the type of quiver I'll describe next.

The Indian-style quiver is quiet and doesn't "flag" game as it allows you to withdraw an arrow with little motion. This one is of brain-tanned moose hide.

This type of quiver also holds arrows securely, even when tipped upside-down. And the arrows do not rattle.

Indian-style Quivers

Many Native American archers carried their arrows in a type of quiver which was slung over their shoulder with a long strap. This allowed the quiver to ride not on the back, but at about waist level. Such a quiver is usually designed to hang at a slant, with the nocks ends of the arrows pointing forward.

No flagging game with this quiver; arrows can be drawn out easily, with a minimum of motion.

For traveling on horseback Plains Indians usually shifted the quiver around so that it rode at the small of the back, with the arrow nocks pointing to the left, for a right-handed archer. When sneaking or crawling through brush, this quiver can be shifted around to the front and tucked tightly up against the body with the bow hand.

The Indian-style quiver was frequently made long enough to protect the entire arrow, leaving only the nocks exposed. Though you might think the fletching would get ruined, being inside the quiver, such is not the case. Instead, the quiver protects the fletching very well. If you do much crawling through thick brush with the fletching exposed, the feathers will definitely suffer some damage.

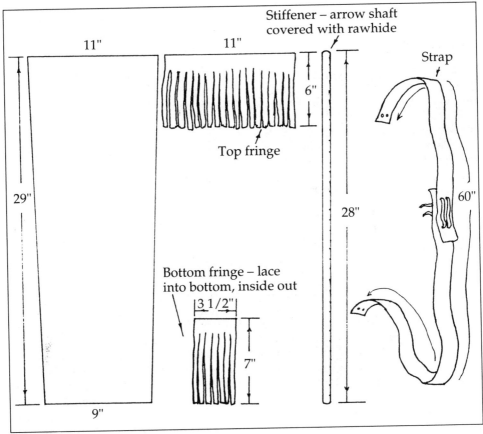

Plans for an Indian-style quiver.

One thing is of the utmost importance when you're making an Indian-style quiver: the skin or leather must have the proper stiffness even though this type of quiver has a stiffener running its entire length. Most chrome-tanned leathers are not suitable for the Indian-style quiver because the leather is too limp. The leather must have the correct "body" so that it will accept arrows without folding in on itself.

Brain-tanned leather — particularly thicker buckskin, elk or moosehide — is perfect for this quiver, because it's not only soft and flexible, but has some "body" or substance to it. Brain-tanned hides — properly speaking, they are "dressed," rather than tanned — have a soft, but rough texture. They hold arrows both quietly and securely, even though the quiver may be tipped nearly upside down. I've made such quivers from both brain-tanned moosehide and brain-tanned buckskin, and found each to work well. I prefer the heavier moosehide because it's more rugged but brain-tanned buckskin makes a quiver which is as light as a feather.

For some reason, the Indian-style quiver has never caught on with archers — yet. But I'm predicting that as more become aware of its attributes, they will switch over to it.

After hunting with one for several seasons I find that I like this type of quiver more and more. In my opinion, it's as close to the perfect quiver as any I've seen. It's absolutely quiet and your arrows do not rattle. It is traditional and it looks great. It holds your arrows safely and securely, and it permits you to withdraw a shaft with almost no hand motion. It doesn't seem to get in your way like a belt-type quiver; you can slip quietly through the woods without knowing it's even there. Plus, it can be made to hold even a dozen arrows.

ARM GUARDS, GLOVES & TABS

Unless you're a masochist who enjoys getting whacked repeatedly on the left forearm (assuming you're a right-handed archer), you're going to need some sort of protection from your bowstring. It amazes me how many people switch from a modern recurve bow to a traditional wooden bow and then remark, "This dang thing whacks me on the arm!"

Small wonder. Some of the laminated recurve bows have a brace height of nine inches or more — which means that the string rarely even comes close to your forearm. No experienced traditional archer would brace a self-wood or sinew-backed wood bow so high; it would place the limbs under unnecessary stress.

Instead, we adjust our shooting technique and equipment — bending our arm slightly at full draw, bracing the bow lower and so on. And we always wear an arm guard on our bow arm. If you're ambidextrous like Art Young or Ron LaClair you could wear one on each arm.

Like the quiver, your arm guard must fit just so. You want it to fit perfectly, so that you can take off through the woods and never even know it's there.

Some archers use those cheapie arm guards made of two little steel-reinforced leather strips running lengthwise down the arm and held on by two elastic bands. To lower oneself to using such an affair with a traditional bow is, to use an old English expression, "A truly hawful thing." I advise you to use a good

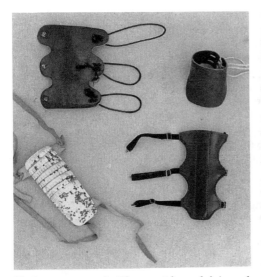

Various arm guards. The one at lower left is made from an armadillo shell.

This unique arm guard, designed and made by well-known Oklahoma artist Ron Owen, fastens to the arm quickly by means of a sliding ring made of antler.

one or not at all — an arm guard which is worthy of association with your other traditional archery gear.

The most common mistake archers make in building an arm guard is to make it too long. A bracer which is too long jams you in the bend of your arm. One made of leather which is too thick will also be uncomfortable. Most good arm guards are made of medium-heavy latigo leather and fitted with speed hooks, which makes it easier to lace.

A shooting glove or tab is necessary to protect your fingertips from the bow-string. Most traditional archers prefer the shooting glove, but I prefer an Old English-style leather tab, for several reasons. First, the tab puts me in closer contact with the bowstring and gives a cleaner release. Second, the tab leaves your fingers free to perform more delicate tasks — building a fire, tying knots, sharpening broadheads, and so on. And third, a shooting tab is much easier to make than a glove. I can cut out a tab in a fraction of the time it would take to cut and sew and fit a leather shooting glove. I use two pieces of leather for my tab, with a slicker piece of leather for the fingertip section.

For traditionalists who prefer the Asiatic composite bow, a thumb ring may be the answer, for it is ideal for short bows which would produce finger-pinch when shooting with the Mediterranean draw. I have experimented with thumb rings made of bone and sheep horn and have shot bows up to 65 pounds with this method. However, I've not persevered enough to become really proficient

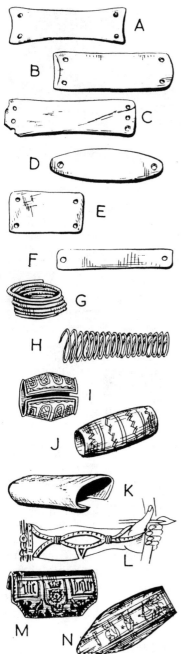

A) Greenstone, with gold studs and a bronze buckle. From a burial at Kellythorpe, Yorkshire. Bronze age. (An account of this can be found in *Ancient Stone Implements of Great Britain*, Evans, 1897).

B) Slate, from Aldington, Worcestershire. Bronze Age. Similar examples have been found at Cruden, Aberdeenshire; Tring Grove, Hertfordshire; Fyrish, Rosshire; Czechoslovakia and Italy.

C) Stone, from Brandon, Suffolk. Bronze Age. (See the British Museum *Guide to the Antiquities of the Bronze Age*, 1920).

D) Stone, Bronze Age. Found at various sites including: Broadford, Isle of Skye; Andalusia and Sardinia.

E) Stone, found at Broadsford, Isle of Skye. Bronze Age. Also similar pattern found in Wiltshire.

F) Bone, found at Everley, Wiltshire. In Devizes Museum.

G) Coiled reed, Egyptian, circa 2700 B.C. (See *The History of Archery* by E. Burke).

H) Bronze, Danish. Bronze Age. In Copenhagen Museum. (See *An Illustrated History of Arms and Armour* by A. Demmin, 1877).

I) Bronze, Danish. Bronze Age. In Copenhagen Museum. (Ibid).

J) Bronze, German. Bronze Age. In Sigmaringen Museum. (Ibid).

K) Copper, from burial, California. (From a photograph by Dr. C. E. Grayson).

L) Assyrian, 7th century B.C. Sketched by W. E. Tucker from a sculptured slab in the British Museum.

M) Embossed leather. Originally belonged to Henry VI (See *Archery*, the Badminton Library, etc.).

N) Ivory, engraved with St. Sebastian scene. Possibly French, 16th to 18th century. In Pitt Rivers Museum, Oxford.

Arm guards from around the world (courtesy The Society of Archer Antiquaries).

O) Padded leather, Japanese (called "tomo"). From Vol. 5 of *Archery of Old Japan* by Masatomo Takagi, 1838. (Ref. W. E. Bishop).

P) Plaited fibre and pierced shell discs, Solomon Islands. (From a sketch taken in Exeter Museum by W. E. Tucker.)

Q) Woven Cane, New Guinea. (From a photograph supplied by the University of Aberdeen).

R) Wooden, New Hebrides. (From information supplied by Pitt Rivers Museum, Oxford).

S) Ivory, Damaraland, Africa. *(Ibid)*.

T) Ivory, South Africa. *(Ibid)*.

U) Padded Leather. Pygmy. (Powell-Cotton Museum, Birchington).

V) Silver with turquoises, leather back. Navajo, Arizona. (From a photograph supplied by Dr. C. E. Grayson).

W) Leather, with tin plates attached. Zuni, New Mexico. (From information supplied by Pitt Rivers Museum, Oxford).

X) Sheep Horn, Point Barrow Eskimo. (See *The Annual Report of the Bureau of Ethnology*, 1887-88, Smithsonian).

Y) Ivory, Kuki tribe, Assam, Indian. (From information supplied by Pitt Rivers Museum, Oxford).

Z) Wood, Cachar Hill, Manipur, India. *(Ibid)*.

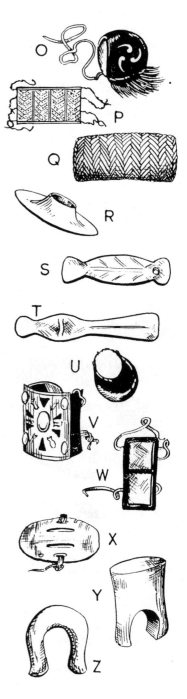

Arm guards from around the world (courtesy The Society of Archer Antiquaries).

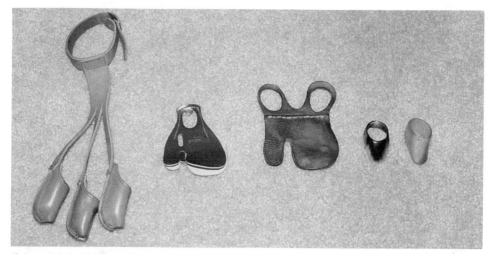

(left to right) A leather shooting glove, a target-style tab, the old English "two hole" tab, and two Asiatic thumb rings made of horn.

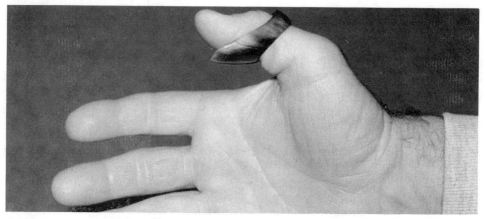

Getting a proper fit is extremely important when using an Asiatic thumb ring.

and comfortable with the style. Getting a proper fit with the thumb ring is of utmost importance. If the thumb isn't fitted correctly you will experience excruciating pain when drawing a heavy bow.

✧ ✧ ✧

After spending so much time and energy making that perfect bow, a linen string, and a dozen arrows with scimitar-like points, it's easy to head for the woods without giving much thought to quivers and armguards. But purchasing, or better yet constructing, the right accessories makes a big difference in safety and comfort when using that beautiful new tackle in the field. And, as I have discovered the hard way, the right accessories can also make the difference between filling a tag and waiting for next year.

"OLD UGLY" AND THE LITTLE BUCK

Jim Hamm

"The deer meander right through here," Paul Crow whispers, gesturing along the crest of the gentle slope. He explains that they travel toward the winter wheatfield whose bright green peeks through the brush a quarter mile in the distance.

He glances toward my Osage orange self bow, "Old Ugly". "Reckon you can hit anything with that?"

I shrug, well accustomed to his friendly sniping. "Doubt it. But maybe I can club one with it."

Paul is a long-time compound shooter, and a good one, and my fascination with wooden bows has always been a fertile source for arguments.

"If you run out of arrows, holler," he declares, "and I'll bring you some of mine."

Before I can come back with a suitably devastating reply, he turns, heading in the direction of the wheatfield where he's been playing tag with a ten-point buck all season long.

The cool wind gusts briskly from the west, down the slope. I ease toward the bottom of the hill to watch back into the breeze. Several scattered groups of live oaks stretch drooping branches nearly to the ground, and I choose a clump and disappear, hopefully, into the brush which surrounds the twisted, snarly trunks.

At first glance, this part of western Texas doesn't promise much in the way of deer hunting. Or any kind of hunting, for that matter. Rolling grassland stretches away in every direction, dotted with live oaks, thickets of mesquite, and clumps of prickly pear cactus. Thicker brush parallels the dry watercourses, and a low mesa, its sides sprinkled with dark cedars, squats on the northern horizon. There is little green, the frost long since sending most plants into dormancy for the winter.

It seems practically a desert — in summer it *feels* like a desert — but first appearances are deceiving. Having hunted near here before, I know the low brush, cactus, and cured grass support a surprising number of deer — up to thirty or forty per square mile. And droves of turkeys, rabbits, and quail.

Among the crooked trunks of the liveoaks, I kick a couple of fallen branches out of the way to prepare a place to stand. Bowhunting is difficult here and normal hunting tactics are seldom practical. A tree-stand hunter would be hard-pressed finding a tree to support a stand, nevermind whether it was in a good place or not. Stalking becomes a lost cause, with the grass and leaves brittle and dry and most of the country so open. And hunting over any type of bait, such as the corn which most hunters in Texas use, would be practically sacrilegious with a wooden bow.

So I settle down to wait, knowing Paul is a keen observer of wildlife and hoping he's right about the deer moving along my hill. I can't help remembering the game warden we saw a couple of days ago. He seemed surprised when we told him we were bowhunting, commenting that with six weeks of gun season already past the majority of hunters were having trouble killing a deer with a rifle. No lie, I'm thinking. In the two days we've hunted here the deer have been spooky and more alert than usual, which means they are practically invulnerable.

As my eyes slowly scan the surroundings, my thoughts drift back to the first deer I ever shot at with an arrow from a wooden bow, now almost twenty years ago. After suffering several early bow failures — the only thing I knew at that point about wooden bows was that they were made from a tree — I stumbled across a short Osage orange bow in a pawn shop in Oklahoma. Indian-made, it was at least a couple of decades old, but stayed in one piece when the shop owner let me pull it. I bought it for $20.

That fall, perched on a branch ten feet up a tree, I watched a nice eight-point buck trot toward me. The term buck-fever does little to describe the sensation which enveloped me. Though I had hunted for years with rifle, .45 pistol, and fiberglass bow, I had never encountered such a flank-speed deluge of adrenalin.

As the deer passed twenty-five yards away, broadside, I let fly with one of my four homemade flint-tipped arrows. The arrow flew well over his back but a curious thing happened. The sound of the arrow striking the ground beyond scared him *toward* me. Silently sliding another arrow from the quiver, I shakily nocked it on the string and launched it. That one whisked under his chin, and *again* he leaped toward me, only fifteen yards away, staring suspiciously at the arrows which had appeared from nowhere.

By then, I was trembling so hard it was a wonder I didn't fall from my perch. After nocking another arrow I shot at him yet again, with no further pretense at aiming, and incredibly, the same thing happened. He stopped ten yards away, broadside, stamping a foot at the odd happenings.

What little remained of my composure turned to cerebral guacamole. I can't swear that I wasn't drooling. With my fourth and last arrow I managed to hit the ground about halfway between us. This was finally too much, and the buck bounded away, tail flagging in alarm.

I held the tree trunk in a death-grip for ten minutes, until the shakes finally subsided. Though I had badly blown the shots, a smile began, then blossomed into laughter. I knew with absolute certainty that my days of hunting with modern weapons were over. Somehow, no matter how long it took, no matter how discouraging the failures, I was going to figure out how to make a wooden bow...

An odd motion fifty yards away catches my attention. It takes a moment to realize what it is; a Pope and Young skunk, ambling through the tall grass and cactus. Experimentally, I draw an arrow at him, then slowly relax the string.

The sun nears the horizon, looking strangely diluted from the blowing dust kicked up by the West Texas wind. A quail whistles off to the right. The hum of truck tires on a distant highway fades, then returns on the surging breeze.

I can't help pondering what makes an allegedly rational person hunt with a bent stick. For the time and cost involved it would be cheaper to eat pickled hummingbird tongues than arrow-killed venison. But dollars and common-sense never enter the picture. If it did, I could have spent all the years since those first fateful shots working for minimum wage instead of struggling with recreating these contrary, captivating weapons. Then I could probably afford to buy this ranch instead of hunting as a guest on Paul's lease.

I finally decide the inner compulsion boils down to the challenge involved. There are few wild frontiers left to conquer today, and the only way to face new frontiers, to face new challenges, is through self-imposed limitations. Each of us chooses the degree of challenge through the degree of limitation: compound instead of rifle, recurve instead of compound, handmade wood bow instead of fiberglass. As Professor Comstock says, wooden bows return us to a time when bows were bows and men were men...

I'm jolted out of the musings as a deer suddenly appears, calmly walking past, travelling away from the wheatfield instead of toward it, as I expected. When less than fifteen yards away I realize it has horns. The bow's draw begins without any conscious effort on my part. Automatically, my eyes lock on a tuft of hair just behind his shoulder. The arrow is drawn, anchored, and released as if performed by someone else. It instantly and miraculously vanishes into the deer's side, precisely where I'm looking.

He gives a great bound, bolts a few yards, then tumbles in mid-stride.

I notice my mouth is hanging open. The shot happened so quickly there wasn't even time for the standard knee-quaking flood of adrenaline. Lowering the bow, the blood pounds in my ears. I glance about in amazement, scarcely believing a deer, slain by my hand, is laying dead in the grass less than thirty yards away.

My mind is suddenly filled with a familiar sharp, clean feeling of peace and wonder: it can only stem from being a Zen-level participant in life, rather than simply a spectator. I savor the sensation.

A coyote yaps in the distance, his haunting cry hanging in the air. The crimson globe of the sun on the horizon sends golden shafts of light flickering among the branches of the trees.

After a few moments, I creep over to the deer. As I kneel down next to him, the emotion of making a kill, a combination of satisfaction and sadness, fills my heart. There is no joy, at least not yet. And certainly no jubilant shout of triumph over a slain adversary. For the deer is no adversary, but an ally. There is only the profound feeling of peace.

I quickly field dress him, noting he is young and the rack is not large. In fact, most rifle hunters would have killed this deer with no more emotion than that of a housewife selecting a cut of meat at the supermarket. He would have no connection with the buck, other than as his executioner.

But I decide I wouldn't trade the little buck for anything, not for the ten biggest deer I've killed with more modern weapons. He and the other deer I've

taken with wooden bows have been a lot of trouble; twenty years spent making sawdust from bowstaves, tens of thousands of practice arrows shot, and months spent alternately freezing or roasting in the woods. But given the satisfaction for a hunter armed with one of these hand-made weapons, I also decide he's been well-worth every minute of it.

I notice Paul moving toward me in the gathering twilight, and quickly step away from the deer. Adopting an air of nonchalance, I cross my arms, hiding the blood, as he walks up, oblivious to the buck lying in the tall grass a few yards away.

"Run out of arrows?" he asks.

"I still have a couple left."

He peers at me closely. "See anything?"

"Not much," I tell him, stifling a smile, then give a jerk of my chin, "just that one."

His eyes widen. "All right!" he blurts, rushing to the deer.

"Nice shot," he says after examining him, then turns to pump my hand. An outrageous grin plastered across his face, he's just as thrilled as I am, the mark of a true friend.

And, as a true friend, he quickly pronounces, "I guess we can settle up for my unerring guide services later." With a satisfied smirk, he hooks a thumb in his front pocket.

"If you'd known a buck was coming through here," I protest," you'd have been sitting on my shoulders all afternoon."

He hesitates, but I notice he doesn't deny it. He tries a different approach. "No bigger'n that deer is, throw him over your shoulder and let's head for camp."

I give a snort which might pass for a laugh. "No amount of pestering's gonna do you any good. I'm insult-proof tonight."

"I would be, too," he finally confesses, reaching down to grab a horn.

As we begin dragging the deer toward camp, Paul asks, "How hard is making one of those wood bows, anyway?"

"If you've been living clean, not hard."

He just rolls his eyes.

"But in this case," I continue, "maybe between the two of us we can turn one out."

He nods. "You're having way too much fun by yourself with those crazy bows. Maybe I'd better start helping you out."

Another convert, helping assure that the days of adventure and self-reliance aren't over just yet. And they never will be, not as long as the ancient lure of wooden bows still holds men within its magical grasp.

BIBLIOGRAPHY

BOOKS

Allely, Steve, Baker, Tim, Comstock, Paul, et. al., *The Traditional Bowyer's Bible, Volume 1*, Bois d'Arc Press, Azle, TX, 1992.

Ascham, Roger, *Toxophilus; The School of Shooting*, 1544.

Bishop, Morris, *The Odyssey of Cabeza de Vaca*, The Century Co., New York, 1933.

Carter, H. R., *Rope, Twine, and Thread Making*, John Bale and Sons, London, 1924.

Catlin, George, *Letters and Notes on the Manners, Customs, and Conditions of North American Indians*, two volumes, London, 1844.

Chou Wei, *A History of Chinese Weapons*, first published in Chinese in 1637, translated into Japanese in 1789 by Mokei Botsu. Partial English translation by Charles D. Swinford.

Comstock, Paul, *The Bent Stick; Making and Using Wooden Hunting Bows*, Delaware, OH, 1988.
— *Hit the Mark! Shooting Wooden and Primitive Bows*, Delaware, OH , 1992.

Elmer, Robert P., *Archery*, Penn Publishing Co., Philadelphia, PA, 1926.

Faris, Nabih Amin, and Elmer, Robert P., *Arab Archery*, Princeton University Press, 1945.

Hamilton, T.M., *Native American Bows, 2nd Edition*, Missouri Archaeological Society, 1982.

Hamm, Jim, *Bows and Arrows of the Native Americans*, Bois d'Arc Press, Azle, TX, 1989.

Hardy, Robert, *Longbow, A Social and Military History*, Bois d'Arc Press, Azle, TX, 1993.

Herrin, Al, *Cherokee Bows and Arrows*, White Bear Publishing, Tahlequah, OK, 1989.

Hickman, C.N., Nagler, Forrest, and Klopsteg, Paul E., *Archery: The Technical Side*, National Field Archery Association, 1947.

Hill, Howard, *Hunting the Hard Way*, Wilcox & Follett Co., Chicago, IL, 1953.

Hunt, W. Ben, and Metz, John J., *The Flatbow*, Bruce Publishing Co., New York, 1940.

Kroeber, Theodora, *Ishi in Two Worlds*, University of California Press, Berkeley, CA, 1961.

Klopsteg, Paul E., *Turkish Archery and the Composite Bow, 2nd Edition, Revised*, Evanston, IL, 1947.

Latham, J.D., and Peterson, W.F., *Saracen Archery*, The Holland Press, London, 1970.

Laubin, Reginald and Gladys, *American Indian Archery*, University of Oklahoma Press, 1980.

Maximilian, Alexander Philip, *People of the First Man, The Firsthand Account of Prince Maximilian's Expedition up the Missouri River in 1833-34*, illustrated by Karl Bodmer, E.P. Dutton, New York, 1976.

Massey, Jay, *The Bowyer's Craft*, Bear Paw Publications, Girdwood, AK, 1987.
— *The Book of Primitive Archery*, Bear Paw Publications, Girdwood, AK, 1990.

McLeod, Wallace E., *Composite Bows from the Tomb of Tut'ankhamun*, University Press, Oxford, England, 1970.

Nagler, Forrest, *Archery - An Engineering View*, 1946.

Pant, G.N., *Indian Archery*, New Delhi, 1978.

Pope, Saxton, *A Study of Bows and Arrows*, University of California Press, Berkeley, CA, 1923.
— *Hunting With the Bow and Arrow*, G.P. Putnam's Sons, New York, 1925.

Payne-Gallway, Sir Ralph Bt., *Projectile-Throwing Engines of the Ancients*, Longman, Green and Co., London, 1907.

Roberts, T., *The English Bowman*, London, 1801.

Rausing, Gad, *The Bow, Some Notes on its Origin and Development*, Acta. Arch. Lundensia, Bonn, Germany and Lund, Sweden, 1967.

Wilbur, C. Keith, *Indian Handcrafts - How to Craft Dozens of Practical Objects Using Traditional Indian Techniques*, Globe Pequot Press, Chester, NH, 1990.

PERIODICALS

Adler, Bruno, *Der Nord Asiatische Pfeil* (The North-Asian Arrow), Supplement Int. Arch. fur Ethnographie, Bd 15, Leiden, 1901.
— *Die Bogen Nordaisens* (The Bows of Northern Asia), Int. Arch. fur Ethnographie, Bd. 15, Leidon, 1902.

Anon., *The Turkish Bow*, The American Archer, Vol. 1, No. 6, N.Y., 1940.

Balfour, Henry, *Remarkable Ancient Bow and Arrows Believed to be of Assyrian Origin*, The Journal of the Royal Anthropological Institute of Great Britain and Ireland, London, 1897.
— *The Archer's Bow in Homeric Poems*, The Journal of the Royal Anthropological Institute of Great Britain and Ireland, London, 1921.

Birket-Smith, Kaj, *The Greenland Bow*, 1915.

Brown, F.E., *A Recently Discovered Compound Bow (Iraq)*, Ann. de L'Institut Kondakov, Praha, 1937.

Case, Roy, *Broadheads*, Archery, April, 1958.

Clark, J.G.D., *Neolithic Bows from Somerset, England, and the Prehistory of Archery in Northwestern Europe*, Proceedings of the Prehistoric Society for 1963— Vol. XXIX.

Comstock, Paul, *Throwing Darts with the Baton de Commandment*, Bulletin of Primitive Technology, Vol. 1, No. 4, Fall 1992.

Cosson, Baron de, *The Crossbow of Ulrich V, Count of Wurtemburg, 1460*, Archeologia, 1893.

Discover Magazine, January, 1992.

Donato, Franco Di, *Italian Prehistoric Bows*, Journal of the Society of Archer Antiquaries, Vol. 34, 1991.

Eliott, Milan E., *Korean Archery*, Archery, Vol. 35, 1963.

Fabian, G., *The Hungarian Composite Bow*, Journal of the Society of Archer Antiquaries, London, 1970.
— *The Avar Bow*, personal correspondence to Dr. Charles Grayson, 1984.

Fisher, Anders, Hansen, Peter Vemming, and Rausmussen, Peter, *På jagt med stenalder-våben" (A Hunt with Stone Age weapons), or "Macro and Micro Wear Traces on Lithic Projectile Points"*, Journal of Danish Archaeology, Volume 3, 1984.

Harmatta, J., *The Golden Bow of the Huns*, Acta. Archery 1 (English translation), Budapest, 1951.

Hein, Joachim, *Bogenhandwerk und Bogensport beiden Osnamen*, Der Islam, 14, 15, Leipzig, 1925-25.

Jochelson, Waldemar, *The Jessup N. Pacific Expedition*, Memoirs of the American Museum of Natural History, N.Y., 1926.

King, Duane H., *Cherokee Bows*, Journal of Cherokee Studies, Fall, 1976.

La Flesche, Francis, *The Omaha Bow and Arrow Makers*, Smithsonian Institution Annual Report, 1926.

Mason, Otis T., *North American Bows, Arrows, and Quivers*, Smithsonian Institution Annual Report, 1893.

Matthiassen, Dr. Therkel, *The Eskimo Archeology of Greenland*, Smithsonian Institution Annual Report, 1936.

Murdoch, John, *A Study of the Eskimo Bows in the U.S.* National Museum, Smithsonian Institution Annual Report, 1884.

Nagler, Forrest, *Broadhead Notes*, The Archery Review, Feb., 1933.

Nelson, Edward William, *The Eskimo about Bering Straits*, Bureau of American Ethnology, 1896-97.

Paterson, W.F., *The Archers of Islam*, Journal of the Economic and Social History of the Orient, Vol. IX, Leiden, The Netherlands, 1966.
— *Archery in Moghul India*, Islamic Quarterly, Vol. XVI, Oxford, England.

Pope, E.F., Ye Sylvan Archer, Sept., 1927.

Robinson, Eugene, *The Egyptian Composite Bow*, Archery, Vol. 23, No. 4, April, 1951.

Rohrer, R., *Der Chinesische Pfeilbogen*, Jahrbuch des Bernischen Historicschen Museums in Bern, Bern, Switzerland, 1942.

Suhm, Dee Ann, and Krieger, Alex D., Bulletin of the Texas Archeological Society, Vol. 25, 1954.

Tan Tan-chien, *Investigative Report on Bow and Arrow Manufacture in Chengtu, China*, Bulletin of the Institute of History and Philology, Vol. 23, Taiwan, from the original translation of Charles D. Swinford, 1950.

Wilke, Philip J., *Bow Staves Harvested from Juniper Trees by Indians of Nevada*, Journal of California and Great Basin Anthropology, 1988.

Wilson, Gilbert L., *Notes on the Hidatsa Indians*, Anthropological Papers of the American Museum of Natural History, New York, 1979.